A
Broader
Vision

Other Books by Richard H. Drummond

A History of Christianity in Japan
Gautama the Buddha, an Essay in Religious Understanding
Unto the Churches
Toward a New Age in Christian Theology
A Life of Jesus the Christ

A
Broader
Vision

Perspectives on the
Buddha and the Christ

by Richard Henry Drummond, Ph.D.

"All places that the eye of Heaven visits are
to a wise man ports and happy havens."
William Shakespeare
Richard II, Act I,
Scene iii, 275-276

A.R.E. Press • Virginia Beach • Virginia

A.R.E. Press
Sixty-Eighth & Atlantic Avenue
P.O. Box 656
Virginia Beach, VA 23451-0656

The Scripture quotations contained herein are from the New Revised Standard Version of the Bible, copyrighted 1989 by the Division of Christian Education, National Council of the Churches of Christ in the U.S.A., and are used by permission.

Quotations of translations from the Pāli are those of the Pali Text Society, Broadway House, Newton Road, Henley-on-Thames, RG9 1EN, England, and are used by permission.

Edgar Cayce Readings © 1971, 1993 by the Edgar Cayce Foundation.
All rights reserved.

Library of Congress Cataloging-in-Publication Data
Drummond, Richard Henry, 1916-
    A broader vision: perspectives on the Buddha and the Christ
/ by Richard Henry Drummond.
    Includes bibliographical references and index.
        p.   cm.
    ISBN 0-87604-348-1
    1. Christianity and other religions—Buddhism. 2. Buddhism—Relations—Christianity. 3. Jesus Christ—Person and offices. 4. Gautama Buddha. I. Title.
BR128.B8D69   1995
261.2'43—dc20   95-19151

Cover design by Lightbourne Images

To Pearl, with whom I have walked
the way to this faith-understanding

Contents

Contents

Guide to Pronunciation

The oldest source materials for the Buddhist tradition are found in two related Indian languages, Sanskrit and Pāli. Since, however, the Sanskritic forms are more familiar to English-speaking readers, I regularly use them with an occasional addition of the Pāli reading in brackets. Exact quotations may contain the Pāli form, as *Dhamma* for the Sanskrit *Dharma* or *Nibbāna* for *Nirvāṇa*.

The vowels of Sanskrit are generally pronounced as in Italian; the long *ā* as in the English f*a*ther, *ē* like the *a* in ev*a*de and *i* like the *i* in mach*i*ne. Short *a*, however, is a colorless sound comparable to the vowel of the English b*u*t or s*o*n. There is in Sanskrit an untrilled r-sound that is used as a vowel and transliterated sometimes as *r*; I prefer, however, to transcribe this sound as *ri*. There is also an *l* that may be pronounced as a vowel.

As for the consonants, *h* when it follows another consonant regularly effects an aspirated diphthong. *Bh* is pronounced somewhat as in the English clu*bh*ouse, but it issues as a single diphthong without pause between the parts. Palatal *c* is pronounced about like the *ch* in *ch*eese. *J* is approximately as in *j*udge. The nasal *n* is like the *ny* in can*y*on. The sibilant *ś* is similar to the English *sh* but pronounced more in the front of the mouth; *ṣ* is a variant of this sound uttered from farther in the back.

Ḥ is a final *h*-sound articulated from the position of the preceding vowel.

Ṃ, to be distinguished from the labial *m*, is a resonant-vocalic nasal pronounced with the mouth open.

Ṅ, to be distinguished from the dental *n* and the cerebral *n*, is a guttural nasal pronounced like *ng* in si*ng*ing.

English Equivalents to the Pāli Buddhist Texts Referred to in the Endnotes:

The Book of the Discipline (Vinaya-Piṭaka)
The Book of the Gradual Sayings (Anguttara-Nikāya)
The Book of the Kindred Sayings (Sanyutta-Nikāya)
Dialogues of the Buddha (Dīgha-Nikāya)
The Minor Anthologies of the Pāli Canon (Udāna, etc.*)*
The Collection of the Middle Length Sayings (Majjhima-Nikāya)
Milinda's Questions (Milindapañha)
Psalms of the Early Buddhists (Therī-gāthā, Therī-gāthā)
Sacred Books of the East
Woven Cadences of the Early Buddhists (Sutta-Nipāta)

Preface

This book is the product of many years' study of the life and teaching of Gautama the Buddha and of Jesus the Christ. It is an academic work, inasmuch as I endeavor to make full use of historical-critical methods, pertinent literature, and other appropriate materials. The focus, however, is on the main themes of both life and teaching, and hence many subordinate critical issues or problems are only lightly considered, or not at all, in order to delineate more clearly and emphatically the larger picture. I have felt that the limitations of space as well as the need for better understanding require such a proportionate approach.

This book, however, is in a number of ways exploratory

somewhat beyond the usual academic understanding of the adjective. I greatly respect the contributions of scientific historiography—"scientific" in the sense of the social or human sciences—and literary as well as textual criticism in biblical studies over the past two centuries and more. These methods have also been employed in Buddhist studies in the West and in Japan and elsewhere, even if not with the same degree of thoroughness, since the discovery and translation by Western scholars of Sanskrit, Pāli, and then Chinese, Tibetan, and other Asian religious texts beginning in the eighteenth century. I do not, however, totally restrict my methodology to that of empirical-historical research. There is not a little in human experience, I believe, that is knowable through the use of methods other than these, methods that may have their own critical disciplines and criteria of truth and authenticity. We shall consider later problems of the legitimacy of these "other methods," as well as the possible contributions that they may make to our study. At this point I shall say only that this is a religious study—we are considering two persons who, at least in some quarters, are regarded as the greatest religious figures in the whole of human history—and, as I define religion, it necessarily considers realities and events that cannot fully be comprehended by empirical-historical methods.[1]

If I may speak more of my personal background, I should say that I have been a student of Buddhism now for over forty years. I have been an adult participant in biblical and historical studies related to Christianity for over fifty years. This book, therefore, represents a distillation of these years of study and experience with the result that I may say that it is far more than a citation and comparison of the work of other scholars. Not only is the selection and organization of material my own. Even as I have been instructed by others too numerous to mention here, I have not hesitated to make use of my own insights and to draw my own conclusions. I leave it to my readers to evaluate these on the basis of their own best insights and standards. The point is that this is an original work.[2]

I should add that a major speciality of my adult life has been Japanese studies. In all I have lived and worked in Japan for nearly eighteen years, serving as both a field and educational missionary of the Presbyterian Church (U.S.A.). My study of the Japanese language began in earnest in the summer of 1948, and only rarely since that time have I let a day go by without some use of the Japanese language. In my years of service in Japan by far the bulk of my personal relationships, as of my teaching and preaching, has been in that language. I mention this fact because not a little of my understanding of both Buddhism and Christianity has been aided—that is, aided in the sense of both instruction and correction—by Japanese Buddhists and Christians.

With reference to textual matters, apart from translations of Chinese and other Asian languages, I have used as much as possible for verbatim quotations of Buddhist materials the translations of the Pali Text Society. As for biblical materials, all verbatim quotations are from the New Revised Standard Version. Permission to use these materials has been granted in both cases. My use of Buddhist texts, moreover, has been significantly influenced by the works and persons of noted Japanese Buddhologists, whose names will appear in the course of this work and in the endnotes. Similarly, I have been instructed by both Buddhists and Christians in Japan who in more recent years have been engaged in various kinds of interreligious dialogue. With reference to my use of biblical and related historical materials, I may add that my doctoral studies were in classics, in the study of Greek and Latin literatures, history, and thought. I have taught at various times classical Greek, New Testament Greek, and both classical and ecclesiastical Latin. In seminary my major area of study was Hebrew and Old Testament studies.

A primary purpose behind the writing of this book has, of course, been the intent to make some contribution to worldwide interreligious dialogue. It is widely recognized that such dialogue has over the past several decades increasingly become a "primary topic of discussion among scholars representing all disciplines of religious studies."[3] A great amount of theoretical, as well as specifically theological, discussion has been carried on over this period. I believe that at the present time there is need for more specific historical data and reflection thereon to give additional content and color to the dialogue. Hence this fresh presentation, analysis, and comparison of the rich data available on the life and teaching of Gautama the Buddha and Jesus the Christ.

I write this book as a person of Christian faith. This fact does not mean, I trust, that I work from a narrow or exclusive posture of faith. Quite the contrary, my own position, as best I understand myself, is somewhat akin to that of the "Broad-Church" movement, to use a term from the history of the Church of England in the nineteenth century. My faith-position, I believe, is close to that of major theologians of the early church, such as Justin Martyr, Irenaeus, Clement of Alexandria, Origen, and others, who were theologically more inclusive than had been commonly realized until a series of recent studies has shown them to be such.[4] Furthermore, it has increasingly become clear that no one, in academic context or not, operates from a life posture that can be called completely impartial or objective. The complete objectivity posited in the positivism of Auguste Comte is no longer seen as a viable goal in contemporary scholarship, even as an ideal. A wise missionary, I may add, knows that no one with whom he/she may dialogue is ever a "blank sheet of paper" with regard to "the things of God," to use Christian terminology. Every person has had some previous life experiences of Ultimate Reality, has some sort of worldview, whether implicit or explicit, some standard of values, usually some sense of cosmic as well as personal meaning in life.These can and must be respected; they are not infrequently noble indeed.

I believe, then, that the issue is clarified if a writer acknowledges with specificity his or her own position of religious faith and consequent orientation. In this context of candor the dangers as well as the advantages of a particular position can be identified and subjected to critical discourse. This is to say that no one functions without some kind of value system, and in the context of religious studies such is usually a religious value system. A religious value system, of course, need not be Christian—certainly not in the context of contemporary global academia—in order to be legitimate. Any posture of authentic faith and coherent reflection may have its own legitimacy. But, as the Dutch-American scholar Kees W. Bolle has put it, "it is only a *specific theology* that can assist and reprimand the historian of religions in his own conflict situations." This is to say that while history of religions as a social and historical science must continue to maintain focus upon the methodology of historical investigation, it needs to transcend the traditional limitations of the discipline if scholars are to deal responsibly with the full spectrum of the data of religion in their entirety. Concretely, this means that each historian of religions, perhaps best in community, will need to enter into some kind of interdisciplinary cooperation with theology, or whatever term may be appropriate as we encounter varying perceptions of the Transcendent, or Ultimate Reality, posited in most views of Reality that can be called religious. The writer's own theological position may then properly play its appropriate role.

It is fitting at this point, I believe, to indicate, at least in outline, the methodology or methodologies that I use to identify for my understanding—and I hope for that of others—the relative authenticity of source materials supportive of my conclusions in this book. I offer here, then, a brief summation of fuller discussion in subsequent chapters. With reference to the materials on the Buddha, I am significantly indebted to the distinguished Japanese historian of religions Hajime Nakamura for identification and structuring of primary sources. I have focused, however, on these sources, examining each one carefully in its context, using primarily the translations of the Pali Text Society. With reference to larger issues of interpretation, I have drawn upon a wide range of secondary sources, including my own perceptions.

As one example of the last point, I assign a relatively greater significance to the role of the Dharma in the life and teaching of the Buddha than does Professor Nakamura. I believe that I am able to support my conclusions with a sufficient array of primary source materials. It is gratifying to me to note, however, that a number of scholars in the tradition of the Japanese Pure Land Schools of Buddhism *(Jōdo-Shū, Jōdo-Shinshū)* have recently been moving in the direction of "renaming" Amida Butsu, the primary object form of their historic "trinitarian theistic" faith, as one with the Dharma of early Buddhism.

I should like to add a few words on the personal role of the individual scholar—even when working in community—in the processes of this kind of work. To downplay this role, I am convinced, is to deceive ourselves as to the actual state of affairs in historical studies, above all in the case of history of religions. As an example, one may gain an initial impression in perusing John Dominic Crossan's important book *The Historical Jesus, the Life of a Mediterranean Jewish Peasant* (San Francisco: Harper Collins, 1991), especially the detailed appendices, that is misleading. That is, that in evaluating the relative historical authenticity of items allegedly pertaining to Jesus of Nazareth in either intracanonical or extracanonical materials, we have reached a stage of almost mathematical certainty.

But in keeping with his aim of "attainable honesty," Crossan admits that in following through with his suggested process "almost every step demands a scholarly judgment and informed decision." This is also to say that at every step on the way the personal evaluative judgments of the scholar—with their potential flaws as well as excellencies— are brought into play. A concrete example is to note that in Chapter 12, "Kingdom and Wisdom," Crossan cites more supportive evidence (as quotations) from the Gospel of Thomas than from all th canonical gospels put together.[5]

I should like to bring this point of the personal role of the scholar even more to the forefront. This is not to put down the personal role, but to recognize its very great and indeed necessary significance. Historical studies of every kind deal largely with what would be considered anecdotal material in a modern court of law. Even the artifacts of archaeological excavations must be identified, interpreted, and evaluated. Crossan himself, furthermore, summarizes the historical formation of the Jesus tradition as involving "the continuing presence of the risen Jesus and the abiding experience of the Spirit." Although Crossan does not use precisely my own following words, presumably he also allows himself the right to work within the larger parameters of these potential transhistorical "influences." I would like to claim that right for myself and place it in the context of being a longtime participant in communities of faith—as well as in cooperative scholarly and academic activities. I referred above briefly to my background of academic studies. I would add at this point a note of my longtime interest and participation in the history of Christian spirituality, to which I have later been led to include the history of Jewish and Muslim as well as Buddhist spirituality. All these factors have their proper role in the development of what I call "religious understanding" in my work of Buddhological research. They certainly play their role as I work in Christological research.

The use of these factors is by no means intended to downgrade the importance of what Crossan calls the "*formal* moves" of academic scholarship. But what he calls a subsequently necessary "*material* investment" actually includes both personal and transhistorical spiritual reality-factors. In any case, as Crossan says of his work, it is "one scholar's reconstruction," with the possibility of divergent interpretive conclusions that can be drawn even with the use of similar methodologies and "material investments." E.P. Sanders, professor of exegesis of Holy Scriptures at the University of Oxford, at the conclusion of his even longer introduction on methodology, admits to the large numbers of hypotheses that can be constructed with the varying methodologies that can be used.[6]

The preceding discussion is not intended to posit a situation of completely chaotic hyper-individualism in biblical studies or in Buddhological research. We do read and influence each other. I myself in this work am committed to use the "formal" procedures of historical critical methodology as these are currently understood. Also I have no objection to the methodological complex that Crossan sets before us, except perhaps that it is too complex and tends overly to limit that which is "acceptable." My own preferred methodology is to focus on themes in the materials available. This is to focus more on kind and quality of content rather than on form. It is to find authenticity more on the basis of coherence of moral and spiritual content than in counting numbers.

The above is not to say that I consider the "received text" as without variations or even inconsistencies. Nor do I ignore the process by which the authors of the dozen or more gospels that circulated in the first and early second centuries of our era, as Helmut Koester has put it, "did rewrite, edit, revise, and combine, however he saw fit" the materials they had available.[7] And I agree with Crossan in rejecting pejorative language for this process. My contention, however, is that in the case both of the Buddha and of the Christ there is a consistent thread, or rather stream, of coherent content discernible in the extant materials that enables us, using historical critical methodologies in combination with "religious understanding," to draw very credible outlines of the life and teaching of these two great figures. Details will be treated in the course of the work.

I wish to thank most warmly various friends and colleagues who have consented to read and critically evaluate this manuscript. They are also persons from whom I have learned much over long years. These are, in alphabetical order, Benedict M. Ashley, O.P., professor of theology, Aquinas Institute of Theology, St. Louis; James L. Bailey, professor of New Testament, Wartburg Theological Seminary, Dubuque, Iowa; Donald G. Bloesch, professor of theology, University of Dubuque Theological Seminary; William D. Bray, professor emeritus of New Testament, Kwansei Gakuin University, Japan; Harmon H. Bro, theologian and psychotherapist, formerly dean of Drake University Divinity School; Charles Thomas Cayce, president, Association for Research and Enlightenment, Inc., Virginia Beach, Virginia; John F. Jansen, late professor of New Testament interpretation, Austin Presbyterian Theological Seminary, Austin, Texas; Minoru Kiyota, professor of Buddhist studies, University of Wisconsin; Paul F. Knitter, professor of theology, Xavier University, Cincinnati; James I. McCord, late chairman, Center of Theological Inquiry, Princeton, New Jersey; Donald K. McKim, formerly associate professor of theology, U.D.T.S.; Lyle D. Vander Broek, professor of New Testament, U.D.T.S.; C. Howard Wallace, professor of biblical theology, U.D.T.S.; James C. Windsor, formerly president, Atlantic University. I myself assume, of course, full responsibility for any remaining errors or inadequacies.

I should like to thank in a special way my wife Pearl for her help in proofreading and, above all, for both aiding and sharing the developments in my personal understanding that are reflected in this book. Our sons, Donald and Lowell, both graduates of our seminary, have also been most helpful in proofreading and especially in the work of preparing the bibliography. I also wish to thank warmly Mrs. Debra Lovett for her careful typing of the manuscript and sensitive concern for the accuracy of its content. Finally, I wish sincerely to thank Dr. Walter F. Peterson, formerly president, now chancellor, of the University of Dubuque, for his leadership in the creation of the climate of intellectual and spiritual openness in our school that has made the writing of this book a pleasurable adventure. I wish also sincerely to thank the former dean of our school, Dr. Arlo D. Duba, for his generous openness and other help that have both allowed and encouraged the exploratory kind of work that gives this book, I believe, a certain special quality. The present officers of the university, the president, Dr. John J. Agria, and the dean of the seminary, Dr. C. Howard Wallace, have carried on this tradition in exemplary fashion.

Richard H. Drummond
University of Dubuque
Theological Seminary

PART

Gautama
the
Buddha

1

The Background of the Buddha

The way to begin a consideration of Gautama the Buddha is, of course, with his time and place. A consensus of modern scholarship focuses on a small range of dates around 560 B.C.E. (before the Common Era) as the time of the Buddha's birth.[1] The place was Kapilavastu, capital of the small aristocratic republic of the Śākyas, which lay in a rich irrigated plain between the foothills of Nepal and the present Indian border. The Buddha's personal name was Siddhārtha ("he who has achieved his goal"). His father's name was Śuddhodana, who as rāja ruled the district in a kind of vassal status under the king of Kośala, the largest of the four chief kingdoms of northern India at the time. The dominant and likely tradition states that the Buddha's family was of the Kṣatriya or warrior-kingly caste, although Gautama was more commonly a name of the Brāhman or priestly caste.

Both the time and the place of the Buddha's birth and later activity are highly significant for a proper understanding of his religious role. The time of his public ministry made him a later contemporary of Ezekiel in Israel, as of the writer of Deutero-Isaiah. He was almost an exact contemporary of Confucius (551?-479? B.C.E.) in China. If we accept the date traditionally held by Zoroastrians, the last years of Zarathustra's life (618-541 B.C.E.) coincide with the early youth of Gautama. Karl Jaspers used the term "Axial Period" to denote the activity of formative religious personages who appeared in India, China, Persia, Israel, and Greece between 800 and 200 B.C.E. In a somewhat mysterious way these figures shared in a respective promulgation of a "desacralized" or spiritually independent worldview which enabled them to make constructively intended, but sharply radical critiques of religious concepts and social practices in their respective societies.[2]

A particularly significant comparison of the Buddha's situation may be made with the Greek-speaking coast of Asia Minor during this period. The focal point of the Buddha's adult environment in northeastern India, the larger Ganges River basin, manifested in the early and mid-sixth century B.C.E. a burst of spiritual and intellectual activity that at several points resembles that of the pre-Socratic Greek philosophers. Thales, Anaximander, and Anaximenes were all active in the first half of the sixth century. Pythagoras and Xenophanes were roughly contemporaries of the Buddha in the second half. As I have written elsewhere, "A spirit of critical inquiry, love of abstract speculation, remarkable skill in syllogistic and other forms of logical thought, and, as the background suitable for this activity, a politico-social con-

dition that greatly favored freedom of thought characterized both Ionia and northeastern India at this time."[3]

As we shall see, the Buddha tended to see less value than
the Greeks, or indeed than many of his Indian contemporaries, in abstract speculation as a tool for solving the basic
dilemmas of human life, but he otherwise clearly shared in
the ethos of intellectual and spiritual sophistication of his
time and place.

Both the Ionian Greeks and the Indians were earnestly
concerned about the relationship in the universe of parts to
the whole, about the nature of physical matter and above
all about the nature of human thought. The chief problem
that concerned Indian thinkers, however, was that of human destiny, especially after death. Furthermore, we may
recall that the interest of the Greek pre-Socratic philosophers turned increasingly in the direction of study of physical nature. The Indian emphasis tended toward the spiritual
and metaphysical, and its methodology was largely intro-
spective, that of meditation. And yet it is of no little significance that Socrates, whose birth in 469 B.C.E. occurred
hardly a dozen years after the death of the Buddha, was, like
the latter, primarily concerned for the ethical life of human
beings.

The larger situation of northeastern India at the time of
the Buddha may properly be viewed as the product of a long
political, social, and cultural development that can be identified with some precision as extending back for over a thousand years. And yet we are now able to begin the study of
the Indian tradition even earlier, with the Indus Valley civilization, whose physical remains were first discovered in the
second decade of the twentieth century and of whose geographical extent and high cultural achievements no literary
tradition had come down to us. This extraordinary culture,
comparable in time and quality with those of Sumer, Egypt,
and the Yangtze River in China, constitutes one of the earli-

est known high achievements in human civilization. And among these it was the most widely extended geographically, possibly the widest cultural unit to exist in the pre-classical world.[4]

Well before 2500 B.C.E. a Bronze Age civilization had emerged on the flood plain of the Indus River and its five tributaries. Commercial contacts show that it reached its prime in the twenty-fourth century B.C.E. This civilization was characterized by populous cities, highly skilled industries, far-flung commerce, and a pictographic script. The cities of Mohenjo-daro and Chandhu-daro in the lower Indus Valley and Harappā, 400 miles to the north, were each as large as Sumer and were built almost entirely of kiln-fired bricks. They show an advanced knowledge of town planning, as evidenced by many well-planned streets and a magnificent system of drains, which were, from the archaeological evidence, regularly cleaned out. The skills of the citizens were highly developed in sculpture and other arts as well as in the making of bronze tools, the construction of buildings, and, evidently, the creation of an exact science based on mathematics.[5]

The decay of this great civilization in the middle of the second millennium B.C.E. coincided with the invasion of a tall, light-skinned people who called themselves Aryan (Ārya).[6] There is considerable archaeological evidence, however, of internal decline before the arrival of the Aryans, who may have come in waves and, like their distant kinspersons, the Dorians in Greece, brought sporadic destruction and the gradual replacement of a high grade of culture with a low one. They seem to have been ignorant of letters and of many peaceful arts. The more southernly towns of the Indus Valley civilization evidently escaped the kind of destruction experienced by Mohenjo-daro, and some continuity of culture was possible there.[7]

The Aryans, speaking an Indo-European language from

which classical Sanskrit developed, poured in from the northwest upon the racially mixed—with Dravidian as possibly the dominant ethnic element—dark-skinned and highly civilized inhabitants of the Indus Valley with the energy and contempt for urban civilization generally possessed by vigorous, illiterate nomads. This event or, more likely, series of events brought to a climax the decline of a great civilization, but it did not bring about the destruction of its people. The consequent political and social dominance of the Aryans coupled with a long process of cultural cross-fertilization, however little intended, has constituted the primary cultural-social framework for the whole of subsequent Indian history, including its religious history. Indeed, historic Hinduism has been described as "a combination of pre-Aryan [Dravidian] and Vedic Aryan elements inextricably fused into a composite system of belief and practice."[8] Much of the subsequent cultural history of India consists of the gradual expansion of this process from northwestern India across the whole of the subcontinent with varying degrees of thoroughness of permeation and transformation. Throughout much of the northern and central parts of the country linguistic displacement occurred, with Urdu, Punjabi, Hindi, Bengali, and other languages being the modern developments of early forms of Sanskrit. In the South the ancient Dravidian and other languages were able to survive in the forms of modern Tamil, Telugu, Malalayam, etc., in the context of generally less thorough permeation of Aryan cultural influence.

Our knowledge of the religion of the Aryans in northern India is largely derived from their sacred literature, which first became known in the West in the eighteenth century. This corpus of texts is recognized by the generic term *Veda* (knowledge) and consists of various materials composed largely by professional religionists over a period of a thousand years and more, its origins evidently extending to the

period before the migrations into India. Aryan religious self-
awareness combined with differences of skin color and general disdain for the conquered peoples to create the
specificities of the later Indian caste system. There are many
indications in Vedic literature which reveal Aryan disdain
for the older inhabitants because of their "disbelief," their
failure to sacrifice in the Aryan way, their impiety as contrasted with Aryan practice.[9]

The age of this Vedic literature may be regarded as extending from the early second millennium B.C.E. to perhaps 800-700 B.C.E.[10] The latter part of this period clearly
shows emphases which merge with the literature of the next
period, literature called the Upanishads ("that which lies
under"), and which bring us closer to the time of the Buddha. The Upanishadic materials (ca. 800-500 B.C.E.) reveal
much of the background situation of the Buddha and also
enable us to see something of the specific contributions
which he was to make.[11]

It is both customary and proper to distinguish with some
sharpness between the general religious postures of the
Vedas and the *Upaniṣads*. The Vedas are generally considered as expressing a kind of "polytheistic" worldview because of their many hymns addressed to various gods and
goddesses of the Aryan pantheon. The dominant ethos of
worship was sacrifice of animals about a fire in the open, a
rite seen primarily as constituting a propitiatory offering.[12]
But the anonymous authors of the Vedas were by no means
unaware of the subtle and the abstract. Moreover, there appears early in the *Vedas* a belief in a basic principle of unity
in the universe which the multitude of gods and natural
phenomena both serve. This belief was in fact perception
of a cosmic causal order both physical and moral (*rita*, ety-
mologically related to the English "right" and the German
"Recht"), and much early Aryan religious activity was directed to the maintenance and/or restoration of this cos-

mic order. Indeed, the "polytheism" of the hymns may in some cases be more apparent than real. In the *Rig-Veda* the statement occurs several times that "He is one, [though] wise men call him by many names."

The *Upaniṣads*, however, constitute a distinct ethos and represent another stage in the development of the Indian religious tradition. The religion of the Vedas, with its elaborate ceremonies based on sacrifices about a fire, gradually gave way, at least in some classes, to a worldview and practices that were profoundly different. The earliest *Upaniṣads*, the *Brihadāranyaka* and the *Chāndogya*, show close connections with Vedic speculations about the origin and nature of human beings and the universe and the mysterious identity that was felt to exist between them. Continuity with the Vedic past was maintained especially through the Brāhman or priestly caste. But in the circles which gave rise to the Upanishadic literature, largely in northeastern India and within the Kṣatriya caste, developments of the profoundest significance came into formal expression.

Much had been happening to the Aryan conquerors as a result of their centuries of living in the Indian climate and in contact with the Dravidian peoples. Even as Vedic-Aryan civilization expanded in ever-widening circles, the activism and naive confidence in the externals of life and in the empirical human self of the early Aryans tended to weaken. The climate itself helped to make the sacrificial fires irrelevant and perhaps absurd; the bathing places of Dravidian worship increasingly commended themselves. The seeking of favorable cosmic results and personal advantage by sacrifices that cause injury to other creatures evidently began to offend the ethical sensitivity of many and seemed to them only to tighten the knots binding human beings to the sufferings of life on this earthly plane. This perception of the human situation increasingly came to be sensed in an acutely poignant way.

The central preoccupation of the Upanishadic literature was with Ultimate Reality, seen as unitive, and the nature of its relationship with the empirically human. The religious goal in particular was seen as a kind of in-depth, existential perception of the essence of the human self as one with Ultimate Reality. But aspiration for this goal was not with intent to affirm or maintain the status quo of the empirical self; such has never been the way of "normative" Hinduism. The primary intent was to know Unitive Reality and that aspect of the human self which was seen to correspond with it and thus to participate in it (the *Brahman-Ātman* syndrome) to the end of the transformation of human character and thereby of its destiny. The writers of the *Upaniṣads* were profoundly concerned with the problem of human destiny after death and with the possibility of attaining a mode of immortality through a proper orientation of the human self to Unitive Reality. But they were as convinced of the need for human ethical transformation in this process as they were of the efficacy of the methodology of introspection and meditation. The historic change represented by the *Upaniṣads* signified in the large a change of emphasis from the outer to the inner, from Vedic sacrifice and external ritual to intuitively derived religious knowledge and interiorly directed ethics. It constituted a shift of religious focus from the many to the One.[13]

In order to clarify, however, the further transition involved in the historic phenomenon of the Buddha, it would be well to specify with more precision the developing sociological and economic situation of northeastern India toward the end of the Upanishadic period. As we have noted, this area enjoyed a notable cultural flowering in the middle of the sixth century before our common era. Commercial activity had developed especially along or near the Ganges River, and larger towns were being created. As a consequence a merchant class of increasing wealth and social power emerged that was composed significantly of Vaiśyas, the third caste accorded to formal Brahmanic distinctions. The older ruling groups of the towns and rural areas, generally classified as of Kṣatriya caste, shared in the growing wealth and cultural self-confidence of the time and place. We should note that the social and personal status of women was also affected. In the Vedic ceremonies women evidently played a relatively inferior role. In the *Upaniṣads*, however, women, although not often appearing as prominent figures, are generally accorded a dignity comparable with men.[14]

The provenance of the *Upaniṣads* appears to have been primarily in the courts of the rājas of northeastern India, who themselves evidently contributed seminally to the thought as well as gave financial and moral support to the activity of the movement. The content of the literature seems to suggest with considerable specificity sociological developments of great significance at work in Indian life. The performance of the Vedic sacrifices was a monopoly of the Brāhman caste, and their role was central in the expansion of Vedic-Aryan civilization from its home in northwestern India in ever-widening circles in the form of what we may properly call Brahmanic civilization. The *Upaniṣads*, however, reveal a new and bold kind of religious and larger cultural self-confidence among Kṣatriyas vis-à-vis the Brāhmans.[15] They seem to constitute the religious expression of groups newly conscious of political, economic, and social power. Their activity, therefore, constituted a significant critique of the religio-cultural forms and content of much of developing Brahmanism.

This activity, however, is hardly to be termed a religious revolt, because neither in the *Upaniṣads* nor in later teachers is there any overt attack on the older ways. We note that neither the Buddha nor his great contemporary Mahāvira, the Jain teacher, attacked Brahmanism as a system to be done away with nor urged their followers to refrain from participating in its rites. But both Buddhism and Jainism, and somewhat later the Ājivakas, shared with the authors of the *Upaniṣads* a critical stance toward certain basic religious and social principles of Brahmanism, albeit in different ways. The Buddha differed from the Upanishadic authors in that he did not accept the authority of the Vedas even in theory and hence came to be regarded as heterodox by Hinduism proper. The *Upaniṣads*, however, as Vedānta (that in which the Vedas reach their *anta* or culmination) came in existential fact to constitute for most of subsequent Hinduism, especially among the educated classes, the highest stage in an ascending religious development.

There are certain basic presuppositions of thought which underlie the whole of the *Upaniṣads*, and a brief consideration of aspects of these assumptions will enable us to move directly into consideration of the life and teaching of the Buddha. As we have seen, the authors of the *Vedas* had a strong sense of cosmic order, of cause and effect at work not only in the realm of physical phenomena but also in the personal lives and social activity of human beings. This principle, however, came to be perceived with new clarity and richness of color in the Upanishadic period. For the first time in the extant documents of the Indian tradition we meet with the doctrine of reincarnation (reembodiment) or the rebirth of "souls" upon the earth, a phenomenon technically termed metempsychosis or palingenesis. All Hindus and Buddhists hold some form of this concept, which appears in distinct form first in the early Upanishadic *Brihadāranyaka* (6:2, 15-16). Within the context of Vedic-Aryan civilization the emergence of this concept may be considered a later or post-Vedic development, but it is highly likely that it represents the appropriation of an ancient Dravidian tradition, perhaps a tradition of the Indus Valley civilization itself.

Various attempts have been made to explain the origin

in human life of the concept of reincarnation; one is that it developed out of the animistic notion of the presence of *mana* or sacred life force in all things. From this understanding may have come the idea that something like a "soul" with aspects of individuality and continuity exists in all sentient beings. In the passage of the *Brihadāranyaka* cited above, the understanding is clearly that the human "soul" may return to this earth in higher or lower forms of life, human or nonhuman. In this passage human beings are threatened with the possibility of becoming "insects and moths, and those creatures which often bite." This is the form of the concept of reincarnation which is generally termed transmigration and which persists to the present day in popular Hinduism and Buddhism. This mode of rebirth is seen as part of a larger process of change called *samsāra*, whereby the whole of phenomenal existence—including that of gods *(devas)*, human beings, demons, animals, and all lower forms of life—is believed to be involved in a cycle of continued rebirth (reincarnation) either on earth or in other realms.

The Brāhmans and related circles of the laity, following in the ethos of the Vedic tradition, generally regarded this samsaric process in a relatively optimistic way, believing that proper performance of or participation in Brahmanic rites would ensure their rebirth in favorable conditions. The *Vedas* do not lack positive ethical teaching nor a sense of the cosmic consequences of wrong ethical behavior; indeed, their rites were designed with special focus to cope with such consequences. But it appears that the Brahmanic hermeneutical emphasis upon the correct performance of sacrificial rites and ceremonies as central elements in the ensuring of human welfare in this world and any other tempted the less earnest to a relative neglect of ethical concerns. The relatively wide extent of this kind of "worldliness" may have been a significant factor in the emergence

in India from before the time of the Buddha of the class of
religious seekers whom we may call wandering recluses
(śramaṇa) and who were, in comparison with the older
Vedic ethos, relatively ascetic, generally celibate strivers for
religious knowledge and liberation. They had abandoned
the life of the householder for the apparently complete freedom of the homeless, mendicant way of life, and by this
means they strove to solve the deeper problems of human life
as generally perceived in their time and place. Apparently
no early human civilization outside of India had anything
like this practice whereby relatively large numbers of young
men—we shall later find instances of women living celibate
lives as Buddhist nuns in more protected environments—
left the normal life of the world, their home, family, occupa-
tion, and society as such, to seek spiritual liberation and
peace either singly or in groups in secluded forests and caves.[16]

The authors of the Upaniṣads apparently without exception did not belong to this category of ascetics, but they
shared with most of them a tendency to understand the
process of rebirth in ethical terms. This is to say that the
mode of rebirth—the time and place, the condition of body
and mind, the social and economic position of parents, in
sum, the whole complex of human conditions and opportunities—came to be seen as largely determined by the ethical quality of human conduct in previous lives on earth.
This understanding took deep root and has remained an
integral part of the anthropological as well as cosmic worldview of India and the rest of southern and eastern Asia to
the present day. We shall see that the Buddha essentially
shared this view, but gave the understanding of it a deeper
interiority. Almost all groups saw the causal process as continuing to operate within the present life even though their
understanding of liberation-salvation allowed for varying
perceptions of freedom vis-à-vis the process.

The basic cosmic principle involved came within the first

millennium B.C.E. to be associated with the Sanskrit word
karma (karman), which originally meant work or action. In
time, however, the term came to denote the linkage of action, the relationship of cause and effect, particularly as a
process operative in human life, both individual and social.
The ethical quality of human action, both mental and
physical, was seen as bearing fruit, producing consequences, in human character as well as in externals of life in
accordance with the principle of causal connectedness.
Thus we note in the literature of early Buddhism use of the
term *samskāra* to denote predispositions or tendencies of
character which inhere within sentient beings and condition their given state of being as the result of past action.
The main thrust of the Indian religious tradition—Hindu,
Buddhist, Jain, or other—was in some way to alter or
achieve liberation from the bondage of this condition-situ-
ation—it was generally experienced and interpreted as constituting a mode of "bondage"—so as to open up the destiny
of human beings both in this life and in the life to come.
This thrust was, of course, based upon a fundamental conviction of faith, a worldview, that such liberation is cosmically possible.

A final point should be added here with reference to the
Upanishadic and also popular Hindu and Buddhist teaching of rebirth (reincarnation) as possibly entailing transmigration, namely, the rebirth of human beings into
subhuman forms of life on earth. To my knowledge, there is
no passage in early Buddhist literature which gives us reason to believe that the Buddha himself taught reincarnation in this sense of transmigration.[17] It is significant that
the early Alexandrian Christian theologian Origen, who like
the Buddha apparently assumed some form of reincarnation as part of the givenness of human life on earth, was
also opposed to the concept of transmigration of human
souls into subhuman forms of life.[18]

$\boxed{2}$

The Life of Gautama

An initial word is in order with reference to the problem of the source materials on the life of Siddhārtha Gautama. There is no formal "Life of the Buddha" in the older Pāli or Sanskrit Buddhist texts. These materials generally contain only incidental and fragmentary references to events in his life. Apparently neither his immediate disciples nor those of subsequent early centuries had any pressing interest in such matters. Their primary concern was to understand and follow the Buddha's teachings as handed down in the traditional Indian mode of oral transmission and thereby to participate in the experience of liberation and transformation to which his life and teachings pointed.

The person of the Buddha was not seen as the key factor in the ongoing possibilities of this experience-process. Revered as the person and the role of the Buddha were, the developing Buddhist community increasingly came to see his significance as archetypal. The Buddha was perceived as representative of a mode of spiritual manifestation which appears on earth at different times and places and of which particular "names and forms" are of only secondary importance. This perception came to be expressed in the conviction that many Buddhas (Enlightened Ones) had appeared in the long eons of the past as envisaged in Indian cosmology, and at least one more (Maitreya) is expected to appear in the future.[19]

This kind of worldview is one reason for the relative lack of interest in historiography or even in the chronicling of events which has long been a characteristic of Indian society in general. We may note that the earliest extant texts of the Buddhist Pāli linguistic tradition, whose content is focused on the teaching of the Buddha and the rules of the monastic community, were written down first in the reign of King Vattagāmani (90-77 B.C.E.) in what is now Sri Lanka. They are the products of a long process of oral transmission that however aided by mnemonic devices evidently included some revision and much addition, all in the name of the Buddha. We should also note that while the Pāli texts which form the Theravāda canon constitute by far the largest quantity of extant early Buddhist materials, they represent only one of several canons of texts which are known to have existed in the first four or five centuries of Buddhist history. Of the eighteen different schools whose names are recorded, perhaps the best known, beside the Pāli, are the Sarvāstivāda and the Mahāsanghika, which both belong to the Sanskritic linguistic tradition. There were certainly ideational differences of some consequence among these groups, as that the Mahāsanghika developed the concept of universal buddhahood, a notion that we do not find in the Pāli texts. All traditions, however, seem to have included in their respective canons of texts essentially the same content material with regard to the life and teaching of the Buddha which we find in the Pāli.

The first instance of a formal "biography" of the Buddha is the Sanskrit Buddhacarita of Aśvaghosa composed probably toward the end of the first century C.E. The largely legendary work *Lalita-Vistara* (The Pleasurable Biography) has its origin in approximately the same period. Both are replete with legendary and mythical material and represent a later development in the Buddhist communities in the direction of an exaltation, even a kind of "deification," of the person of the Buddha. This was a development, however, that was to have abiding, but not necessarily decisive influence in the history of Buddhism, either in the Theravāda or the Mahāyāna. We may note as perhaps the most influential of the later biographies the *Nidāna-Kathā*, written by the great Ceylonese scholastic Buddhaghosa in the fifth century C.E. The problematic nature of the source materials on the life and teaching of the Buddha has occasioned various degrees of skepticism in the scholarly community, especially in the West, over the past century and more. An extreme reaction has been to dismiss the historic Buddha as in fact the projection of a solar myth. Heinrich Zimmer, from a somewhat different perspective, has said that there is not a single word in even the oldest texts that can be ascribed with unqualified certainty to the Buddha himself.[20] This statement as such cannot be specifically disproved, but it does not adequately summarize the present state of Buddhological studies. There is, in fact, fairly wide agreement that certain main lines of the teaching derive from the Buddha. This is because a consistent thread of coherent content runs through the otherwise somewhat mixed and uneven materials and strongly intimates a primary source.

If we combine the methodology of scientific historical and paleographical research with a due measure of "religious understanding," there is reason to believe that we can give an account of Gautama the Buddha which is coherent and faithful to the textual and archaeological data as well as to the historical probabilities.[21]

As we have noted, Siddhārtha Gautama was born near the year 560 B.C.E. as the first son of the rāja of Kapilavastu, in a fertile plain of modern Nepal near the Indian border. His education was most likely one in accord with the standards of a martial aristocracy with emphasis upon the active life. The portrayals of extreme luxury and magnificence in the style of his early home life found in the later biographies probably represent the authors' wish to heighten the contrast with his later sacrificial renunciation. Some accounts indicate that he learned to read and write, but even if such be true, the fact was of only minor cultural consequence since probably little more than tax records, merchants' accounts, and the like were written down at this period. In the Vedic-Aryan tradition religious teaching was considered too precious to be communicated other than by word of mouth. The long life and arduous missionary journeys of the Buddha suggest a sturdy physical constitution formed by a hardy early training. Later stories that credit the boy with manifesting extraordinary mental as well as physical ability probably err only in degree. In his adult life, according to the early texts, the Buddha indeed showed remarkable mental acumen and skill in argument.[22]

The Pāli texts describe Siddhārtha as marrying at the age of sixteen or seventeen; there is little reason to credit later sources that speak of his having several wives and concubines. His only wife, named Yaśōdharā, bore him a son, who was given the name Rāhula ("hindrance"). The name suggests that the birth of the child occurred either shortly before or after Siddhārtha left his home and family. For at the age of twenty-nine, he left his externally most attractive home situation for the homeless religious life. As we have seen, this kind of a decision was neither an isolated one nor out of keeping with an important stream of contemporary religious ideals. It was, however, evidently the result of aspiration for a higher good that had long been in the process of development.[23]

The background of this critical event is given focus in a story which is perhaps legendary in its form but probably true at least in a symbolic sense. Siddhārtha is said to have visited Lumbini Park in Kapilavastu over a succession of days. Here he beheld in turn a decrepit old man, a diseased man, a dead man, and a religious ascetic. The last, in spite of his few possessions, is described in one account as "carefully and decently clad," as one inwardly happy and in possession of spiritual victory. The story suggests by this means Siddhārtha's growing perception of the frailty and impermanence inherent in all forms of phenomenal existence and at the same time an intimation of the possibility of a solution of the dilemma of human beings living in this situation.

We have an account in the early texts that purports to relate Gautama's reflection on the experience later in his life. Disenchantment with the external forms of ordinary human existence was clearly an elemental part of the experience. But at this later time he recalls the inappropriateness of his earlier shame and disgust over the pathetic situation of others when, as a human being, he was destined to meet the same fate. Even more significantly, he recalls his pride in the externals of his youthful vigor and its comparable inappropriateness in the face of the larger human situation. The experience seems to have constituted something akin to what in the Judeo-Christian tradition would be termed repentance, regret over what is perceived to be a basically wrong life-attitude and a determination to turn from it.[24]

Siddhārtha left his home to travel south and eastward toward the cultural centers of northeastern India in the Ganges River basin. The texts record frankly the grief and resentment of Yaśōdharā at her husband's departure, although in the context of the extended family system characteristic of the time—all the more in the case of the family of a rāja—she was, of course, not left without economic sustenance or personal care.[25] Siddhārtha visited, learned from, and evidently practiced meditation exercises for a time under certain prominent religious teachers of the Ganges basin area, notably Arāda Kālāma of Vaiśāli and Udraka Rāmaputra of Magadha. Possibly the later threefold structure of the Buddhist movement—Dharma (law, teaching), Vinaya (discipline), and Sāngha (community)—was derived from the practices of these teachers. Furthermore, while differing somewhat between themselves, these two teachers evidently conceived of their religious goal and methodology of attainment in a way closer to later Buddhist understanding than was true of either the Upanishadic or Jain tradition. They aimed at a mode of enlightenment *(bodhi)* and transcendence *(Nirvāṇa)* through the cultivation of deepening stages of mental awareness or consciousness. Siddhārtha, however, was not satisfied to become a permanent disciple of either of these two or of other teachers.[26]

Siddhārtha then began a regimen of religious discipline on his own with increasingly severe ascetic practices. One text tells how from the extremes of fasting he was able, when he touched the skin of his belly, to take hold of his backbone. The hair fell off when he rubbed his limbs, and his complexion became unhealthily sallow. In the course of his regimen Siddhārtha acquired five disciples who were evidently attracted by his sincerity and the heroic style of his austerities. Yet however energetic his efforts, this methodology, while enabling him to gain a certain measure of mental self-control, gave him neither inner peace nor spiritual enlightenment.[27]

At this point of frustration over the futility of the methods of extreme asceticism, Siddhārtha is recorded as reflecting as to whether there was not a better way of awakening to the happiness that does not depend upon sensory pleasures, to the knowledge and vision which a true Aryan may aspire to achieve. He recalled how in his youth, while still living in his father's home, he had meditated in a simpler way without austerities and had experienced unusual self-control, insight, and even a certain rapturous awareness. He decided to try this method again as a better way. It is important in this context, however, to note that Siddhārtha neither at this time nor later divorced the practice of meditation and consequent religious experiences from strenuous moral and intellectual discipline. His turning at this point in his life was away from harsh austerities to the "Middle Way" of moderation and balance, which was also the way of faith, faith in the cosmic possibilities of liberation and transformation. It was supremely the way of openness to the relational aspects of the religious life, the nature of which we shall soon discuss. We note that as he began to eat in moderation and in other ways to prepare for entering upon this different lifestyle, his five disciples left him in disgust that he had wavered in his ascetic striving and had reverted to an easier way.[28]

According to the traditional accounts, Siddhārtha found a suitable spot under a large tree—the place was Uruvilvā, not far from the modern Bodh-gāya in the state of Bihar. Here, as he meditated in the early evening, the experience came to him that was ever afterward to be known as the Enlightenment and that Christmas Humphreys has called "the womb, the heart, and *raison d'être* of Buddhism."[29] The central significance of the experience lies not in its vicarious nature—the early texts do not use language suggestive of a vicarious or substitutionary significance for others as inherent in the event—but in its role as the model for others who seek to solve the basic problem-dilemma of the human situation. The nature of the event was such as to make personal experience—as distinguished from either doctrinal formulation or institutional allegiance—a primal element in the entire Buddhist tradition.

Major texts describe in considerable detail, largely with the use of the categories of later Buddhist scholasticism, the several stages of consciousness which Siddhārtha experienced at this time, although the earlier poems of the Sutta-Nipāta make no reference to the first four stages of awareness.[30] The so-called three stages of knowledge which are described as following the four stages of deepening consciousness and moral purification are more significant for the later teaching. The first knowledge was the state of awareness wherein, as the text puts it, "ignorance was dispelled, knowledge arose, darkness was dispelled, light arose, even as I abided diligent, ardent, self-resolute." In this condition of mind Siddhārtha was able to recollect his former lives "in all their modes and detail" to the extent of a hundred thousand births.

In the middle watch of the night, at the second stage of knowledge, Siddhārtha was able to perceive the workings of the process which we have identified with the term *karma*. He saw all sentient beings as they pass away and are reborn. He perceived that this process, the primary characteristic of phenomenal existence, functions in a precisely measured chain of cause and effect, a process specifically denoted in the Buddhist tradition by the term *pratītyasamutpāda*, translated variously as dependent origination, interdependent coexistence, Kausalnexus des abhängingen Entstehens (Helmut von Glasenapp), the universal concatenation of all things (Raimundo Panikkar). All human beings reap consequences of good or evil character

and favorable or unfavorable life circumstance in their rebirth according to the ethical quality of their action—
whether of body, speech, or thought—in previous lives. The
texts indicate that the volitional aspect is of primary significance. The Buddha himself, as we have noted, does not suggest that this process works precisely the same way in the
case of animals or other subhuman creatures. The point of
Siddhārtha's perception, however, with reference to human
beings, was that the structures of experience of the present
life of persons occur not by chance nor may they be altered
significantly by the performance of religious rites in the
Vedic-Brahmanic sense. They arise solely in consequence
of the ethical quality of human action in this or prior lives.
And the solution therefore lies not in anything as superficial and inconsequential as external religious rites. We shall
discuss later how "cause and effect" may relate to the ambiguities regarding continuity of being or self.

Something of the existential quality of this experience
may be seen in the various references in early texts of
Siddhārtha's temptation during his struggle for enlightenment by Māra, the tempter, a spiritual figure who functioned variously as the personification of evil, transitory
pleasure, and death. Most of the sources confine this encounter to the period immediately preceding the enlightenment experience, but the oldest materials suggest that
this kind of spiritual struggle also occurred earlier and, indeed, in his subsequent life as well. The nature of the temptation was in essence to give primary concern to physical
life and health at a vitalistic level and to follow the Vedic-
Brahmanic way of sacrificial rites. Siddhārtha's response—
and supremely so as the Buddha—was in effect to give
priority to the higher values of spiritual truth and moral
goodness and to commit himself unreservedly to this way.[31]

Then in the last watch of the night Siddhārtha attained to
the third knowledge, which seems to have been an experi-

ence combining both perception and attainment. He came to a knowledge of how to solve the basic problem-situation of human existence, which is to heal what the texts call the cankersores of human life, to change the negative fruit-producing direction of the karmic process into a direction that produces positive, that is, good fruit—in human life and in the cosmos. The perception was of what later came to be known as the Four Noble Truths. These are to see the nature of empirical human existence as suffering, to see the cause of suffering, the possibility of its cessation and the way that leads to cessation. The attainment was that Siddhārtha understood and experienced himself as freed from attachment to sensory pleasures, freed from ignorance of the way life is, and indeed from the process of rebirth. This is to say that he felt himself freed from himself and his past, not totally freed from the effects of his past, but from the binding or constricting aspects of the workings of the karmic-causal process. He was now able to cope with them, as we would say in modern terminology. A major text relates his own description of the experience: "I am freed; and I comprehend: Destroyed is birth, brought to a close is the Brahma-faring (the doing of what is Right), done is what was to be done, there is no more of being such or such . . . ignorance was dispelled, knowledge arose, darkness was dispelled, light arose even as I abided diligent, ardent, self-resolute."[32] Siddhārtha Gautama had become the Buddha, the Enlightened.

It is important to realize that we have to do with highly stylized, indeed scholastic, accounts of the Buddha's experience of enlightenment in the traditional texts. It is necessary, therefore, in order better to understand the event to bring to bear other data from related materials in the early texts to illumine these standard accounts. An initial problem for many modern minds is that of alleged perception of former lives. We have space only to give this matter the barest kind of treatment. Firstly, it is unwise to be distracted by the traditional Indian predilection for large numbers in cosmological accounts, such as the one hundred thousand births allegedly perceived by the Buddha. As Westerners, however, we do well to remember with humility that the stupendous numbers common to older Indian accounts of the age and size of the present physical universe are indeed closer to the vistas shown by twentieth-century astrophysics than are those of medieval and early modern Western scientific speculations.[33]

Secondly, the initial reaction of probably most academically trained persons in the West to alleged perceptions of former lives of human beings would be to consider such statements as essentially mythical. This is not to say that these persons consider the accounts as entirely fictional, but, as is now common as a result of the study of pre-literate religions where myth is a "living thing" and constitutes "the very ground of the religious life," myth may be held to reveal truth in an exemplary way.[34] Nevertheless, this is generally to consider at least the form of the myth as indeed fictional, and I would contend that in the case of alleged perceptions of former lives the possibility that such an event can happen both as a phenomenon of human perception and as a phenomenon with referents in historical fact should not be ruled out on the basis of *a priori* philosophical assumptions. To do so would be tantamount to ignoring a substantial body of data in the phenomenology and history of religions. We do not have the space here to adduce quantities of supportive data, but Westerners are morally obligated, I believe, to take seriously at least some of the instances of perception of former lives recorded of the two perhaps greatest visionaries of the twentieth century in the Western world, Rudolf Steiner and Edgar Cayce. Steiner (1861-1925) is the Austrian philosopher, Goethe scholar, and pioneer in new methodologies of education, the arts, medicine, and biodynamic agriculture of whom the British philosopher Owen Barfield and the American Nobel Prize-winning novelist Saul Bellow have not hesitated to call themselves disciples.[35] Edgar Cayce (1877-1945) is the American Protestant seer best known for his phenomenally accurate clairvoyant medical diagnoses and wide-ranging methodologies of healing.[36] The recorded past-life perceptions of these two men have become part of the most significant data of the phenomenology of religion in the twentieth century.[37]

In the case of the experience of the Buddha, however, perception of former lives of human beings and even of the essentially ethical referents in the working of the karmic-causal process was evidently no more than perception of the human problem-situation as it is. It was not the solution or cure. Perception in the last watch of the night of the Four Noble Truths and personal appropriation-experience of their reality constituted the healing and transforming event. And the key element therein as identified in the early texts was the element of liberation. A statement that may go back to the Buddha himself is this: "As the great ocean has one taste, the taste of salt, even so, monks, does this *dhamma* and discipline have one taste, the taste of freedom."[38] This means to be set free, liberated from one's (empirical) self and one's past, liberated from the bondage of the karmic-causal process so as to be able to use the process for one's own welfare and for the welfare of others, both in this world and in others. This means that the process *(pratītyasamutpāda)* is dynamic rather than static. It is flexible, open-ended, permitting change in persons.

A second element or aspect of the enlightenment experience which can be identified in the early texts is that of integration. In early Buddhism the empirical self of human beings, the "natural man," is seen as basically self-centered and selfish. The self in this sense is depicted as characterized by evil desires, indeed as "in the thrall of evil desires," the begetter of its own snares. The self is characterized by self-exaltation, wrath, faultfinding, temper, ill will, sulkiness. It is envious, grudging, treacherous, deceitful, stubborn, proud. From the standpoint of the Buddha's experience, the root of the problem is what those of the Judeo-Christian tradition would call a kind of idolatry, "seizing the temporal, grasping it tightly, not letting go of it easily."[39] And yet the other side of this coin of idolatry is self-will, which is one of the major elements of evil. Self-will is also self-centeredness, self-in-isolation. The two sides of the coin thus constitute at once a problem of human perception and of relational ethics. From one point of view to perceive the self as isolated or independent is delusion, but from another point of view it is morally wrong. Therefore, in the context of the operation of the ethically qualified principle of *karma*, or *pratityasamutpāda*, human sorrows, vain longings, suffering are self-bred. Hence it is the self that hurts the self, that keeps it subject to the ongoing process of birth, aging, decay, and rebirth on earth.[40] In consequence, essential to the experience of enlightenment is integration, integration of the self with the Self, the empirical self with the higher Self, transformation of the self-centered self by means of integration with higher Reality. One picture of the goal in early Buddhism, which is the "wisdom of the still," is the self-at-one *(ekatta)*, which is the self integrated, not attached to nor distracted by the "many," but finding itself in the "One."[41]

The third element or aspect of the experience is actually what may be termed a more precise identification of the second, integration seen in its relational aspect. For fundamental to true integration is the establishment of right relationship with what I have provisionally termed Ultimate Reality. And for meaningful human discourse it is necessary to identify this Ultimate Reality with a certain measure of precision. This the Buddha did not hesitate to do. Going beyond the otherwise important methodologies of ethical effort, meditational practice and attitudinal (psychological) analysis, the Buddha stressed the relational aspect of the religious life and experience as primary, and he identified the "Other" of true relationship as being supremely *Dharma.* We shall consider this matter in more detail in the next section on the teaching of the Buddha.

There is little, if any, indication of ongoing development in spiritual understanding or practice in the life of the Buddha that can be discerned in the early texts. It is as if he were full-born spiritually and ethically, clothed with all maturity, from the moment of his enlightenment experience. In the later "biographies" development is seemingly confined to the process constituted by his early lives. Thus we find in the first recorded sermon after the experience a relatively full statement of his teaching in the form of the Four Noble Truths, including the Noble Eightfold Path as descriptive of the ethical conduct proper to the "Middle Way." This sermon was addressed to his former disciples, the five ascetics who had left him in disgust after his decision to turn to this way of moderation. They were now converted to the faith-understanding of this way and are said to have achieved enlightenment in precisely the same way as the Buddha. They became the nucleus of the community *(sangha)* of Buddhist monks.[42] A related order of nuns was formed later.

The Buddha evidently had remarkable success from the beginning of his public ministry in winning followers, both lay and monastic. In organizing into a separate monastic community those who were willing to follow him with full seriousness into the homeless life, the Buddha, as we have seen, made use of a practice common in Indian life in his time. It was common for teachers, such as Kālāma and Rāmaputra, to gather disciples for corporate living of the homeless, mendicant way, even as there were others who

preferred the more isolated, individual lifestyle. Differently
from the Vedic-Brahmanic tradition, wherein "young men
of good family" studied under a teacher for perhaps as
much as twelve years and then were married,[43] many of the
ascetics committed themselves to lifelong celibacy. We
should note that among these "ascetics" were also not a few
charlatans who scandalized their contemporaries by their
misdeeds and immoralities. At the same time there were
many sincere and noble men who were honored by the laity of every class, in no small part because supernatural
powers were believed to accrue to the life of renunciation of
worldly ties and pleasures. This belief was an important factor in the willingness of the laity to contribute to the mendicants what they needed for their daily sustenance.

There were appreciable differences, however, in the general tone and lifestyle of the Buddhist monks as compared
with other followers of the homeless way. In keeping with
the model of their teacher, they were expected to manifest a
dignified and pleasing, even if simple, exterior in contrast
with naked or unkempt ascetics. Another characteristic of
the Buddhist monks can be seen in a comparison with the
followers of the Jain Mahāvira. The Jain monk was expected
to clear the way before him with a little broom to avoid
harming any living thing, however small. The Buddhist
monk, on the other hand, was primarily concerned to exercise watchfulness over the ethical quality of his intentions
and attitudes.[44]

From the earliest period it seems that the Buddha proclaimed his teaching to lay persons as well as to those who
wished to follow him into the homeless life. As we have
noted, the initial group of five converts are all alleged to
have attained enlightenment. The same is not said, however, of all the subsequent monastic followers. Ānanda himself, the "beloved disciple" of the early tradition and younger
cousin of the Buddha, evidently did not achieve enlighten-

ment during the lifetime of the Buddha. It seems clear from the early texts that the Buddha believed that householders, both men and women, and those of every caste could achieve liberation in this lifetime as fully as any monastic. The heart of the matter, religiously speaking, was the renunciation of attachment to the things of this world, the abandonment of overweening desire for sensory pleasures, not their complete abandonment. The laity were able to progress in the religious life, in moral growth, in commitment to *Dharma*, even as the monastics.

The Buddha probably believed that the homeless way was the "better way," even though it was in no wise a condition for the higher reaches of the religious life. The monastic order, however, was the object of his special concern, but not just for its own sake. True, it was with the monks that he normally shared the deeper levels of his understanding, but this was in large measure because they were expected to be the primary agents of missionary activity. At a relatively early period, the Buddha gave his initial direction to the monks to enter upon what was in principle a universal mission. They were to go out singly—later, two by two or in larger groups. And as the heart of their message, they were to teach *Dharma*, which is "lovely at the beginning, lovely in the middle, lovely at the ending." They were to explain to "the manyfolk... with the spirit and the letter" the religious life of complete fulfillment and entire purity.[45] The lifestyle of the monks could, therefore, be described as mendicant, meditative, and missionary.

The monastics were under one leader, the Buddha, who was, however, more their teacher and spiritual guide than commander. Throughout his lifetime he remained the final court of appeal in all disputes of doctrine or discipline, but he disavowed the role of leader in a formal sense and exacted no vow of obedience to himself. The leader and refuge of all was *Dharma* and their higher Self.

The Buddha did not only send out others in missionary service, he also went himself. For the remainder of his long life he went from place to place throughout the larger Ganges River basin, usually accompanied by a band of his disciples, teaching whoever would hear and accommodating the content of his message to the readiness and spiritual capacity of his hearers. The three months of the rainy season were usually spent in fixed abodes, which soon came to include donated grounds and buildings. During the rest of the year he and his monastic disciples traveled, meditating in the early morning, begging their nourishment at noon, teaching the "manyfolk" in the late afternoon and evening. It was on just such a missionary journey that the Buddha died, after a short illness, at the age of eighty. Among his final words was the admonition to his disciples not to depend on him but on *Dharma* and their higher Self. His very last words were, "Decay is inherent in all component things. Work out your salvation with diligence."[46]

If we ask what manner of person this man was, there are a few things that can be said with some assurance from a critical reading of the early texts. One is the sublime assurance of knowing the truth that the Buddha apparently manifested from the earliest period after his enlightenment experience. He was evidently not a worker of miracles, such as healing the sick or raising the dead, but as the alleged experience of perceiving his former lives would suggest, the Buddha evidently had more than usual gifts of what we may term psychic or intuitive powers *(siddhis)*. There are frequent references in the texts to these gifts, such as the power to read the minds of others and to perceive events occurring at a great distance. We may doubt whether in the context of the Indian religious tradition it would have been possible for him to have gained substantial numbers of followers apart from some achievements of this kind.[47]

The scriptural accounts agree that the Buddha not only

taught, but was characterized himself by a remarkable reso-
luteness and strenuousness of mind. This mental vigor,
however, appeared always in the context of calm self-control and serenity. He was the "tamed one," who had tamed
self well.[48] This quality should be coupled with the references, which may be authentic, to the calm and bright expression of his face. There are also references to his courtesy
in discussion and to his fine tact in social relations.[49] His
was evidently a bright and positive spirit manifesting a se-
rene dignity that had been achieved as a result of profound
spiritual and moral victory. But the crown of all was his compassion for those in physical need and his tenderness to
those who were spiritually and morally deficient.[50] The
forty-five years of his public ministry manifested, according to all the accounts, a consistent pattern of selfless concern for and service to others.[51] Even if, as modern persons,
we would prefer to ascribe some degree of growth-process
to the Buddha's moral and spiritual development after as
well as before his enlightenment, we clearly have to do with
one of the great personages of human history.

3

The Teaching of
Gautama the Buddha

1

Some of the teaching of the Buddha has already been given in the account of his background and especially in the discussion of his enlightenment experience. We have space only to indicate the main themes thereof and to discuss the most pressing issues. To begin with one issue, the basic religious posture of the Buddha to be inferred from the early texts has been misunderstood by some in both East and West as human-centered to the point of being "atheistic."[52] Such a view, to my mind, represents an egregious error. I refer not primarily to the fact that the Buddha evidently shared the faith of the early Buddhist community in the existence of gods and various supernal as well as lower spirits. For the Buddha seems to have been one with the writers of the *Upaniṣads* in considering the role of the "gods" *(devas)* of Indian popular faith as of relatively minor significance in making cosmically possible the liberation of human beings from their karmic bondage.[53]

There are, of course, reasons for the misunderstanding. One is the highly significant role of meditation in the practice of the early community and, indeed, in the entire subsequent history of Buddhism in both its Theravāda and Mahāyāna forms. One aspect of meditation as traditionally understood is intellective reflection on particular themes; there are, in fact, a number of references in the texts to the Buddha's being asked by monks to give them specific themes for such meditation. Another reason is the increasingly important role that came to be given to psychological analysis in the Buddhist tradition.[54] A major reason, however, is perhaps the presence in the texts of many instances where the Buddha is recorded as summoning his followers to vigorous exertion of will, especially with reference to states and habits of mind. Strenuousness of mind is clearly a primary characteristic of the Buddhist disciple. One of the items of the Noble Eightfold Path is "right effort," and in the execution of such the disciple "puts forth will, he makes effort, he stirs up energy, he grips and forces his mind."[55]

The fact, however, that the Buddha unhesitatingly called for strenuous human participation, both mental and physical, in the work of salvation, a work involving ethical transformation from beginning to end, does not mean that for him the entire process was one of, to use modern Western terminology, totally human-centered self-help.[56] Precisely the opposite was the case. As we have seen, central to his perception of the experience of enlightenment was its relational aspect. And central to his understanding of the ongoing religious life was this same relational aspect, with reference both to Transcendent Reality and to other sentient beings on this and other levels of existence.

A primary element in the inner life of the Buddha seems to be revealed in his recorded teaching on the theme of friendship or intimacy with the "lovely" *(kalyāṇa)*.

> Monks, I know not of any other single thing of such power to cause the arising of good states [of mind] if not yet arisen, or the waning of evil states already risen, as friendship with the lovely. In one who is a friend of what is lovely, good states not arisen do arise and evil states already arisen wane.
>
> Indeed, friendship with the lovely conduces to great profit.[57]

In another passage we learn that friendship with the lovely is the forerunner and prior condition for both the beginning and the sustained practice of the moral life described in the form of the Noble Eightfold Path. A monk who is a friend of the lovely is expected to practice this path in all earnestness, but the relational orientation in the sense of theological, if not temporal, priority properly precedes the effort. On one occasion the Buddha is recorded to have said to his cousin, the monk Ānanda, that the whole of the holy life he taught "consists in friendship, in association, in intimacy with what is lovely." The primary event of liberation becomes possible "because of my friendship with what is lovely."[58]

The primary question, then, is what is the "lovely." Aspiration as well as association was evidently understood to be part of the relationship implied, and the term *kalyāṇa* evidently meant both moral and physical beauty. Mrs. Rhys Davids has suggested that "lovely" is probably the best translation for the Pāli term and that it is akin to the "lovely" of Paul's exhortation to noble aspiration of thought in Philippians 4:8 *(quaecumque amabilia)*.[59] But the various passages in which the word is used in the early Buddhist texts seem to imply, as integral parts of the meaning, human openness to as well as aspiration for beauty and goodness that already exist, that are in some measure transcendent. We have already noted ascription of the term "lovely" to *Dharma*, and, indeed, for the Buddha the "lovely" seems to have been supremely *Dharma*.

At this point we enter into direct consideration of the basic faith-position and worldview of the Buddha. The early texts clearly indicate that a major motive lying behind Siddhārtha Gautama's decision to enter upon the homeless life was quest for the Good. This he claimed to have found in distinctive fashion in the experience of the enlightenment, and his life was lived from that point on in the light of and, indeed, as a kind of continuation of that experience-relationship. The Good is, however, simply another designation for *Dharma*. Our task then becomes that of attempting to define and relate the two central terms of early Buddhism, *Dharma* and *Nirvāṇa*.

We must first note, however, that the Buddha consistently refused to define either word in intellectual terms. In fact, a primary characteristic of his manner of teaching was what we may call reserve with reference to the practice of metaphysical speculation, a practice which was widespread in India in his day and since, to the extent of becoming a notable aspect of the historic Indian character. The Buddha was by no means anti-intellectual. He employed careful reasoning and was indeed highly skilled in disputation, which he apparently always conducted with calmness and courtesy. He also considered certain knowledge—in the sense of perception of cosmic truth-reality—as essential. But knowledge for him was to the end of practice. He was concerned for the establishment of primary relationships and for ethical transformation, and religious knowledge or philosophical speculation that did not lead to this end he believed of little use. His famous parable of a man pierced by an arrow who insisted on knowing irrelevant details of the event before he would let a physician treat him is illustrative of the futility of failing to distinguish between the more and the less important concerns of life.[60] The Buddha, however, gave various directions as to how to reach the goal, and from the manner of usage of the two basic terms we are able to gain a fairly clear idea of what they meant in the early community and probably to the Buddha himself.

Nirvāṇa was the goal of early Buddhist vision and effort, the Ultimate, the One, an end, however, perceived as Reality more religious than ontological. As we have seen, the Buddha understood the primary cause of the human dilemma to be misplaced desire, greedy desire, and grasping for things and persons in phenomenal existence as if they constituted ultimate values in themselves. He did not consider either things (matter) or persons in this category to be evil in themselves, but they were not worthy, to use the Tillichian phrase, of "ultimate concern." They were not the Ultimate in themselves, and to regard them and to relate to them as if they were was to act-be in a way fundamentally disruptive of the integrity of human life in both its interior and exterior aspects. The solution lay in reorientation, which is also reintegration, of the self to and with what is Ultimate and One.

Differently from various perceptions of later Mahāyāna philosophy which tended to see the Ultimate, the One, as the cosmos itself, rightly perceived—a kind of philosophical monism which was usually affirmed with important ethical and religious qualifications—the Buddha's worldview was essentially dualistic in the sense of affirmation of a radical religious distinction between the Ultimate and all else. Because of his reserve with reference to metaphysical speculation, he did not discuss this distinction philosophically, and therefore it does not emerge specifically as an ontological difference. But he made the religious distinction—in the sense of clarification of the religious goal, the primary "Object" of human life orientation—sharply and radically. The Buddha perceived the whole of phenomenal existence as operating under the single integrative principle of *karma* or *pratītyasamutpāda*, but this was neither the proper "Object" of ultimate concern nor the means of human liberation-transformation.

Nirvāṇa has the etymological meanings of a condition of being "blown out" or "extinguished," "become cool," "extinct." The image is of the unfed flame, no longer given the materials by which its formal continuity may be sustained.[61] These meanings, in early Buddhist context and in consideration of the empirical human psycho-physical condition, refer primarily to liberation from the mental defilements of craving, ill will, and delusion. The issue is not one of annihilation of the self but of its transformation. *Nirvāṇa* is where there is no-thing ultimately separate—a religious affirmation—and where there is naught that is grasped for—an ethical statement.[62] Use of the term implies cooling of the otherwise uncontrolled fires of feeling, of anger, fear, and grief as much as of sensual passion. Coolness of mind, however, is not dullness of mind; rather, its clarity, alertness, and creativity are enhanced.[63]

The coolness of *Nirvāṇa* is also not coldness. We find many references in the texts to the happiness, bliss, and boundless peace of *Nirvāṇa*. Not only griefless, it is that in which men and women delight.[64] *Nirvāṇa* is deliverance from every tie but not the abandonment of concern or indifference.[65] "Detachment" from phenomenal existence is one side of a coin whose obverse is the spirit not only of joy but of friendliness and compassion. Control of mind is not merely the repression of ill will, but its transformation into these positive qualities.[66]

Nirvāṇa in the early texts seems morphologically corre-

late—in the sense of its cosmic reality and function—with
the Kingdom of God in the teaching of Jesus. It was both
spiritual condition and "realm," both religiously transcendent and realizable in this world—as well as maintainable
beyond.[67] *Nirvāṇa* was not merely a state of human consciousness. It did denote liberation of human consciousness from its bondage to karmic process, but this was an
event as much cosmic in its consequence as of personal
consciousness. Furthermore, *Nirvāṇa* was frequently spoken of as if it were an independent Reality with its own dynamic.[68] In one Sūtra the Buddha is recorded as flatly
affirming his conviction, a conviction shared by his Brāhman
interlocutor, that *Nirvāṇa* is, even as the way (which we
shall see to be *Dharma*) to it is, the unchanging goal.[69] In
the Udāna Sūtra we find the clearest affirmation of the religious otherness as well as soteriological necessity of
Nirvāṇa.[70]

The Udāna passage would seem to indicate that for the
Buddha *Nirvāṇa* was not only a transformed mode of human consciousness—which no longer sees itself as totally
separate—but also and primarily Ultimate Reality itself. As
the later Ceylonese scholastic Buddhaghosa phrased it in
more philosophical language, *Nirvāṇa* is causeless, whereas
the whole of phenomenal existence is characterized by subjection to the chain of causation. It is unconditioned,
whereas existence is conditioned.[71] It is of another or further world *(lokuttara)*.

Dharma (Pāli: *Dhamma*) was the way by which human
beings may attain *Nirvāṇa*, in both its present and its future
modes. *Dharma* was a term already in use in Sanskrit-
speaking India before the time of the Buddha. Its primary
meaning, from the root *dhr*, was "to hold or support." Probably before the Buddha it had begun to be used to express
the concept denoted earlier in Vedic literature by the term
rita, the principle of moral order in the universe with per-

sonal, societal, and cosmological implication. It clearly had something akin to the meaning of a universal principle of righteousness; it was that which ought to be done.[72] But in the larger Indian context, *Dharma* came to mean any established—as if with cosmic sanctions—law, condition, or fact, either of nature or of human institution.[73]

In the teaching of the Buddha, however, we find no such association of *Dharma* with particular societal structures, whether of caste or sex or other. For him *Dharma* was particularly the cosmic force that "makes for righteousness," that leads to *Nirvāṇa,* a Reality not to be identified in any total way with phenomenal existence in part or whole, yet at work and available to human beings within such existence.

Like certain other terms in the early community, *Dharma* had to carry the burden of several meanings. It later came to be the technical term for Buddhist doctrine. It was also used to denote not only the proper but also the actual condition of beings and things. In the plural number, the term was used to designate all the elements of phenomenal existence, and all living beings and crafted products were considered as combinations of *Dharmas.* But the Buddhist disciple was taught to be carefully observant of these elements of being, in particular of the interdependent process of their causation and cessation, to the end that he might grasp after none of them.[74] Neither any one of them nor all together constituted Ultimate Reality, and the negative aspect of human liberation consisted in nonattachment to any or all. The positive way to liberation was dependent relationship to *Dharma* in the singular number, *Dharma* as the "lovely," as the force in the world that helps human beings to be and to do what is right.

Mrs. Rhys Davids wrote over a generation ago that when the Buddha began to teach, the term *Dharma,* which he deliberately chose as the focus of his message, as yet meant "no formulated doctrine, code of teaching, collection of sayings." She insisted, without the excessive reserve of many later Buddhologists, that this was the term which he deliberately chose—the texts tell us this "with utmost emphasis"—to designate "Whom alone he held meet that he should worship."[75] There is good textual warrant that the Buddha's posture toward *Dharma* was indeed that of worshipful honor and respect, the posture of one who lives "only under *Dharma*."[76] It is significant that the text in question should identify *Dharma* as that with reference to which the Buddha came to be "supremely enlightened" and that the creator god of the Vedic tradition, Brahmā Sahampāti, who points the Buddha in the direction of this focus of worshipful commitment, emphasizes that the Arhants (also Arahants-perfected saints), Buddhas Supreme, Exalted Ones of both past and future "live only under" *Dharma*, honoring and respecting it (him).[77] We may recall as among the last words of the Buddha before his death the injunction to his followers to live with *Dharma* "as your island, as your refuge, and no other."[78]

We must take care, however, not to understand this focus of the teaching in the Christian post-Reformational, ideological sense of *sola gratia*. That is to say, the theological priority of dependent relationship with *Dharma* is not to be understood as if it removed human responsibility to relate to one's higher Self and to practice the religious life in all earnestness, both in its interior and exterior aspects.[79] A monk, or any other, must remain "ardent, self-possessed, and mindful" with reference to matters of the body, feelings, thoughts, ideas if he or she is to "overcome both the hankering and the dejection common in the world."[80] Ethical aspiration and effort on the human side properly belong to the religious life, as we have seen, from beginning to end.

We do not have space to communicate all the richness of

content and nuance given the term *Dharma* in the early texts, but we may conclude this section with a few central items. *Dharma* is not only the Truth principle by which persons may grow; it seems specifically to be the quality and power of *Nirvāṇa* manifested in phenomenal existence. We note language used of *Dharma* that is reminiscent of that used with reference to both the Law and Wisdom in the Hebrew Scriptures. "The gift of *Dharma* exceeds all gifts; the sweetness of *Dharma* exceeds all sweetness."[81] The connection of the way with the goal is suggested by the statement that the monk, and any other, who behaves with kindness and is happy in *Dharma* will reach *Nirvāṇa*.[82] Perhaps we can say that *Dharma* in its relationship to *Nirvāṇa* shows subordination to a higher integrative principle comparable to that of Wisdom subordinated to the Lord God in the tradition of Israel.[83] In later Jewish literature, such as The Wisdom of Solomon (first century B.C.E.), we find Wisdom described as a kindly Spirit, the veritable equivalent of the Spirit of the Lord, more precious than all things, the guidance of the Lord. "In kinship with wisdom there is immortality, and in her friendship there is pure delight." Wisdom is said to know the works of God, to have been present when he made the world.[84] Here we see not only kinship with the concept of the Logos in the Johannine literature of the New Testament, but also an ambivalence with reference to personalism that is surprisingly similar to early Buddhist perceptions and statements about *Dharma.*

In what may be the earliest of extant Buddhist literature, the *Sutta-Nipāta,* we find reference to *Dharma* as the way by which persons may cross the flood waters of human life. *Dharma* "reigns" over the enlightened man or woman. *Dharma* is their delight; they take their praise from *Dharma* and also know its corrective judgments. Such persons order their conduct by *Dharma* as norm lest *Dharma* reveal their guilt. *Dharma* is the ancient, deathless word of Truth, and

Truth is one. It is near us and yet at the same time a lofty goal, a Reality inwardly perceived, not merely handed down by tradition. The Buddha was at least as critically selective with reference to the past of the Indian tradition as the early Christian movement was to that of Israel.[85] He was as insistent that the issue is primarily one of spiritual Reality and power rather than the transmission of oral teaching. For *Dharma* is that which ends human craving based upon a misplaced system of values, that by which he or she "who finds and knows and fares alertly may cross over the world's foul mire."[86]

Dharma in the teaching of the Buddha clearly suggests his belief in and awareness of the presence in phenomenal existence —and yet not to be identified with phenomenal existence—of a Force that "makes for righteousness." There is, therefore, in the "Object" of this perception-understanding that which is akin to the universal Spirit of God as the latter was intimated by the prophets and the writers of wisdom literature in Israel and forthrightly proclaimed by the theologians of the early Christian church. We find the same normative and corrective role, the same accepting and healing role. We note the transcendent dimension as well as the unitive.[87] It is not without reason that a distinguished contemporary Thai Buddhist scholar wishes, while maintaining some reserve with reference to the issue of personalism, to equate *Dharma* with the Christian concept of God.[88] *Nirvāṇa*, together with its expression in *Dharma*, forms the "still point," which is yet more dynamic than static, of early Buddhist aspiration and devotion.

2

We may properly conclude this account of the teaching of the Buddha with a brief consideration of the Four Noble Truths and the early Buddhist perceptions of the self. The

Four Noble Truths, simply put, are affirmation of the universal fact of suffering, the cause of suffering, the overcoming of suffering, and the way of overcoming, which last is the Noble Eightfold Path. The formulation is similar to the four divisions of ancient Hindu medicine and is, in effect, a diagnosis of the human malady, identification of its cause, proclamation of its cure, and description of the remedy. "Faith" in early Buddhism meant, among other things, belief that such a cure is cosmically and personally possible.

The term *suffering (duḥkha)* in this formulation meant pain of mind and feeling as well as of body, including grief, anxiety, frustration, and despair. The all-pervasiveness of this condition, as characterizing the "natural" life of all sentient beings, especially human beings, is stressed in the texts. A sense also of the transitoriness of all the "names and forms" of human life as well as of all phenomenal existence looms large in these materials. The "natural" state of all beings was perceived as having the character of impermanence, overall inadequacy, purposelessness, as lacking true reality or ultimate value.

This teaching, however, is not to be understood as meaning that the whole of phenomenal existence is one totally unrelieved mass of suffering. Certain forms of provisional or temporary happiness are allowed to human life both on earth and in supernal realms for limited periods of time. Also, and most significantly, the Buddha held the present human situation on earth as the one potentially most productive of good. To be born a human being means that one has the opportunity to hear the Truth and to attain *Nirvāṇa*. And in this present context of "being," it is good to help others and to enjoy the doing of good. "The accumulation of good is delightful." Friends are not only objects of virtuous action, but pleasant to have. Indeed, any number of experiences may be enjoyable and pleasant. Not only is moral virtue pleasant in its effects in human life, but so is "faith firmly rooted," "attainment of intelligence," or the "avoiding of sins."[89]

The purpose behind the negative analysis that is the First Noble Truth was actually in order to affirm positive religious values, a style of teaching widely used in India at least from the period of the *Upaniṣads*. Gautama's search for the Good led him to find it not in changing phenomena nor in the vagaries of the empirical self, but in that which changes not and is "other" than the flux of phenomenal existence, that is, in *Nirvāṇa* and its dynamic manifestation as *Dharma*.[90]

The cause of suffering was seen as thirst *(triṣṇā),* which is craving or inordinate desire for aught that is not worthy of such desire. The issue was primarily one of determining ultimate values. As we have seen, the Buddha did not totally deny value to the persons and things of phenomenal existence. Indeed, he was reproved by some of his contemporaries as "living in abundance" because of his abandonment of extreme asceticism for the Middle Way.[91] His point was to affirm that they lack ultimate value and dependability and hence are not worthy of ultimate religious aspiration.

There appear to be two primary aspects of this teaching. One would seem to be that the event of liberation-integration is made possible only by human committal to the One, which is the only supreme value as well as focus-origin of human salvation in the fullest sense of the term. The second aspect, in ways akin to the issue of idolatry in the Judeo-Christian tradition, is ethical. In the early texts the understanding of craving was in the widest sense of what human beings normally yearn and strive for: health, wealth, power, fame, or sensory pleasure, but the Buddha apparently saw the primarily evil aspect of this craving in its self-centeredness.[92] It was thus evil in its selfishness as well as foolish in its misdirection. Even desire for separate self-identity in this world or any other, if fundamentally self-centered, is both evil and foolish.

In some passages in the early texts the primary evil of the human "natural" condition is traced from craving back to ignorance *(avidyā)*. The methodology of tracing is through the principle of dependent origination, which, as we have seen, was used as a technical term for the karmic or linkage process in phenomenal existence.[93] But ignorance and craving are evidently two sides of the same coin. Ignorance is not primarily cognitive want of facts, but a misplaced system of values. It is not to know that all the elements of phenomenal existence lack Ultimate Reality and value. Craving is foolish inordinate desire for any of these elements based on the misapprehension that they are worthy of such grasping.

The Buddha is recorded as having thought through the process of dependent origination *(pratītyasamutpāda)* in both direct and reverse order. As the whole mass of human ill arises, so may it cease. And thus we come to the Third Noble Truth, the cessation *(nirodha)* of suffering. It is the complete cessation of and disengagement from craving, "giving it up, renouncing it, emancipation from it, detachment from it."

At first glance this approach appears exceedingly negative, as if it were to take the emotive quality out of life. But as we have already intimated, the negative perception that nothing among all the elements of phenomenal existence, either person or things, is ultimately real or worthy of ultimate aspiration is for the sake of a positive reorientation of self. The obverse of the negative aspect of the Third Noble Truth is reorientation of self from selfish, separate self-centeredness, from misplaced, inordinate infatuation with all that has "form and name" to find a mode of being in dependent relationship with that which is other than all these, *Nirvāṇa* as the goal and *Dharma* as the way. Only these are worthy of ultimate aspiration. In the whole of subsequent Buddhist history, in every tradition of which we have knowledge, there has always been a "focus" of ultimate aspiration, however differently this focus may be termed.

And the cessation of craving for things or persons of this world does not mean the cessation of right relationships with persons or of right use of things. The goal is such relationship and use that we are no longer "hooked" (a term actually used in the texts), infatuated or carried away by them. Only then are we free to be unselfishly benevolent and kindly toward other persons and discretely wise with reference to use of things.[94] An expression frequently found is that of the liberated one who "abides independent, grasping after nothing in the world whatever." The end result of this posture, however, is not negative or weak but an attitude "ardent, self-possessed, and mindful." Such a person has "overcome both the hankering and the dejection common in the world."[95] The overcoming of craving is thus not only the way to conquer the discouragement and despair of ordinary human existence. It also frees one to love, to exercise benevolence, without being possessive or otherwise harmful. We note in the texts the association of passion, or possessive emotion, with malice.[96] Conversely, the practice of goodwill becomes possible only by freedom from possessive emotions.

The religious quest is thus directed toward aspiration for and dependent relationship with Ultimate Reality and its values, but the profoundest ethical implications are involved at every step of the way. As we have seen, the Buddha perceived inordinate desire for lesser values as both cognitively mistaken and morally wrong. Hence the methodology of cure was inextricably linked with the ethical life, with ethical striving and exertion of will to that end. I have stressed that a basic element of both liberation-integration and the subsequent religious life was relational—friendship or intimacy with *Dharma*. But *Dharma* as the lovely was impregnated with ethical qualities. For this reason the

Fourth Noble Truth is none other than the Noble Eightfold Path, the somewhat scholastically structured ethical path of early Buddhism.[97] Religious aspiration or reorientation of life to the One is not to be separated at any point from ethical aspiration and strenuous effort of will, mind, and body.

The Noble Eightfold Path consists of "right view, right aim, right speech, right action, right living, right effort, right mindfulness, right concentration." The word for "right" (samyak; Pāli: sammā) is cognate with the Latin summum, the highest or best. It also has the meaning of "real" or "true." Study of the Buddha's teaching in the context of his time shows that he did not differ appreciably from his contemporaries in his understanding of what constitutes right ethical conduct. Indeed, we may properly recall that there has been strong emphasis upon ethical conduct throughout the religious history of India from the Vedic period onward.[98] The Buddha, however, emphasized to a degree beyond almost all others in the Indian tradition the inner aspects of human behavior. Not only the Noble Eightfold Path but the whole of the Buddha's teaching is concerned to insist that the ethical quality of human intent and motives, thoughts, and attitudes is as important personally and cosmically as external words and deeds. Indeed, the range of the teaching makes clear that the Buddha perceived the inner dimension to be primarily significant and determinative. In one of the texts, the Buddha is recorded as saying that in rootage karma is volition, "when one has willed, one does a deed (karma) by body, speech, or thought" (Anguttara-Nikāya III, 415).

In an account of his early struggle with Māra, the evil one, Gautama is described as already perceiving that strong mental watchfulness and concentration are more effective in the human situation than the Vedic ideal of a pious life characterized by the faithful observance of ritual sacrifices that Māra urged.[99] A classic Buddhist expression of the primary importance of human interiority in the functioning of the karmic process is that of the opening verses of the Dhammapada:

> All that we are is the result of what we have thought: it is founded on our thoughts, it is made up of our thoughts. If a man speaks or acts with an evil thought, pain follows him, as the wheel follows the foot of the ox that draws the carriage ... If a man speaks or acts with a pure thought, happiness follows him, like a shadow that never leaves him.[100]

The ideal, however, is not self-centered mental self-control. Negatively understood, proper control of thought for the Buddha consisted of overcoming the mental defilements of craving, ill will, and delusion. But positively considered, right thought meant the consistent practice of benevolence *(mettā)* toward all sentient beings, active concern for their welfare, and a tranquillity of mind that is at the same time characterized by mental alertness and energy, the opposite of sloth and torpor. Such thought is also characterized by friendship with the lovely, which is singularly *Dharma*.[101] The mind of such a person is free and empty of self-centeredness, free of clinging to aught in this world as if it had immortal substantiality or ultimate value in itself, free to aspire to that which is truly valuable and eternal and to express its qualities in this world without the distractedness begotten by a multitude of ultimate concerns.

We may classify the eight items of the path under three headings: the first two under the category of wisdom or understanding, the next three under moral conduct, the last three under mental discipline. All parts, however, are suffused with ethical qualities. In one sense, all elements of the path are to be practiced simultaneously. In another sense there is an aspect of progressive development envisaged, for all parts are designed to lead to right concentration *(samādhi)*, which is both liberation *(vimutti)* and experience of *Nirvāṇa*, or integration of self with the Highest. In the process of development both the practice of meditation and work over the wider ranges of the ethico-religious life are seen as interdependently and inextricably intertwined.

A brief word is in order at this point to inquire as to what further "theological" explanation the Buddha gave toward understanding in larger cosmic terms the reasons for the possibilities of human liberation-transformation which he and the early community clearly believed to lie before all human beings.[102] Actually, very little more can be said on this point. The Buddha claimed no "vicariously redemptive" role for himself, although he clearly believed that his teaching was helpful to others. To be sure, from any impartial evaluation, his public ministry of forty-five years would be considered sacrificial in the sense of unselfish service to others.[103] We may note, however, that a vicariously redemptive role came in the later Mahāyāna to be assigned to the Buddha himself, particularly as a singularly exalted cosmic Being able to help all other sentient beings, to Bodhisattvas, somewhat similarly exalted Beings of merciful character and helpful activity, and supremely (in terms of historical significance and influence) to Amitābha (Japanese: Amida), who came to be the supreme figure in the trinitarian faith of the Pure Land schools of Buddhism.[104]

We have also noted that while the Buddha and the early community clearly had a coherent view of the world, as of human psychology, he himself regarded metaphysical speculation as of little moment in the way to liberation-integration. This means that we are not to expect elaborate discourses on whether "grace" is antecedent to human actions or how liberation from past karma is cosmically possible. What is clear is that there is help "from above" available to human beings who sincerely strive to follow on the way, supremely from *Dharma* but also from the *devas* and, in a sense, from fellow human beings.

At the same time, the Buddha apparently taught that a human being should take the initiative on his or her own part to try to change, to turn from doing evil to doing good, to orient his or her whole self toward *Dharma-Nirvāṇa*. "Hatred ceases by doing good . . . good people fashion themselves." We also read in the Dhammapada that "He whose evil deeds are covered by good deeds brightens up this world, like the moon when freed from clouds."[105] This all seems to mean that they who would, can. That is, here is faith that the cosmos is so constituted that help is available to human beings who aspire to deal victoriously with the most radical of human dilemmas, including the accumulated effects of a bad past. The Buddha clearly believed that every human being can make a new start regardless of his or her past. Even though there may be certain consequences from the past which the liberated person may have to cope with, perhaps with some suffering, these no longer have power truly to harm the person. That is, these consequences no longer have the power to cause moral or spiritual disintegration. They are not able effectively to block the building of good *karma*. Such a person is truly liberated, free.[106]

A final word needs to be said with regard to the Buddha's teaching on the self. Even in recent years we meet with views that Buddhism, and the Buddha in particular, deny any significant reality or continuity of individuality to the human self. Such a view, however, is not true of the Buddha nor of the early community, even though some contemporary Buddhists of the Theravāda School do state that the Buddha taught that there is no such thing as the human self or personal entity with continuity.[107] Mahāyāna philosophy, we may note, especially in the tradition of Zen, has often approached the problem from a monistic ontological perspective and has held salvation to lie in perception of the essence of the self as identical with the cosmos, or more particularly with the essence of the cosmos which is perceived both as the Whole and yet religiously transcendent.[108] For example, the Avatamsaka Sūtras (ca. 150-400 C.E.) emphasize the reciprocal relationship and interpenetration of the absolute Buddha-nature and all phenomenal existence. But this penetration-identification of the whole with the part does not rob phenomena of their particular character. Each individual thing or person has its special meaning in the universe.[109] Furthermore, enlightenment with reference to such truth is not to be taken for granted. To know "things as they are" is the consequence only of a profound spiritual-ethical conversion, a basic reorientation of the whole self.[110]

In some ways these Mahāyana views seem to represent a development of the Upanishadic equation of the human self (*ātman*) in its essence with absolute Reality *(Brahman)*. This latter understanding, a development from the *Rig-Veda* concept of *ātman* as wind or breath (cf. the Hebrew *nephesh* and the Greek *pneuma*), then self or essential nature of a thing, posited a metaphysics of an eternal and unchanging "substance" that the true or essential Self of human beings shares with *Brahman*. This Upanishadic view, as we have seen, held the basis of religious salvation to lie in some kind of in-depth, existential perception-experience of this identity, a perception properly—indeed, necessarily—to be achieved in the context of a regimen of ethical striving and meditative prayer. The Buddha, however, evidently taught something other than either of these two positions.

The word *anātman* (Pāli: *anatta*), which appears in the early texts and means "not-self" or "non-self," is, as com-

monly found in early Buddhism, a negative term employed
to teach positive truth. As we have seen, central to the
Buddha's teaching was his intent to help human beings re-
orient their primary life-direction and aspiration from that
which is ephemeral and ultimately undependable to that
which is eternal and changeless, the Good, the truly dependable. For him this latter was not any part of phenomenal existence, physical or mental or spiritual, nor was it the
human self. He never identified the self in any form, not
even as consciousness, with *Nirvāṇa*.[111] But the true Self,
the self-at-one *(ekatta),* the self transformed, is a part of the
larger goal of human beings.

   We can better understand the meaning of the term
anātman if we note its use in connection with the early Buddhist analysis of human existence as consisting of five aggregates or elements *(skandhas)* of existence. These are the
material qualities *(rūpa,* material form, or the physical
body) and four nonmaterial aspects: feeling, perception,
habitual tendencies (also translated as predispositions),
and consciousness. The Buddhist affirmation is that all five
aggregates are conditioned, impermanent, not the self.
They are characterized by impermanence *(anicca),* suffering *(duḥkha),* and lack of substantive reality *(anātman).* Indeed, one element of the Buddha's understanding of
religious salvation was liberation from the domination or
the "calming" of the tendencies or predispositions of character with which persons come into this world and which
they "naturally" continue to develop.[112]

   Clearly the term *ātman* continued to be generally used
in India in the Buddha's time in the sense of the human self,
at least in its essence, as identical in some sense with Ultimate Reality and, therefore, as being in itself eternal "substance." The Buddha's intent was to direct persons to what
is truly eternal and changeless—and, therefore, ultimately
dependable—and, because of his perception of the nature

of the human empirical self, he insisted that no element of the human self, physical, mental, or psychic, can be identified with eternal "substance" in this ultimate sense. It is not the proper religious goal of human beings.

There appear to be three distinct meanings assigned to the term *self (ātman)* in the early texts. These are the selfish or self-centered self, the self that is the responsible agent of action, and the higher Self. The first is part of the samsaric process and hence subject to birth, aging, decay, dying, sorrow, and stain. An important element of liberation is to be "void of self and what pertains to self." This teaching means, of course, to be void of self in the first sense,[113] but we find the texts giving us other intimations with reference to the meaning of the second and third modes of self.

The self as responsible agent of action is urged to take the initiative to "look after self." This is the self that reflects on self, that measures self against self, the self that is to take action to be purified, freed, awakened. There are many references to the self-awakened ones.[114] The worthy person is "poised-of-self."[115] The self is responsible for taking the path to utter cool; the self-resolute monk purges the self. For his or her self ill is quenched.[116]

We note references to the self as self-blaming agent. Also the awakened person, "poised amid the restless," is neither soiled by the world nor blamed by self.[117]

We clearly have to do in these texts with an understanding of the human self as in process of transformation, a process in which the self as conscious and responsible agent has a specific role to play, but is not in itself the goal nor is in itself constitutive of Ultimate Reality. The goal, which is the "wisdom of the still," is the self-at-one, the self integrated, not attached to nor distracted by the "many," finding itself in the "One." In this context the Buddha could speak of the "calm of the self within" and of the self as an island, a refuge. Persons of such experience have uprooted the false view of self, which means that they regard the self-in-isolation and all phenomenal existence as void of substantive or Ultimate Reality; thus, they are victors over death. In the person-of-calm there exists neither self *(attam)* nor non-self *(nirattam)*.[118] This is to say that the human self in its true condition is not describable by the language normally used to describe the empirical human self, but it is by no means to be denied. Actually the self in the true sense and what belongs to it "although actually existing are incomprehensible."[119]

In a discussion with the ascetic Vacchagotta the Buddha is recorded as refusing to affirm whether the Tathāgata, a term which in the later part of his life he evidently preferred above others to designate himself,[120] "is" or "is not" after death. This would be to enter into unprofitable speculation. But the Tathāgata, when "freed from denotation by material shape," is "deep, immeasurable, unfathomable as is the great ocean." Such a person is no longer in process of being; he has become.[121] In this context we may recall the suggestive observation of Reinhold Niebuhr that "The self in its freedom is too great to be contained with the self in its contingent existence."[122]

The use, we should note, for the Tathāgata—after physical death—of the phrase "unfathomable as is the great ocean" is not to be understood in the sense of the concluding verse of Sir Edwin Arnold's famous poem *The Light of Asia*, "The dewdrop slips into the shining sea."[123] That is, the Buddha's perception of the state of the integrated self, the self-at-one, after physical death is by no means that of the loss of all individuality in the "undifferentiated unity of the Absolute." Such may be the conclusion to be inferred from certain forms of Hindu Vedānta philosophy, but it is inappropriate for the Buddha's teaching. We have an account of a significant conversation between a monk named Yamaka and Sāriputra, one of the leading disciples of the Buddha. Yamaka had imputed to the Buddha the doctrine that the

Arhant (one who has attained, correlate to Tathāgata) upon death "is broken up and perishes . . . becomes not." Sāriputra forthrightly termed such a notion an "evil heresy." He went on to say that while none of the elements of existence is permanent, including the human body, the self is not to be identified with the body. Yet it is. The texts speak indeed of "evolving consciousness," as also of going beyond the sphere of infinite consciousness—whatever that may mean!—but still "knowing."[124]

We find in the early texts not only repeated statements that terminology primarily used to describe transitory phenomena is not adequate to denote the nature of a Tathāgata's "life" after physical death. We also find, particularly in parabolic or metaphorical speech referring to punishment of evil, references that clearly imply belief in a continuity of the responsible agent—self in the context of reincarnations both in this world and in other realms. One account tells of a man who had lived an immoral life and was reborn in the realm of waste and woe. Brought before Yama, the lord of death, he is told by Yama that his evil deeds were not done by relatives, friends, or any others. "By yourself alone was it done. It is just you that will experience the fruit thereof."[125]

> But what he doth, by act or word or thought:
> That is the thing he owns; that takes he hence;
> That dogs his steps like shadow in pursuit.[126]

This is all to say that the Buddha saw human beings-in-process in terms not of static being but of activity in awareness of self and others, all charged with value. He preferred to think of human beings more as moral, religious beings rather than in terms of their ultimate nature or reality. But any notion of the annihilation of human existence after death was specifically a Buddhist heresy. Raimundo Panikkar has used the term "dynamic points" to denote "selves" in this early Buddhist anthropology; such are the "subjects of intelligibility" on the plane of human history. What may be beyond this plane and the entire samsaric process is envisaged in the texts as even more wondrous.[127]

This line of thought naturally leads us finally to consideration of the issue of personalism, whether the Buddha thought of *Dharma* or *Nirvāṇa* in personalist terms, comparable to the ascription of personal aspects to the Deity in the Judeo-Christian tradition. The Buddha would probably have answered such a question with the answer that "it goes too far"; that is, the question is more of the speculative order than that which is pragmatically helpful to human beings caught in the bondage of their selfish selves. Indeed, there are not a few Christian theologians of the present day who prefer to speak of personal elements in God as transpersonal rather than to delimit him by overly tight associations with human experiences of the personal.[128]

There are, however, important qualifications to be made to the widespread notion that the personalist dimension is utterly lacking in the Buddha's perception of the Ultimate *(Dharma-Nirvāṇa)*. I have already laid considerable emphasis upon the significance for the inner life as well as for the teaching of the Buddha of friendship or intimacy with *Dharma* as the "lovely." Obviously a sustained as well as intimate relationship was meant, one that could at least be called "quasi-personal." We note the use of the expression "come and see" *(ehipassikam)* for *Nirvāṇa* as something to be seen for oneself, presumably as manifested in persons, particularly in the Buddha himself, a reality beyond time but leading persons onward.[129] The coolness of *Nirvāṇa* was not expected to make life cold or lonely. Furthermore, as we have seen, the Buddha taught and practiced concern and responsible interpersonal relationships among human beings. In fact, such conduct was an integral, a necessary part of the life of "Dharma-persons." The Buddha seems to have aimed not at the annihilation, but at the transformation of the personal. Indeed, as Lama Govinda has put it, "it is just the anatta-idea which guarantees the possibility of development and growth of the individual."

We may say in sum that the Buddha perceived the transformed self as in relationship, supremely with *Dharma-in-Nirvāṇa*, secondarily with all else in the cosmos—in benevolent cooperation, without fixed boundaries. Differently from some thinkers in the later Mahāyāna tradition, he refused to discuss in ontological terms this relationship, this connectedness, with all else in the cosmos. Perhaps he could agree with the anthropology of Raimundo Panikkar, who writes in this context of the human person as "that knot in a network of relationships woven ad infinitum." And yet, the Buddha perceived the liberated person—who continues to be involved in such a network—as truly free.[130]

The German Roman Catholic scholar Paul Hossfeld, to whom we have made reference earlier (endnote 52), stresses that for himself the essence of authentic religion consists of a relationship involving movement from the human being to the most High and Holy and from the latter to the human being. With reference to the second aspect of the relationship, Hossfeld holds that it properly exists only when there is a prior self-opening and active acceptance on the part of the most High and Holy. He concludes that such a taking of initiative toward human beings is never ascribed by the Buddha in any of the early texts to either *Dharma* or *Nirvāṇa*.[131]

Hossfeld is probably right. Language precisely akin to Francis Thompson's *Hound of Heaven* is not to be found in the early texts as descriptive of the activity of *Dharma* or *Nirvāṇa*.[132] But as I have suggested above, the Buddha comes close to such language. And if my readers will peruse with care the pages in Karl Ludwig Reichelt referred to in endnote 104, they will find weighty evidence of develop-

ments within Mahāyāna Buddhism precisely in this direction of an actively gracious, initiative-taking, self-sacrificial
activity on the part of the Ultimate, however the latter be
termed. Some may feel that this development has been a
deviation from the original complex of faith-understanding of the Buddha himself. It is at least equally possible to
say that the Mahayanists understood the Buddha's essential intent very well and only strove to express it with new
creativity of thought and language. I am inclined to agree
with the latter view.[133]

What, then, as Christians or as Jews or as Muslims, should
we make of all this? We shall attempt a fuller answer in the
next chapters. At this point, however, let us content ourselves with notable—even if they require some qualifications from our present perspectives—words from the
distinguished German Roman Catholic theologian of the
past generation, Romano Guardini:

> There is only one whom we might be inclined to
> compare with Jesus: Buddha. This man is a great mys-
> tery. He lived in an aweful, almost superhuman free-
> dom. Yet his kindness was powerful as a cosmic force.
> Perhaps Buddha will be the last religious genius to be
> explained by Christianity. As yet no one has really un-
> covered his Christian significance. Perhaps Christ had
> not only one precursor, John, last of the prophets, but
> three: John the Baptist for the Chosen People, Socrates
> from the heart of antiquity, and Buddha, who spoke
> the ultimate word in Eastern religious cognition.[134]

PART

Jesus
the
Christ

1

The Background of Jesus

1

A few preliminary words are in order, as in the case of the Buddha, with reference to the authenticity and reliability of source materials available on the life and teachings of Jesus of Nazareth. He is the one who came to be called the Christ, the Messiah or Anointed Agent of God, a name and role of historic Jewish expectation. Since the beginning of modern historical-critical studies of the Jewish-Christian Scriptures in the late eighteenth century, the four gospels of the New Testament have been considered the source materials most worthy of consideration both for their substantive content and general reliability.[1] These documents, however, are not precisely biographies in the modern sense of the word. They are rather testimonies of faith, profoundly affected by the personal faith and understanding of the authors themselves and of the communities of faith to which they belonged and which they in considerable part represented. The authors certainly wished to know the truth and to tell it, truth of historical fact as of the surmises of faith (cf. Lk. 1:1-4). Yet the literary genre is closer to that of the Greek moralist-historian Plutarch (ca. 46-120 C.E.), author of the famous *Lives of Noble Greeks and Romans*, than of modern critical biography. This may be said even though the authors of the four gospels were far closer to their data in both time and place than was Plutarch to his. In short, the gospel writers were interpretive historians, writing from faith to faith. Hence almost no contemporary biblical scholar would presume to write a biography of Jesus on the basis of these gospels. And there are really no other substantive materials available.

Yet we are able, I believe, as in the case of the Buddha, to discern relatively clear lines indicative of the person, the activity, and the teachings of Jesus of Nazareth. Some scholars would dispute this statement. A majority, I am convinced, would tend to agree. Let us consider possible evidence for this assertion and discuss the larger context.

Leaving aside for the present questions of interpretation, we may say that our current text derived from the original Greek New Testament, and that of the four gospels in particular, as accepted and published by the United Bible Societies of North America and Europe, is remarkably accurate. If we may calculate the death of Jesus to have occurred in 30 C.E.—assuming his birth in 4 B.C.E., shortly before the death of Herod the Great—the public appearance of the four gospels is generally seen as occurring between the years 65-95 C.E. The Gospel of Mark, commonly held to be the earliest of the four, has also been assigned, as a minority opinion, a date as early as the later fifties or early sixties of the first century of our era.[2] The Gospel of John, by a wide consensus, is considered the latest, at least in its final form, appearing thus in the last decade of the first century. Matthew and Luke are generally seen as products of the preceding decade, the eighties of the same first century.

There are basically three kinds of source materials from which we are able to obtain our text of the Greek New Testament. The first is manuscripts in the Greek language, all of which are copies of early or later date; we have extant no original autographs. In all, there are about 5,000 Greek language manuscripts that contain the whole or parts of the New Testament, an almost intimidating plethora of materials.

The second kind of materials available to us is the extant translations from the Greek into ancient languages made mostly by Christian missionaries. The earliest extant translations into Syriac, Latin, and Coptic are highly regarded because of their origin in the second and third centuries of our era. Next in importance are translations into the Gothic, Armenian, Georgian, and Ethiopian languages in the fourth and fifth centuries.

The third class of materials of particular significance in obtaining the best possible text of the Greek New Testament is the large number of quotations made by early Christian writers, often called church Fathers. It has been said that it would be possible to reconstruct almost the whole of the New Testament text from these source materials alone, so extensive are the quotations from the Scriptures, both the Old and New Testaments, made by the church Fathers.[3]

This plethora of extant materials shows, as is to be expected in the process of human transmission, a large number of variant readings in the text, as well as displacement of individual words, phrases, or sentences. It is necessary, however, for us to see these variations in context, that is, their relative importance with reference to the goal of obtaining a text with a high degree of reliability. As the pioneer

British textual scholars, Brooke Foss Westcott and Fenton John Anthony Hort, put it in the introduction to their edition of the Greek text of the New Testament published in 1881, the various drawbacks in the texts available "do not materially impede the arrival at secure conclusions about the history of the text at large." In fact Westcott and Hort go on to say that "if comparative trivialities, such as changes of [word] order, the insertion or omission of the article with proper names and the like, are set aside, the words in our opinion still subject to doubt can hardly amount to more than a thousandth part of the whole New Testament." In comparison with the transmission of manuscripts of ancient Greek and Latin classical authors, the text of the New Testament, as a result of "the variety and fullness of the evidence" that has led to this high degree of certainty, "stands absolutely and unapproachably alone among ancient prose writings."[4]

2

Interpretations of the text, however, do not admit of the same high degree of certainty as claimed above for the text itself. This is a statement, some would aver, far too gently put, given the wide variety of interpretations of the Bible that have emerged over the centuries of Jewish and Christian history. Since the beginnings of modern historical-literary criticism of the Bible in the late eighteenth century, interpretations in particular have often greatly differed as to whether statements attributed to Jesus in the text of the four gospels were actually made by him, even with some variations arising from the process of transmission, or were the product of the early church. The activity of the church in this regard has been seen to arise out of its needs to formulate and express its faith, or somewhat differing forms of faith, in the various times and places of its expansion and development. Among academically trained scholars using the methodologies of historical-literary criticism, there is actually a very wide divergence of opinion in this area. The German biblical scholar Rudolf Bultmann, for instance, concluded that we cannot be truly certain about a single word or teaching of Jesus found in the New Testament, only the fact that he was an historical person.[5] Bultmann's somewhat later contemporary in Germany, Joachim Jeremias, contended, on the other hand, for a more positive appreciation of the reliability of the New Testament gospels. He long sought, especially through the parables of Jesus, to determine the *ipsissima verba,* the "very words," of Jesus, even in some cases to the point of discerning the Aramaic original used by Jesus.[6]

This is not the place for a detailed discussion of the problem of the historical Jesus nor of the variations in interpretation of New Testament scholarship regarding the historical reliability of the individual sayings of Jesus recorded in the four gospels. I say four because I do not exclude the Gospel of John from the list of those documents that may be used, albeit with careful discrimination, as materials for historical study. I shall give my own opinion on particular sayings or passages in the course of this chapter. As to the reliability of the witness of the New Testament gospels as a whole, I should like to offer as essentially also my own view the position taken by the Norwegian biblical scholar Nils Astrup Dahl in an article that appeared first in Norwegian in 1953.

Dahl contends that even though the gospels of the New Testament are not documentary reports and the writers all wrote from positions of faith, yet even as we fully recognize this situation, "we will the more easily be amazed at how much we still know of Jesus historically. A great part of the tradition consists of brief, pregnant expressions and characteristic episodes which are easily committed to memory. Very early, the tradition must have taken on a relatively fixed form and, of course, in a milieu where it was customary to preserve recollections with great faithfulness." Dahl goes on to conclude that "although we are still far removed from the [modernly] desired degree of exactitude, we may still construct quite a clear picture of Jesus' appearance [historical manifestation] as well as of the content of his proclamation and his teaching, and of the impression which he made on the adherents and opponents among his contemporaries."[7]

When the use of these gospel materials is combined with responsible "religious understanding," as I put it in consideration of the materials available on the life and teaching of the Buddha, we have, I strongly contend, source materials for the life and teaching of Jesus the Christ that can be called "good," even as this term may be understood in academic context.

3

With reference to the facticity of Jesus of Nazareth as an historical person, there are, apart from the documents of the New Testament and other so-called extracanonical works of Christian composition, some, even if few, references to his person and activity in ancient sources. The Roman historian P. Cornelius Tacitus, writing in the second decade of the second century (his *Annals* was published sometime between 115 and 117 C.E.), is one such source. Tacitus's historical account of the reign of the emperor Nero tells of the persecution of Christians in Rome in 64 C.E. Nero himself had been popularly accused of starting a fire that destroyed a large part of the city of Rome, especially much of the poorer sections. Nero tried to lay the blame on the small religious sect of Christians who were by this time coming to be distinguished from Jews and were convicted, according to Tacitus, more for their "hatred of the human race" than for arson. Tacitus explains the name Christian as originating "from Christus, who had been sentenced to death by the procurator Pontius Pilate during the reign of Tiberius" (Annals XV, 44).

A less valuable reference is found in the early second-century life of the emperor Claudius written by the Roman biographer of the Caesars (Roman emperors) Suetonius Tranquillus (ca. 69-150 C.E.). The passage speaks of Claudius's action in expelling Jews from Rome, evidently the event mentioned in the Acts of the Apostles 18:2 in connection with the husband-and-wife team of Aquila and Priscilla, Jewish-Christian friends and co-workers of the apostle Paul. Suetonius writes, mistakenly, of Jews frequently creating disturbances "at the instigation of Chrestus *(sic)*." Since this event of expulsion—Suetonius uses the Latin verb *expulit*—occurred probably in 49 C.E., the author seems to have assumed that this Chrestus—there is no evidence of anyone other than Jesus Christ to whom Suetonius could have referred—was still alive at that time. The Roman biographer evidently also assumed that this same Chrestus was personally responsible for what may have been semipublic disturbances arising out of religious disputes between Jews and Christians in and near the city of Rome.[8]

The Jewish historian Flavius Josephus (37-ca. 100 C.E.), who wrote extensively in Greek about Jewish history, religion, and customs while resident in Rome in the latter part of his life, has only a single brief reference to Jesus that is probably authentic. Josephus had been given Roman citizenship for his services to the empire during the final Roman siege of Jerusalem in the Jewish War and indeed was officially commissioned by the emperor Titus to write a history of the Jewish people. His active support of Rome naturally led to his experiencing strong and abiding antipathy from fellow Jews. His posture as a writer, however, was that of an apologist and supporter of the Jewish faith and people. In his *Antiquities of the Jews* (XX, 9,1) his brief reference to

Jesus is in connection with his account of the condemna-
tion and execution of James, "the brother of Jesus, who was
called Christ." James's death evidently occurred during the
latter period of the reign of the emperor Nero (54-68 C.E.).

The most extensive and weighty evidence in classical literature, however, for both the person of Jesus and the early
Christian movement is found in a letter of Pliny the younger,
nephew of the Roman natural historian C. Plinius Secundus
and then governor of the province of Asia Minor. This letter
was addressed to the emperor Trajan and can be dated 110
C.E. Pliny writes to the emperor to ascertain proper procedures to follow regarding legal prosecution of Christians,
who were evidently liable to criminal charges throughout
the empire for the mere profession of "the name."[9] Trajan's
reply was judicious: Christians are not to be singled out
(Conquirendi non sunt). If accusations are brought by others against persons and they are found guilty, they are to be
punished. If any recant, they are to be pardoned, and no
one is to be charged on the basis of anonymous accusation.

In Pliny's letter itself we find mention of the fact that it
was customary for Christians to meet on a fixed day before
it was light. There "they sang in alternate verses [anti-
phonally] a hymn to Christ as to a god." Pliny further writes,
on the basis of reports from Christians who had recanted,
that they "had bound themselves by a solemn oath" [evi-
dently at baptism] not, Pliny assures the emperor, to commit some crime [as hostile rumors might suggest], but
rather to refrain utterly from theft or robbery, never to commit adultery nor violate their word or fail to return anything
entrusted to them. Pliny reports further that the Christians
then separated, to return later to eat together "food of an
ordinary and harmless kind" [again, Pliny implies, their
conduct gives no evidence to confirm popular rumors of
evil deeds]. Significant also is Pliny's statement that his appeal to the emperor comes from the large number of per-

sons involved, including "persons of all ranks and ages, and of both sexes." What the Roman governor calls a contagious superstition had already spread, he finds, through villages and into the countryside, even to the extent that ancient temples were deserted.[10] Pliny's letter reveals an incontestable background of historical events and at least implies the historical reality of the Christ of this worship as something beyond the mythical figure of a mystery religion.

4

A final preliminary observation should be made, I believe, regarding what we may call the spirituality of Jesus, that is, the nature and scope of his religious faith and practice, including his "worldview." We shall, of course, consider this theme in greater detail later in this and the following chapter, but for now it would seem helpful to attempt an outline of the principles involved, as we may discern them. Once again, we may properly begin by briefly recalling what has been said on this theme about Siddhārtha Gautama.

We noted that basic to the public life and teaching of the Buddha was his religious experience commonly denoted as the Enlightenment. And central to that experience, going beyond perception of human psychology or related cosmic processes, was a new mode of relationship with "the Highest" of cosmic reality, *Nirvāna* with its focus in *Dharma*, the force that makes for right doing and being in human life. Furthermore, as we have seen, subsequent to the Buddha's primary experience there emerged the practice, evidently adhered to quite unfailingly over the forty-five years of his public ministry, of morning meditation of perhaps some hours' duration. This meditation clearly involved more than intellective reflection. Its deepest and most fruitful aspect, as the texts show, was friendship or intimacy with *Dharma* experienced as "the Lovely." Some aspects of this relationship may have involved interior "verbal communication," much of it may not. Raimundo Panikkar is surely correct in suggesting commonalities between the Buddha's devotional practices and the apophatic tradition of Eastern Orthodox Christianity. Indeed, Panikkar sees these commonalities as going beyond the practice of prayer in silence into a sharing of ontological perceptions.[11]

In the context, however, of comparison with Jesus the Christ, I should like at this point to discuss somewhat more fully the larger cosmic realities presumed to lie behind the practice of meditation and prayer in the case of both the Buddha and the Christ. One of the great contributions, in my judgment, made by the distinguished German-British Buddhologist Edward Conze over the past generation and more to the whole field of Buddhist studies has been his continuing insistence that both the Buddha and subsequent Buddhism throughout its history in many lands presume the existence of what we may call at this point a spiritual world. He specifically emphasizes that in early Buddhism "the help of unseen beings had always been taken for granted." Indeed, Conze insists that such is the assumption of nearly all East Indian thought and religious practice. What he calls the experiences of yoga are the chief raw material for both the practice of the religious life and religio-philosophical reflection thereon.[12] He sees the practices of yogic meditation as "the avenues to the most worthwhile knowledge of true reality, as well as a basis for the most praiseworthy conduct." Indeed the yogic vision is "the source of ultimate certainty."

Conze in particular would have us know that these yogic practices are not solely activities of the human mental-psychological complex, although they, of course, may include such. They are aimed at relationship with higher levels of reality, and basic is the faith-assumption that such levels have their own dynamism of activity and self-communication. Hence Conze does not hesitate to affirm that in this worldview "revelation" is the ultimate source of all knowledge. From the perspective of human experience, however, we may also say that "mystical intuition, trance, and the power of transcendental wisdom . . . disclose the structure of the spiritual and intermediary worlds." A basic and integral element of this worldview, Conze affirms—one that presumes various levels of reality in the cosmos—is the conviction that "contact with the higher degrees of reality entails a life which is qualitatively superior to one based on contact with the lower degrees." We have seen that such conviction is one way of describing the nature of the Buddha's primary contribution to the life of India and of the world. For Conze—his perception is singularly appropriate to the life and teaching of the Buddha—the phrase "qualitatively superior" necessarily involves ethical dimensions, as well as being a lifestyle that is "more solid and reliable, more intellectually satisfying . . . much more worthwhile." "For the decisive factor in every event is a 'moral one.' "[13]

Some of this language may seem vague or ambivalent with reference to what has traditionally been called "personal relationship" in Western culture. But clearly a vital, profoundly meaningful relationship of some kind appears to be presumed in almost all cases, in the whole of East Indian and indeed in the whole of Asian religious history. I contend also that perception and affirmation of the superlative significance of relationship with higher levels of reality in the cosmos are characteristic of the Hebraic religious experience, even though at times appreciable differences from Indian or East Asian views may exist in perceptions of the ontologies alleged. I recall that many years ago one of my revered seminary professors, the notable Old Testament scholar Herbert G. Alleman, said in one of his lectures that basic to the worldviews of the whole of the Judeo-Christian Scriptures are two assumptions. These are the fact of God

and the possibility of revelation, seen as the self-communication of God. To be sure, perceptions of the nature of God,
as of the content of divine revelation, show not a little variation, many would say development, in the history of Israel.
However, in that history which is specifically the historical
background of the person and life of Jesus of Nazareth, there
is essentially no variation in the continuity of these two assumptions.

At this point I should like to refer to a recent "life of Jesus"
written by the American biblical scholar Marcus J. Borg and
entitled *Jesus, a New Vision.* I shall later offer one or two critical comments on aspects of his interpretation, but I wish to
say here that I consider the book one of the finest in its genre
that I have read. It is rich in perceptive and balanced insight, replete with a wealth of academic scholarship, as well
organized as it is lucidly written. What Edward Conze has
done for Buddhist studies in his generation, Marcus Borg
has also done, I believe, for biblical studies in his own. I refer to Borg's unusually strong—unusual in the context of the
use of historical-critical methodologies—insistence upon
the need for academic as well as personal concern for the
reality of what he calls "the world of Spirit" in consideration
of the significance of Jesus of Nazareth. Indeed, the entire
first section of his book, consisting of three chapters, is entitled "Jesus and the Spirit."[14]

Borg emphasizes that "the notion of another reality, a
world of Spirit, was the common property of virtually every
culture before ours, constituting what has been called the
'primordial tradition.'"[15] I personally agree with this perception of the historical interiority of the human race. I would
gently disagree, however, with Borg's statement that this
notion of "another world" is quite alien to the modern way
of thinking. It may be alien to our modern way of talking. I
recall hearing in a television program William F. Buckley's
wry comment that in New York City if anyone should men-

tion the word God twice at a dinner party, it is tantamount to insuring that one would not be invited again! But just as modern persons—that is, in industrial societies since the end of the eighteenth century—have hesitated to speak in public society of their dreams and yet often take them quite seriously in more private ways, so, I would contend, awareness or at least the surmise of "another world" is by no means absent in our midst. I would also include in this "midst" well-educated persons who may participate little in the activities of organized religion in either East or West.

Borg, however, I believe to be quite correct in his insistence that basic to the worldview of the Bible, as of most subsequent Jewish and Christian history, is assumption of the existence of another world of "nonmaterial reality, charged with energy and power." This is a world that, at least in some measure, can be known and with which relationship helpful to human beings on earth may be had. Indeed, such relationship may be said to be proper to what it means to be truly human. We may add, however, that in biblical context the distinction between "this world" and "that" is more useful than ultimate. The Bible begins with its account of the creation of "this world" by the prime figure of "that world," the Yahweh who later gave his name to Israel (Gen. 1:1-31; Ex. 3:13-14).

For the people of Israel, however, as for believers in the New Testament period, the unseen world, while dominated by the Most High, was perceived as richly peopled. Monotheism—henotheism may be the proper term to denote the faith of Israel in early periods—did not, does not, mean for Judaism, for Christianity, or for Islam that only God is alive in the supersensible realms. Quite to the contrary, basic to the tradition from earliest times has been awareness of the existence of angels and archangels, of cherubim and seraphim. And for most of Israel those who "had gone to their ancestors" were held to be alive in some sense. As in the case of historic Buddhism, annihilation is not the proper term.

Furthermore, awareness that seems to have increased with some sharpness in later pre-Christian centuries, stimulated at least in part as a result of Iranian (Zoroastrian) influences, awareness of the reality and activity of spiritual forces not altogether benign, indeed even evil, came to be a meaningful part of the faith of Israel, as of Jesus and the early Christian church. If we may describe the worldview of the Judeo-Christian Scriptures with the imagery of a pyramid, the place of God (Yahweh, Elohim of the Old Testament, *the* God of the New) is, of course, at the apex of the pyramid. This is the highest "Point," the Point that is also the center of every circle, the Source and Sustainer of all that is. Human life and history are properly seen as functioning on the bottom line of the pyramid, with angels, archangels, etc., in the spaces above. Just "above" the plane of human history is the "place" of the reality or realities that the writer of the Letter to the Ephesians describes as "the ruler of the power of the air, the spirit that is now at work among those who are disobedient" (Eph. 2:2). This is the figure whose effects extend into and "below" the plane of human history.[16]

It is not always adequately recognized how powerful were the role and influence assigned to these forces by New Testament writers. They see these forces at work in such wise in spite of their strong convictions about the providence of God in human history, about the victory over sin and evil wrought through Jesus Christ, and the expected total victory of God the Father over all opposing forces (I Cor. 15:28). We shall note later the many references in the New Testament gospels to unclean spirits or demons.[17] In the apostolic writings of the New Testament we find surprisingly strong statements about the power of evil forces in human life. Both the Pauline and Johannine literature make this point with language as graphic as it is strong. The apostle

Paul speaks of the "god of this world (*aeon*)" as the one responsible for blinding the eyes of unbelievers (II Cor. 4:4). The present age (*aeon*) is evil, from whose power the work of the Lord Jesus Christ is intended to set us free (Gal. 1:4). In the Letter to the Ephesians, which contains much Pauline material even if it is not the direct product of Paul's dictation, we find that the present struggle of believers is "not against enemies of blood and flesh, but against the rulers, against the authorities, against the cosmic powers of this present darkness, against the spiritual forces of evil in the heavenly places" (Eph. 6:12). With similar concern the author of the First Letter of Peter urges Christians in Asia Minor to discipline themselves and keep alert because "Like a roaring lion your adversary the devil prowls around, looking for someone to devour" (I Pet. 5:8).

Something of the tension, both existential and in faith-understanding, between experience of the power of God in Christ in liberating persons from the bondage of these forces and again experience of their continuing malevolence and effectiveness is suggested in Paul's warning to Corinthian Christians against spiritual presumption, "if you think you are standing, watch out that you do not fall" (I Cor. 10:12). As we shall discuss in more detail later, Paul at once goes on to set this perilous situation within the structured context of God's providence with its promise of both possibility and power. But from the Pauline perspective, the possibility of spiritual and moral failure continues to be real, even for liberated Christians, who are after all still in process of being transformed in their character and lifestyle (cf. Rom. 8:24; I Cor. 1:18; 3:18; II Cor. 5:17).

If we may round out a bit more fully the New Testament perceptions of this situation, there is also very strong language to be found in Johannine literature. In the First Letter of John we note that the author follows his assertion that those "born of God" are protected by "the one who was born

of God [the risen Christ]" with the statement that "the whole
world lies under the power of the evil one" (I Jn. 5:18-19).
This typically Johannine depiction of human life, and indeed the whole cosmos, as a battleground between two
realms—between light and darkness, between faith and
unbelief, between love and hate—emerges again in the
book of Revelation. Here the writer begins his admonitions
to the Christians in the "typical" Asia Minor city of Perga-
mum with the statement that they are persons living "where
Satan's throne is" (Rev. 2:12-13).[18]

The final point to be considered in this preliminary section, one, however, by no means unimportant in the larger
context of our concerns, follows the above in an order of
transition that is perhaps logical in thought but fraught with
difficulty for our understanding. This is what we discussed
in the previous chapter under the rubric of *karma*, or linkage of action, and identified as morphologically akin to the
biblical teaching of cosmic compensation, a process described by the apostle Paul with the imagery of sowing and
reaping, by Jesus himself with the imagery of quantitative
measurement (Gal. 6:7-9; Mt. 7:1-2—the Marcan parallel
suggests that human arithmetic is not necessarily the divine standard of calculation, Mk. 4:24; cf. Lk. 6:37-38). This
process was seen as one of cause and effect, operative in
human life, both individual and corporate, particularly with
reference to the moral quality of action whether internal or
external. That is, the ethical quality of human action, in both
its mental and physical aspects, was perceived as bearing
fruit, producing consequences, in human character as well
as in more external modes of manifestation, all in accordance with a cosmic principle of causal connectedness.

Perception of this cosmic principle-process, I would affirm at this point, plays as large a role in the worldview—
and in the teaching—of Jesus as of Gautama. It is also the
explicit or implicit assumption of the whole stream of pro-

phetic witness and wisdom teaching in the history of Israel of which Jesus, we may say, was the culmination. For both the Buddha and the Christ the functioning of this cosmic process—however views might differ as to the mode or degree of "personal administration" of the process—constituted the background, the operative principle, governing the individual and corporate living of all humanity. Indeed, as we have seen, in the Buddhist tradition this principle has been perceived historically as extending to all sentient beings in the cosmos in ways considerably beyond that common in the Judeo-Christian faith-understanding (but cf. Rom. 8:18-25).

The primary import of the ministry and teaching of both the Buddha and the Christ, as of the long line of Hebrew prophets and wisdom teachers who preceded Jesus, was to proclaim the possibility of the liberation of human beings suffering in bondage to the effects of the karmic process, even though their bondage could be primarily "their own fault," the consequence of their own doing-being. The time span of the working of this process, it would seem, was envisaged by the Buddha in longer terms than has generally been depicted in the Judeo-Christian tradition.[19] In both traditions, however, the primary emphasis has been upon the possibility of liberation from the process even as the process is seen to continue to operate for and in those liberated. Liberation is understood as freeing persons from the binding aspects of the process, not as abolishing the process itself or totally eliminating its past effects. In fact, liberated persons are expected precisely to deal with those effects, but perhaps in a new way, certainly with new power. Through their liberation they are put into a new relationship with the process to the end of "using" it for good and constructive purposes, for the good of both themselves and others—in effect, to serve higher purposes than those commonly operative on the earthly plane. How this liberation is perceived as cosmically possible, we have already briefly discussed in the case of the Buddha. We shall discuss later in this chapter what may be the mind and the role of the Christ with reference to the same issue.

In particular, as we shall see, Jesus the Christ, like the Buddha, was a person of the deepest interiority. This included awareness of and modes of communication with the Person(s) of the world of Spirit. His prayer life, as the New Testament records show, was wondrously profound, consistent, and continuing. These same records do not give us an account of Jesus' daily "schedule," perhaps with wise reserve, because there are indications that his "schedule" was flexible. He was open to "interruptions" (e.g., Mk. 1:35-39, etc.). But we find numerous indications that Jesus prayed regularly, at different times of the day and night, with special intensity and extent before decisive events (cf. Mk. 1:35; 6:4, 6; 14:32, 35-39, and parallels—n.b. the seventeenth chapter of John). The four gospels, we may add, have somewhat differing accounts and emphases in their depiction of Jesus' prayer life. All agree in emphasizing the central reality and importance of prayer in his life and ministry. In the Gospel of Luke, however, we find perhaps the most beautiful and appealing reports of this dynamism of Jesus' person. Only in Luke do we find, for instance, explicit mention that before Jesus' selection of the twelve from among his disciples, "he went out to the mountain to pray; and he spent the night in prayer to God. And when they came he called his disciples and chose twelve of them, whom he also named apostles" (Lk. 6:12-13).

2

The Cosmic
Background of the Christ

The schema of Romano Guardini relating the Buddha to the Christ which I quoted, with implicit approval, at the end of the previous section could be interpreted by some as a "put-down" of the religious significance of the person and work of Siddhārtha Gautama, who became the Buddha. Guardini obviously conceived the schema in conformity with John the Baptizer's perception that the one who comes after him "is more powerful than I" (Mk. 1:7). A "put-down," however, was, of course, not intended, but, as I have already indicated, I write this book from within the context of Christian faith, and my own perception of Christian faith leads me to accept such a schema, however simplistic and in need of significant qualifications it may be in the format quoted. Participants in the Buddhist or Muslim traditions or also the Jewish would no doubt create different schemata of relationship, and I feel that I would have no right to object to theirs. If done with proper respect and sensitivity, theirs would surely not be a "put-down" of the Christ, and very possibly we could all be instructed by the sharing of our various schemata.

Actually, the use of schemata can be helpful in expanding and clarifying understanding in other directions. Jesus of Nazareth, like Siddhārtha Gautama, did not, according to his early followers, come into his person and role without a background of wider cosmic significance. We have seen that a part of Siddhārtha's experience of enlightenment involved a perception of former lives or incarnations. Later followers developed this theme through the composition of the *Jātakas*, or stories of the previous lives of the Buddha. Much previous Indian folklore and popular wisdom came to be incorporated in these tales, but a central theme running through the whole is the steadfastness of purpose of the being, who, beginning humbly as the youth Sumedha, persevered through innumerable lives amidst every kind of trial and difficulty until he finally achieved enlightenment as the man Siddhārtha Gautama. The imagery is of lofty consequence achieved as a result of a long process of development-growth from lesser origins.

Among the followers of Jesus we find not totally dissimilar attempts from the early apostolic generation to understand the background of him who became the Christ (cf. Jn. 17:24; Rom. 1:4; Phil. 2:5-11; Heb. 1:2). As is well known, the physical/legal genealogy of Jesus is traced back from his legal father Joseph through the Davidic line to Abraham in the Gospel according to Matthew (1:1-17); Jesus is called the son of David and the son of Abraham (Mt. 1:1). In Luke, presumably in keeping with the culturally and religiously more inclusive mentality of the author, Jesus' genealogy, evidently following a somewhat different tradition, is traced further back, from Abraham to Adam, who is also called son of God by Luke (Lk. 3:23-38). Both genealogies restrict themselves to the plane of human history. There existed, however, a belief among certain Jewish Christians from at least the second century, and quite possibly from an earlier period, in a series of incarnations of Jesus prior to his birth and manifestation as the Christ in Palestine at the beginning of this era, a concept more akin to the Buddhist traditional view. This is the one "who has changed his forms and his names from the beginning of the world, and reappeared again and again in the world, until coming upon his own times, and being anointed with mercy for the works of God, he shall enjoy rest for ever (cf. Heb. 1:9; 4:3). His honour it is to bear lordship over all things, in air, earth, and waters" (cf. I Cor. 15:28; Col. 3:11).[20] The imagery here is like that of the *Jātaka* stories of the Buddha in seeing lofty consequence achieved as the result of a long process of development-growth but different in its perception of origin. For the origin is that of Adam as son of God, who though he fell was enabled to rise again to serve the highest redemptive purposes of the Father (cf. I Cor. 15:45).

These and like perceptions represent varying attempts to understand the Christ event, some more complementary than different, others perhaps different to the extent of being logically irreconcilable. They all, however, are one in perceiving the person and work of Jesus of Nazareth as occurring within a panorama of divine purpose and activity vast in its cosmic range, unified in its goal. The New Testament itself shows a variety of attempts to understand the background of the Christ event, all one in perceiving a vastness of cosmic scope and meaning but some notably different in modes of conception.

Perhaps the most widely shared consensus in the contemporary community of New Testament scholarship is that the New Testament manifests a considerable variety in its expressions of what then constituted Christian faith. Over against this relatively varied and fluid situation, we find attempts from an early period to create a greater measure of unity in faith and practice. Not a little of the work of the apostle Paul was in this direction, although he was usually not of a mind to compromise his own perceptions of the truth (cf. Gal. 1-6; Col. 1-4). Ignatius of Antioch in writing letters to various churches enroute to his martyrdom in Rome (before 117 C.E.) emphasized the emerging concept-practice of the monarchical episcopate as part of his attempt to procure greater Christian unity. Later theologians, beginning apparently with Irenaeus of Lyons and Hippolytus of Rome in the late second century and responding to the considerable variety of Christian views in their own time, formulated and propagated a particular schema of interpretation which came to have wide currency in later centuries. This was the view that the disciples of Jesus, supremely the twelve apostles, grasped in its entirety the essence of the gospel, with concomitant liturgical and ethical practices, as the original form of the Christian faith and transmitted it without real error or variation from their generation to the next, and then to the following, in a line of "orthodox" bishops and elders (presbyters). This concept came to be identified by the term "apostolic succession" and became, in one form or another, a significant element of the "official" theologies of the Eastern Orthodox Church(es), the Roman Catholic Church, and the Anglican Church(es).

The intensive study, however, of the materials of early Christianity over the past two hundred years and more in the context of emerging "modern" thought and associated methodologies has led to various revisions of this latter picture. For one thing, whether the apostles finally come to understand the gospel in its "entirety" or not, such a fullness or completeness was certainly not communicated as such in the New Testament as we have it. There are various indications in the New Testament itself that not all is being told (e.g., Mk. 4:34; Jn. 20:30; I Cor. 2:6; 3:1-2; cf. Mt. 7:6). Morton Smith, quite apart from his interpretations of larger issues, is probably right in assigning the letter which he found at the Greek Orthodox monastery of Mar Saba in the Judean desert in 1958 to Clement of Alexandria (ca. 150-215). This letter refers to a certain "more spiritual" Secret Gospel of Mark carefully guarded by the church of Alexandria and to the fact of other elements of the tradition than those written down.[21]

We are now in a position to question the long-held assumptions that anything extracanonical that is "similar to the canonical gospels is derivative, and anything not similar, secondary" and probably untrue. We now know that there were varying understandings of Christian faith and practice from the earliest period and that the form/forms which emerged as politically triumphant ("orthodox") in the fourth and fifth centuries are not necessarily the final word on the subject. Operating from within this context of thought, I should like at this point to make a few preliminary observations regarding New Testament understandings of the cosmic background of Jesus of Nazareth and reserve a more finalized evaluation to the latter part of this chapter.

As we have noted, the author of the Gospel of Matthew identifies Jesus as genealogically/legally the descendant of Abraham and of David. He is also the one "who is called the Messiah" (Mt. 1:1, 16). The birth and infancy narratives, however, which he shares, with some differences, with Luke—especially the accounts of Jesus' birth from a virgin—point toward a more than usual background of Jesus' person (cf. Mt. 1:23). In Matthew, as well as in Mark and Luke (less commonly in John), the term which Jesus prefers to

use of himself is "son of man," an appellation which some
scholars understand primarily in the sense of an apocalyp-
tically triumphant figure, but which I am inclined to think
Jesus used primarily to indicate his solidarity with all humankind, as well as to suggest deeper and wider themes (cf.
Ezek. 2:1, 3, 6, 8; 3:1, 3, 4, 10, 16, 25; Ps. 8:4; 80:17; 144:3; Isa.
56:2, etc.).[22] Matthew largely follows Mark in depicting Jesus
as one who during most of his public ministry would hide
from the larger public intimations of an exalted background
and mission (Mt. 8:1-4, etc.; Mk. 1:40-45, etc.); this reticence
of Jesus has been termed the "Messianic Secret," a conscious methodology aptly termed reticence after Jesus' bap-
tismal experience and his temptations in the desert.
Matthew, however, like Mark, thinks of Jesus as son of God
in an exalted sense which yet does not break solidarity with
other human beings (Mt. 3:17; 11:27-28; 16:16-17; 17:5;
22:41-45; cf. Mk. 1:1, etc.). Matthew is concerned to affirm,
for example, that Jesus' forgiveness of a paralytic's sins as an
integral element of that particular healing activity is evidence of God's granting such authority to human beings
generically (Mt. 9:1-8).[23]

The author of the Gospel of Luke is noted for the beauty
of his infancy stories and, with regard to the background of
the "Savior, who is the Messiah, the Lord" (Lk. 2:11), like the
other synoptic writers identifies Jesus as "the Son of the
Most High" (Lk. 1:32, 35; 3:22). But, as we have seen, Luke is
also the gospel writer who calls Adam the son of God (Lk.
3:38).[24] Furthermore, in the Gospel of John, where we find
at once the highest christology and the highest anthropology in the New Testament, there is essentially the same "ontological continuum" as in the synoptic gospels.

The Gospel of John begins its prologue with the most exalted language regarding the background of Jesus "the Messiah, the Son of God" (Jn. 20:31). This is the famous
statement, "In the beginning was the Word, and the Word

was with God, and the Word was God" (Jn. 1:1; cf. 17:24). It would take us too far afield to discuss in detail the various possible meanings and implications of "the Word" *(Logos)*. Suffice it to say that the term *Logos* has a specific history in the Greek language beginning at least with the Greek pre-Socratic philosopher Heraclitus, who used the term in the sense of the integrative principle by means of which the entire cosmos coheres and has order.[25] Like the *Dharma* in the teaching of the Buddha, *Logos* in the Johannine prologue seems to have distinct affinities with the use of the term Wisdom in late pre-Christian Judaism. In John, however, the term is clearly personified with a distinctiveness beyond either of the two instances above. We seem to have to do with a "Being" who was in the beginning, was the agent of creation, was "with God"—the phrase "with" *(pros ton Theon*—Lat.: *apud Deum)* had primarily the relational meanings of either "in the presence of" or "at the home of" in New Testament usage[26]—and yet is not to be totally identified with "the God" *(ton Theon)*. The last phrase "and the Word was God" omits the definite article in the Greek and surely meant primarily an unbroken continuum of relationship with the Father in his very nature as well as activity (cf. Jn. 20:28, 31).[27] The rationale for this conclusion is as follows.

The author of the Gospel of John makes clear in the tenth chapter that Jesus himself, as the author reports him, had what I have called a high anthropology and that he, as the author, had no intent in the prologue to create imagery of an exalted origin and background for the Christ that had no "ontological continuum" with humanity. Here in the tenth chapter we find Jesus in sharp dispute with Jewish (Judean?) opponents. But they are the very ones to whom he quotes Psalm 82:6: "Is it not written in your law, 'I said, you are gods'? If those to whom the word of God came were called 'gods'—and the scripture cannot be annulled—can you say that the one whom the Father has sanctified and sent into the world is blaspheming because I said, 'I am God's son'?" (Jn. 10:34-36; cf. 11:4). It is significant that Martin Luther in writing on John 14:13-14 says of the reconciled that "they will become gods and will be saviors of the world by their supplication" (*"Götter werden und der welt Heilande," Luther's Works* XXIV, p. 87).

Just prior to the above quotation Jesus is cited as, in effect, defining what is the meaning of being "God's son." He says, "the Father and I are one" (Jn. 10:30). We find, however, that "continuum" is probably the proper term to indicate Jesus' meaning here, a continuum of relationship and function as much as, or more than, of ontology. For Jesus did not only pray that the disciples should be one even as he and the Father were one, but also that the disciples may be one in the Father and the Son (Jn. 17:11, 20-23; cf. 15:4-5). The functional aspect of the continuum emerges even more clearly in the application to the disciples of what is actually a basic theme of the Gospel of John, the sending of the Son by the Father. Jesus affirms in his high-priestly prayer, "As you have sent me into the world, so I have sent them into the world" (Jn. 17:18). This continuum of the disciples' mission-function with his own is repeated in the post-resurrection commission statement, "Peace be with you. As the Father has sent me, so I send you" (Jn. 20:21; cf. 4:38).

The author of the Gospel of John makes it clear in various ways that he does not intend by his language to communicate a total identification of Jesus with the Father. For example, we note Jesus himself saying immediately following the accusation that he made himself equal with God, "the Son can do nothing on his own, but only what he sees the Father doing" (Jn. 5:19; cf. "the Father is greater than I," 14:28). Jesus is further cited as saying, "the Father who dwells in me does his works," and he then goes on to indicate the continuum between him and his followers under God with the statement, "the one who believes in me will also do the works that I do and, in fact, will do greater works than these, because I am going to the Father" (14:10, 12).

We thus have to do here with a grand concept of a relational continuum ranging from Father to Son to other children (cf. Jn. 1:11-12; Rev. 21:7; Mt. 25:40—the children appear to participate in the continuum both ontologically and then consciously by act of faith) which is being qualitatively reconstructed through the person and work of the Son as the Father's key mediating factor. The proclamation that God is working at the qualitative reconstruction (restoration) of the relational continuum between him and his creation (especially with human beings)—a work process focused in the person and work of Jesus the Christ but one which in relationship with him has been in operation from the beginning and continues now (cf. Jn. 5:17)—is the essence of the message of the entire New Testament. That this continuum is in some measure already in existence is clear from what has been adduced above and most significantly emphasized in Jesus' parable of the prodigal son, who is a son of his father even though prodigal and errant (Lk. 15:11-32).[28]

We have space only for brief references to comparable views of the background of Jesus in the apostolic writings of the New Testament. The apostle Paul affirms with Matthew and Luke the Davidic descent of Jesus "according to the flesh" and sees him "designated Son of God in power according to the Spirit of holiness by his resurrection from the dead" (Rom. 1:3-4). Paul, however, had his own exalted perception of the pre-existence of him who became the Christ. A key expression of his thought is found in his Letter to the Philippians, where he speaks of "Christ Jesus, who, though he was in the form of God, did not count equality with God as something to be exploited, but emptied himself, taking the form of a slave, being born in human likeness. And being found in human form he humbled himself and became obedient to the point of death—even death on a cross" (Phil. 2:5-8).

This is a difficult passage, and every word needs to be examined with care. But Paul was certainly trying to say that the original nature of Christ Jesus was essentially akin to that of God; it was a "form" *(morphē)* which was consonant with the reality of what God is in himself.[29] The glory of the Christ, however—a glory fully in keeping with his nature—was that he did not try to make this kinship a means of self-aggrandizement. He did not aspire to equality with God in all the ranges of his majesty but, to the contrary, divested himself of his exalted, though described in some passages in the New Testament as derivative,[30] status in order to serve the redemptive purposes of the Most High. This meant the further humiliation—seen by Paul as an act of obedience—of Jesus' death on the cross, which became, however, the very means of the reconciliation of all beings "in heaven and on earth and under the earth" to the Father through him. This mind and activity of Jesus became also the means for God to exalt Jesus' person and name above every other but God's own (Phil. 2:9-11; cf. I Cor. 15:28). And yet Paul tells the Christians of Philippi that they, too, should have precisely this mind and manifest comparable love in action (Phil. 2:1-11).

We also find in Paul language which leads us into the thought of the author of the Letter to the Hebrews. Christ Jesus is "the image of the invisible God, the firstborn of all creation" and also the agent of God in the creation of all things (Col. 1:15-20; Rev. 3:15; cf. Gen. 1:27).[31] But the purpose of his work, both in creation and in redemption, was "that he might be the firstborn within a large family" (in the Greek, "among many brothers"). The destiny of the latter is to be "conformed" *(summorphous*—of like "form" or

morphē) to his image, which is in turn the image of God
(Rom. 8:29). For Paul, too, there was thus a continuum between Father, Son and lesser brothers and sisters which is
ontological, relational, and functional. But his emphasis
was upon the relational and the functional because it was
precisely these elements of the continuum which the person and work of Christ Jesus, under God, were intended to
repair and restore.[32] We may recall, however, that in Paul's
famous speech to the Athenians as recorded in Acts, he
quotes the Greek poet Aratus (b. ca. 310 B.C.E.) with apparent approval that all human beings are God's offspring, of
the same stock (Acts 17:28).

An understanding similar to Paul's but in some ways
more distinctly in the Jewish Christian tradition emerges in
the Letter to the Hebrews. Here Jesus is seen as the pre-exis-
tent Son par-excellence, who is both the agent of creation
and the divinely appointed heir of all things. He is notably
superior to the angels as well as to Moses and the prophets
and priests of old (Heb. 1:1-14).[33] But there is a difference
from Paul, in whom we find the imagery of an exalted Being
who divests himself of the form of his status without moral
fall or any inadequacy in order to serve the redemptive purposes of God. In Hebrews the purpose is also to bring "many
children to glory," but the Son, although he is specifically
said to be without sin (4:15; 7:26), is made perfect through
suffering. A process of moral and spiritual development-
growth is envisaged: "Although he was a Son, he learned
obedience through what he suffered; and having been
made perfect, he became the source of eternal salvation for
all who obey him" (Heb. 5:8-9; 2:10; 7:28; Phil. 2:5-9), and
his solidarity with those for whom he is "the pioneer of their
salvation" is emphasized, "for he who sanctifies and those
who are [being] sanctified all have one Father" (2:10-11).
"He had to become like his brothers and sisters in every respect. . . to make a sacrifice of atonement for the sins of the

people. Because he himself was tested by what he suffered, he is able to help those who are being tested" (2:17-18). Most exalted is the view in this book—perhaps the work of a Christian of Essene background—of Jesus as the Son, the apostle and high priest, the mediator of a new and eternal covenant through his blood, the great shepherd of the sheep, the opener of the new and living way, who sits "at the right hand of the Majesty on high," who ever lives to make intercession for others and to warn from on high. This is also supremely the book of Jesus as the elder brother of many brothers and sisters; like the Gospel of John the theology is theocentric. As Jesus is utterly dependent on the Father in John, in Hebrews God is the originator of all things.[34]

3

The Activity of Jesus in His Public Ministry

A major reason for this somewhat unusual beginning of a consideration of the historical and religious significance of Jesus of Nazareth is my desire to break free of the pedestrian reductionism of not a little academic scholarship in biblical and historical studies over the past two centuries. Even though the strictures may be phrased in terms of what is allegedly possible for "modern man" to accept, the range of personal experiences and expectations of less perceptive persons should not, I believe, become the final criterion of what is historical or "can be" in the case of a person of the spiritual stature of Jesus the Christ. The limitations which have been set up are not confined to the older

issue of "miracles" but often extend to a surprising range of
the biblical data. I myself do not intend, however, to confine our inquiry merely to questions of documents, artifacts,
and other external data—important as these may be in their
own place—but wish to grapple directly with the issues involved in the primary human experiences to which the
documents and other data refer. It is in this context of concern that I wish to consider the issue of clairvoyance.

The term *clairvoyance,* as is well known, is suspect in
some circles. Certain "conservative" Christians tend to classify it in the category of "psychic phenomena," which they
in turn, at least in some cases, identify as of demonic origin.[35] I do not wish to belabor the issue, but I consider it
quite indefensible when such persons denote approvingly
as "the reading of hearts," that is, as a phenomenon of divine inspiration—in the case of those whom they would include in their own religious group or party—precisely the
same kinds of experience that in the case of other persons
they denote as "psychic phenomena" and, therefore, of demonic origin. The point is that, just as in the case of the Buddha, it would probably have been impossible for Jesus to
have been accepted as an authentic prophet in the tradition of Israel if he had not possessed in some measure what
we now frequently identify as extrasensory perception or,
in academic context, transnormal intuition. As one instance we may properly recall the witness in the Gospel of
John regarding Nathanael, the Israelite "in whom there is
no deceit!" The text affirms forthrightly that the one thing
that initially drew Nathanael to follow Jesus as a disciple was
his experience of Jesus' extrasensory perception with regard
to himself (Jn. 1:40-51; cf. 2:24-25). We may say the same
with regard to Jesus' meeting with a Samaritan woman (Jn.
4:1-30). In fact, as we shall see, Jesus possessed such gifts in
abundance, perhaps in more comprehensive measure than
any other person in known human history. We should recall

further, however, that authentically religious clairvoyance need not be dissociated from divine revelation; indeed, clairvoyance in this sense of transnormal perception in an authentically disciplined religious context is properly unthinkable apart from revelation.

It was one of the great contributions of Alfred Guillaume a generation ago in his classic work *Prophecy and Divination* to indicate the significance of these paranormal gifts in the life and work of the prophets of Israel. Evidently the primary criteria that ultimately led to the acceptance by historic Israel of a prophet as authentic were the ethical quality of the person of the prophet and the essential fidelity to the tradition of his teaching. A prophet's capacity to perform miracles or to manifest paranormal gifts was secondary to this primary test.

Yet these admittedly secondary qualities were clearly considered to be significant elements of the prophetic character. Indeed, we may say that there is no prophet in the Old Testament who was not a foreteller of the future as well as a forthteller of the word of God. The writer of Second Isaiah seems to have regarded it as a distinguishing mark of an authentic prophet to be able to foretell the future. Such ability was the basis of the prophet's claim to speak with the authority of Yahweh, who alone knows the future but reveals it to whom he chooses (Isa. 41:21-23; 42:9). Characteristic of First Isaiah was his consciousness of knowing the will and plan of God in quite specific terms (Isa. 6:1-13; 37:7, 33). He was, as Guillaume has phrased it, "the supreme vindicator of predictive prophecy."

Indeed, all the prophets cited as authentic in the Old Testament from Balaam onward were characterized by this kind of supernormal insight. Elisha's gift of clairvoyance was perhaps more strongly developed than most (II Kings 3:15-20; 4:1-9:3), but all the Hebrew prophets who subsequently came to be recognized as authentic by the collective judgment of the people shared in this gift to a significant degree. Not only the early so-called ecstatic prophets, but also the later literary prophets were essentially alike in this respect. As many scholars have noted, to affirm the forgiveness of sins on the basis of presuming to know the mind of God in the case is a prophetic act of this kind (II Sam. 12:13; Isa. 40:2). Jeremiah claimed intimate personal knowledge of the mind of the God of his people's faith (Jer. 23:18, 22). Ezekiel was highly sensitive to the reality of the unseen world; evidently possessing powers of clairvoyance and clairaudience to an extraordinary degree, he was able to see in visions events which were occurring hundreds of miles away (Ezek. 1:1-28; 8:1-11:25). Comparable modes of vision marked and molded the personal lives as well as prophetic careers of Amos, Hosea, and other so-called minor prophets.[36]

In the case of Jesus of Nazareth we find a remarkable variety of such experiences and events beginning with his baptism in the Jordan River at the hands of John the Baptizer, his cousin. I myself tend to take with great seriousness the Matthean and Lucan accounts of the virgin birth of Jesus but prefer not to discuss the issue in this necessarily brief treatment.[37] My point, however, is that I do not intend to be hindered by hesitancy within the academic community to take seriously the scriptural accounts of Jesus' manifestation of unusual powers and, indeed, of his direct relationship with realities of the spiritual world.

To begin with consideration of the external events of Jesus' public ministry, I would contend that there is no *a priori* reason to reject the gospel accounts of Jesus' so-called miracles. It is simply not true that "modern man" cannot accept them. There are those in the larger academic world who still appear to hold to reductive worldviews similar to those of late nineteenth- and early twentieth-century scientism, but the probes and theories of mid-late twentieth-century astro- and subatomic physics, of astrobiology, etc., would seem to have quite ripped away the limits set by that earlier mentality.[38] Furthermore, if the activities recorded of Jesus were utterly unknown elsewhere in all human history, there might be some reason to doubt them. But there is not one, I believe, of the miracles allegedly performed by Jesus, with the single exception of the resurrection event, that has not been duplicated in other well-attested instances in human experience. In the case of Jesus, we simply seem to have an abundance, a rich combination of powers not comparably found elsewhere.

It is nonsense, for example, to say that it was, in the cosmic sense, structurally impossible for Jesus to have walked on water (Mk. 6:45-52; cf. Mt. 14:22-33), when we have extremely well-attested evidence of comparable levitation in the case of Joseph (Desa) of Cupertino (1603-1663), whose flights in ecstasy earned him the title of the "flying friar,"[39] and of the Scottish-American Daniel Dunglas Home (1833-1886), many of whose experiences of levitation were witnessed by some of the most distinguished Europeans of his time.[40]

It is likewise out of order to deny in principle the scriptural accounts of Jesus' feeding large numbers of people (Mk. 6:32-44; 8:1-10), when we have other well-attested records of materialization, even if not as impressive in quantity or as specifically helpful to human need. Rufus Moseley wrote in his remarkable autobiographical work *Manifest Victory* of a Finnish postmistress, "a very intelligent, well-balanced, good-hearted Christian," who was a key person in an incident involving a multiplication of coins. It seems that this lady was in charge of some monies which she and others in her village had raised to build a chapel for worship. The contractor, however, who had agreed to furnish the necessary materials for the building fraudulently added so much to the bill that the postmistress did not have sufficient funds to pay it.

Under what she felt was divine guidance not to resist evil but cheerfully to go the second mile, the lady wrote to the contractor to deliver the materials even as she felt led to pray and keep before her mind the Lord's miracles of multiplication of bread and fishes in his Galilean ministry. She took the money she had in hand for this purpose and carefully counted it before beginning her regimen of prayer. She then began to realize that something was happening to the coins. "When she counted them again, she found them increased and that she had enough and more to pay for the material that had been fraudulently overcharged." It seems that the well-known American devotional writer of the early decades of this century, S.D. Gordon, personally traveled to Finland to make a firsthand investigation of this story and became fully convinced of its truth.[41]

This story, improbable as it may seem, helps to give a certain perspective the better to understand the otherwise astonishing New Testament account of Jesus' telling Peter to get the necessary money to pay the temple tax for the two of them by going to the sea, casting a hook, and taking "the first fish that comes up; and when you open its mouth, you will find a coin" (Mt. 17:27). This latter incident may be more an account of paranormal perception than of physical materialization itself, but like the other miracles of Jesus, it serves to reveal a dual aspect in Jesus' ministry, concrete service to human need in all its particularities and manifestation both of the open-endedness of God's order in the universe and of his work therein.

Since the issue at the moment is of the possibility of miracles of multiplication, it is surely in order to cite an illustration from outside the formal boundaries of the Judeo-Christian tradition. I refer to the contemporary Sathya Sai Baba of the Telugu-speaking area of South India, a man whose life and activity have been strikingly described by the American playwright and screenwriter Arnold Schulman.

Schulman's *Baba* is truly an extraordinary book, noteworthy almost as much for the author as for the person of his account. Schulman, who is of Jewish background, appears as the quintessential modern secular skeptic who at the same time has an ineradicable spiritual hunger which he is willing to try to satisfy even to the extent of enormous personal effort and sacrifice. It is precisely a person of Schulman's background and temperament who can make Baba believable, even more than his close followers of either Indian or Western background. But for our present purposes there is no doubt that in the case of Sathya Sai Baba we have innumerable instances of the materialization of physical objects over a period of more than thirty years, incidents witnessed in some cases by hundreds or even thousands of persons. He is said "to be able to cure the incurable, frequently by materializing a handful of ashes [*vibhuthi*, aromatic ashes allegedly bearing curative power] in his palm and then rubbing the ashes onto the afflicted parts of the body." Schulman writes: "On other occasions he had made it stop raining."[42] I should add as a personal note that I have questioned a number of Indians of various religious backgrounds concerning Baba, and all have agreed in affirming his sincerity and high moral character. The primary content of Baba's religious teaching is simply—some may say simplistically—to urge people to worship God with faith out of the heart and to lead a pure life, never saying "my" or "mine." He tells people to "be gentle and sweet and helpful."[43]

The reference to Baba's apparent power to cause rain to cease or to begin brings to mind, of course, Native American rain dances and similar traditions in Africa and elsewhere. Such events, some of which clearly appear to have effected desired results, bring us to direct consideration of the New Testament accounts of Jesus' stilling a storm on the Sea of Galilee (Mk. 4:35-41; cf. 6:51). Perhaps, however, this is the place to pause and consider more directly what is the point of these miracles, even if true. It would take us too far afield to discuss in detail the various scientific and philosophical problems which inevitably emerge for thoughtful persons who are concerned with the issue.[44] But we are compelled to look for the larger meaning and purpose of miracles in the life and ministry of Jesus.

It may be helpful in this context to cite the rationale given by Sathya Sai Baba, as a contemporary religious figure, for performing what are called miracles. Apparently not a few in India have criticized Baba "for spending so much of his time on physical and mental illness instead of spiritual work," but his answer was that "in order to reach people spiritually it was first necessary to cure their pain." Baba has said that "My miracles are my calling cards. I give the people what they want so that they will later give me what I want, their love of God."[45] It is proper to add that the social welfare and educational work of Sai Baba and his disciples is perhaps quantitatively the most extensive of any nongovernmental work of its kind in contemporary India.

It is clear from the New Testament gospel accounts of Jesus' temptations in the desert at the beginning of his public ministry that he rejected any notion of performing wonders either to amaze others or to win followers on the basis of self-centered motivation (cf. Mt. 4:1-11; Lk. 4:1-13). The evidence for the "Messianic Secret" theme in Mark and the other synoptic gospels shows Jesus as clearly and repeatedly refraining from activity that would unduly draw attention to his own person.[46] The author of the Gospel of John is surely right in using the word "sign" *(semeion)* as the proper term to designate Jesus' miraculous works (Jn. 2:11, etc.). They were not signs designed to attract attention to Jesus himself, but indications of wider and deeper realities. They were signs, of course, of Jesus' own compassion (cf. Mk. 1:41; 6:34; 8:2; 10:16, 45 and par.),[47] but even more significantly Jesus' disciples understood them to be signs of the compassion and caring love of God the Father, the Maker and Ruler of the universe. They were indications that behind and in spite of all the suffering and misery of human beings and other creatures the personal intent-purpose, the "heart," at the center of the cosmos is "most wondrously kind."

The fact of the miracles as "events that happened" was indicative that this divine intent-purpose is clothed with power sufficient to break through the causal chain behind human and other suffering, even when such suffering can be traced to personal as well as corporate human sin and evil. The miracles constitute signs not that natural laws are being abrogated or suspended, but that this universe is indeed open-ended, with authentic possibilities for personal liberation and larger corporate as well as personal changes. They are signs that the God of all is open-hearted, present to human and every other need, and at work in his universe. The creation is, therefore, not locked-in to an irretrievable state or irrevocable process. There are open-ended possibilities for its every part, even for each one of us who call ourselves persons. The whole of the New Testament combines to emphasize this cosmic open-endedness with its use of the word *gospel*, good news, to denote the essence of what its writers wish to say (cf. Mk. 1:1; Rom. 1:1-6). The mighty works of Jesus, however, as of his followers, are not only signs of what is possible. They are, as Krister Stendahl has put it, "acts of redeeming the creation, pushing back the frontiers of Satan."[48] We shall consider the meaning of these words further in connection with the discussion of the meaning of the Kingdom of God in the teaching of Jesus.

In sum, there is no reason of significance—historical, literary, or scientific-philosophical—to doubt that Jesus did perform mighty works, which we may call miracles, largely as reported in the New Testament accounts. It is not without significance that neither Jewish nor pagan opponents of the early Christian movement made any serious effort to discredit the facticity of the miracles recorded of Jesus. The early common position of rabbinic Judaism, which persisted into the Middle Ages, was apparently either to be silent on the issue or to disclaim that the miracles were wrought by the power of God.[49]

The largest number of miracles which Jesus is reported to have performed belong to the category of physical and mental healing. The incidence of such phenomena in every culture and in every age of human history is such that it is quite unnecessary to question or to prove the possibility of their occurrence. With Jesus, however, we have an extraordinary, perhaps a unique, range of healing activity. We find specific accounts of the healing of a paralytic man (Mk. 2:1-12), a paralytic servant (Mt. 8:5-13), an epileptic boy (Mk. 9:14-29), a man with dropsy (Lk. 14:1-6), a man with a withered hand (Mk. 3:1-6), a woman with fever (Mk. 1:29-31), a woman with a long-lasting case of bleeding (Mk. 5:25-34), a woman bent over in body for eighteen years (Lk. 13:10-17), several cases of persons afflicted with leprosy (Mk. 7:32-37; Lk. 17:11-19), a man deaf and with a speech impediment (Mk. 7:32-37), blind persons (Mk. 8:22-26; 10:46-52; Mt. 9:27-31; Jn. 9:1-41), persons said to be possessed by evil spirits and otherwise afflicted (Mt. 9:32-34; Mk. 1:21-28; 5:1-20; 7:24-30; Lk. 11:14-26), deceased persons who were restored to life (Mk. 5:21-43; Lk. 7:11-17; Jn. 11:1-44), a slave with an ear freshly severed (Lk. 22:50-51), and cases where the illness is not specified (Jn. 5:1-18; 4:46-54—perhaps equivalent to Mt. 8:5-13).[50]

We find other numerous references in the gospels to Jesus' healing of large numbers of persons without specification of particular afflictions. To cite references in Mark alone we note: Mk. 1:32-34; 3:7-12; 6:53-56. If we ask why Jesus did not heal all who were sick and otherwise afflicted even within his own then-limited range of contacts, we find an attempt at an explanation from Mark (6:1-6). Perhaps the response of Sathya Sai Baba to similar questions may be of some help here. He would answer by telling his questioner to stop trying to understand him (Baba) and try to understand himself or herself first.[51] We may recall that in Jesus' parable of the prodigal son, the key point of the son's turning is described as that "he came to himself" (Lk. 15:17).

Of comparable significance in the New Testament gospel accounts is the witness to Jesus' clairvoyant powers.[52] We have already noted the significance assigned to these powers by the author of the Gospel of John in his account of the early committal to discipleship of Nathanael and of the Samaritan woman and her friends (Jn. 1:43-51; cf. 2:25; 4:16-20; 11:4). Jesus is also forthrightly affirmed as knowing the mind of the Father (Jn. 5:19-20; 8:28-29). Some biblical scholars hesitate to discuss with adequate seriousness the references to these powers, but a careful reading of the four gospels shows not only a substantial number of instances of their manifestation, but also their importance in the first generation of Christian understanding of Jesus. Even in the Gospel of Mark with its strong emphasis upon Jesus as the worker of mighty deeds, we note distinct identification of this element of Jesus' person and work from an early period of his public ministry. In the healing of a paralytic at Capernaum we read that Jesus "perceived in his spirit" the unspoken criticisms of the scribes present (Mk. 2:6-8; cf. 11:1-6; 12:15; 14:12-16).[53] Mark, followed by Matthew, does not include in the calling of Simon Peter and his brother Andrew the account of an unexpectedly large catch of fish in accordance with Jesus' previous perception of the possibility. But the aspect of Jesus' paranormal perception in this event is fully delineated in both Luke and John.[54] In Luke we find Jesus specifically depicted as a prophet (Lk. 7:16; 13:33; 24:19; Acts 3:22-33) characterized by spiritual discernment, able to see beneath the surface of persons and events, to know both the mind of God and human hearts (Lk. 5:17-26; 6:20-26; 7:36-50).

In keeping with earlier procedures, a few words on comparable experiences of clairvoyance beyond scriptural referents may be in order. Perhaps I may be permitted to refer to the unusual clairvoyant powers of Rudolf Steiner and Edgar Cayce in the twentieth century. It was said of Steiner that commonly after his public lectures on tour in various countries of Europe, men and women would follow him to his hotel and line up to wait for interviews—to the extent that the lines frequently extended along the corridor and down the stairs—because he was clairvoyantly able to perceive the inner realities of their lives and give accordingly appropriate advice.[55] Extraordinary reports, of apparently reliable authority, have been made of Edgar Cayce's being able to know and communicate facts quite beyond the normal experience of human beings.[56] The abilities of the Italian monk Francesco Forgione, best known as Padre Pio, in reading the thoughts of persons who came to him for confession are well known over the past two generations.[57] Similarly extraordinary abilities to discern the thoughts and feelings of others, also unhindered by geographical distance, are reported of Sathya Sai Baba.[58] The above is in a sense only to be expected because the witness of the New Testament is clear that the enlightening and empowering Spirit of God would impart to Jesus' disciples—including those who follow him "from afar"—at least a measure of the spiritual discernment and the power to do good that the Master himself possessed (Acts 5:1-11; 9:10-16; 13:1-3; 16:9-10; 20:29-30; I Cor. 2:10-16; 12:8).

A final word in this category of the activity of Jesus in his public ministry may properly be said with regard to the gospel records of the transfiguration of Jesus. Once again, it is appropriate to recall that there are reliable historical accounts of similar experiences in the case of others, few, to be sure, but apparently authentic. We note that the skin of Moses' face is said to have shone "because he had been talking with God" (Ex. 34:29-30). We are told that at his death the body of Francis of Assisi "shone with a dazzling whiteness."[59] The face of Teresa of Avila is also reported to have shone with a light when she was writing her mystical works.[60] The artistic tradition of depicting saints in many religious traditions with halos suggests that the experience was relatively widespread in persons of authentic religious experience and noble character across all the centuries of human history. In the case of Jesus' transfiguration, however, we have to do with a particularly awesome event which was accompanied by a vision or "materialization" of Moses and Elijah perceived also by the three disciples who were present (Mk. 9:2-13; cf. Mt. 17:1-13; Lk. 9:28-36). Incidentally, with reference to the issue of talking with "the dead," which is, of course, a basic element of the transfiguration event, one may profitably reflect on the meaning of II Peter 1:12-15. In Jesus of Nazareth, then, there was a richness, an abundance of these gifts, deeds, events, experiences such as has, I believe, been found comparably in no other single person in human history. But all were utterly human, human in the sense of being part of the potentiality of what it means to be a human being in the fullness of God's will.

We may note that throughout the lifetime of Jesus and later there is abundant evidence that both Jews and pagans generally regarded miracles as pointing to the presence of transcendent or divine power. Performance of miracles *(terata, terastia, semeia)* was seen as giving a mode of divine legitimization to the word or status of a person as prophet, rabbi, or healer. At the same time, among the thoughtful who shared this belief, there were also those who were quite aware of the existence of charlatans and imposters. The

Alexandrian Jewish historian, Flavius Josephus (37-100
C.E.) clearly shared the belief (*Antiquities* II, 272-274; IX, 23;
X, 28-29), but was equally conscious of the activity of de-
ceivers (*ibid.*, XX, 168-172).

After the Council of Jamnia (i.e., after 90 C.E.), we note
the emergence in rabbinic Judaism of a more distinct hesitancy to accept miracles as evidence of divine legitimization
than had been the case before. The change was probably
due, at least in part, to a reaction against the occurrence of
miracles in the ministry of Jesus and in the early church. Yet
in subsequent centuries we find miracles and various kinds
of "occult" practices playing a significant role in Jewish life.
An interesting example is seen in the Jewish community in
Medina before and during the lifetime of Muhammad.

In later antiquity we find in the midst of widespread
credulity occasional sharp critiques of charlatanism in alleged performance of miracles, as in the case of Lucian (fl.
160-180 C.E.), who has been called the Voltaire of antiquity
(see his *Lover of Lies* and *Alexander the False Prophet*).
Philostratus, whose *Life of Apollonius of Tyana* was published about 220 C.E., felt compelled to defend the heroic
sage and miracle-worker (ca. 7-100 C.E.) of his account
against charges of being a magician or sorcerer whose primary goal was fame and financial gain (VIII, 1-3).

Then as now sensitive persons were keenly aware that
the manifestation of miraculous powers can never be dissociated from the issues of ethical life and character. The
gospel accounts of Jesus' temptations at the beginning of
his ministry make clear that essential to that ministry was
rejection of physical indulgence, worldly power, or reputa-
tion, and, specifically, the performance of miracles for any
purpose other than helping others on God's terms (Mt. 4:1-
11; Lk. 4:1-14; 23:35-43; cf. Mk. 1:12-13). The gospel accounts are one in their witness that Jesus never used his
powers to harm any person or other living thing; the appar-

ent exceptions are the causing of a fig tree to wither (Mk. 11: 12-25; Mt. 21:18-22; Luke omits the incident, cf. 13:6-9) and the sending of evil spirits out of a possessed Gerasene into a herd of swine with the result that the man was healed and the swine were drowned (Mk. 5:1-20; Mt. 8:28-34; Lk. 8:26-39). We should note that the NRSV translation of the Johannine account of Jesus' cleansing of the temple rightly follows the Greek text in stating that Jesus used a whip of cords only to drive out the sheep and cattle (Jn. 2:15). There is no indication in the Greek that Jesus used the whip upon the money-changers. The later Christian community insofar as it wrought miracles of healing regularly did so in the name of Jesus and, as they believed, in conformity with his Spirit and teaching (cf. Mk. 6:7-12; Acts 3:1-16; 15:12).

4

The Teaching of Jesus

1

There is wide scholarly agreement that much of Jesus' teaching was focused upon the term and concept of the Kingdom of God (in Mt. regularly the Kingdom of Heaven). Since the work of Johannes Weiss in the last decade of the nineteenth century and of Albert Schweitzer in the first decade of the twentieth, there has been a strong tendency, especially among Germanic scholars, to emphasize the presumably eschatological aspects of this concept in Jesus' teaching. This is to understand Jesus' teaching as primarily focused upon the end of the world or of human history, as we know and experience it. Increasing interest in and study of Jewish apocalyptic literature—materials which apparently find their literary starting point in the biblical book of Daniel, their most important expression in I Enoch (ca. 200 B.C.E.), and include such works as *Jubilees* and IV Ezra— served to strengthen this tendency.[61]

This emphasis has been, to be sure, by no means entirely mistaken. The religious faith and understanding of Old Testament prophecy, although its primary concern was for contemporary issues and the obedience of faith, came to have an eschatological orientation, at least from the eighth-century prophets Amos and Hosea onward.[62] The Hebrew prophets believed in the universal rule of Yahweh and in a certain onward progression of religiously meaningful (i.e., as under Yahweh) events toward their divinely appointed end.[63] In particular, beginning perhaps with the prophet Isaiah of the southern kingdom of Judah, also in the eighth century, Hebrew prophets came to see the universal rule of Yahweh as a reality to be established comprehensively on earth through the agency of a unique historical figure. This would be a person of the lineage of David, anointed by the Spirit of the Lord and filled with all wisdom, power, and joy in his relationship with the Lord Most High. His rule would be characterized by true justice, above all by concern for the poor and meek of the earth, by gentleness toward the weak and small (Isa. 11:1-9).

From this perspective the concept of the Kingdom of God came to embody hope for the future, when "the holy ones of the Most High shall receive the kingdom and possess the kingdom forever—forever and ever" (Dan. 7:18). This was hope for the effective kingship of God over the whole world, God who is, however, already and always "eternally King" (Ps. Sol. 17:3). But this development as it came to be expressed in Daniel, a book that is now generally regarded as the product of the period of the Maccabean rebellions against the Greek Seleucid rulers of Palestine in the early second century B.C.E., took a divergent turn. The messianic (anointed) inaugurator of full divine rule upon earth, who was still perceived by Deutero-Isaiah in the sixth century B.C.E. as an historical, even a servant figure (whether an individual or all Israel—Isa. 42:1-25), has become a personage of heavenly origin called "one like a human being" (Aramaic: "like a son of man"). Differently from the earlier use of this term by the sixth-century prophet Ezekiel with primarily earthly referents, this figure will come "with the clouds of heaven" and to him is given dominion over all the earth, a "kingship . . . that shall never be destroyed" (Dan. 7:13-14). The context of events leading to this eternal rule is seen as involving destructive wars, troubles untold, and as culminating in the resurrection of "many" of the dead (Dan. 7-12).

Late pre-Christian Judaism generally seemed to be able to combine these notions, which in some circles verged on a totally deterministic predestinarianism, with the conviction of a certain measure of personal freedom and moral accountability before God.[64] The apocalyptic writers, in spite of their tendency to veer off into exclusivist concerns for a righteous remnant that seem heedless of the welfare and destiny of the "many," perceived that the experiences of human beings have connections with beings of unseen worlds. They believed that behind the political, social, and economic forms of human conflict rages a world struggle which is "essentially of the spirit and cosmic scope." This is to say that there is an ongoing battle between God the good Creator and the forces of chaos.[65] We should recall our earlier discussion that significant elements of this worldview and mentality are carried over into the New Testament. In John 1:5 we note that the light is said to shine in the darkness, and even though the affirmation of faith is that the darkness has not overcome (or comprehended) the light (cf. I Jn. 5:4-5), in the First Epistle of John we read that "the whole world is in the power of the evil one" (I Jn. 5:19; cf.

Eph. 6:12; I Pet. 5:8—Paul prefers more abstract modes of expression: Gal. 1:4; Rom. 8:22-23; II Cor. 5:2-4).

It is fashionable in contemporary academic circles to speak of these things, but not to take them seriously for one's own understanding of faith. In his otherwise brilliant and courageous address to the Melbourne World Conference on Mission and Evangelism (May, 1980), Ernst Käsemann exemplified this approach with his statement that we must "criticize and demythologize the language and ideas of an antique worldview as out of date ... since only in this way can we have a true perception of the reality of our contemporary life and present world."[66] Käsemann would have us become even more sensitive than first-century Christians and Jews to the referents in human experience which called forth the older "mythical" language. I myself, however, do not think that it is helpful for our understanding either of Jesus of Nazareth or of the actual nature of our universe to reject out of hand either this language or its referents in other dimensions. It may be appropriate to correct certain ancient concepts of astronomy or of other aspects of physical science on the basis of modern scientific perceptions, but developments in the Western world over the past two or three centuries hardly qualify modern persons to pronounce as incorrect older perceptions of the nature of the invisible world. And unless there is acknowledgment of the reality of other dimensions and the fact that God is (cf. Heb. 11:6; Jas. 2:19), even though our understandings of God may require considerable change, our entire discourse, that of this book and of many others, becomes meaningless.

Actually, as we shall see, Jesus was neither a religious apocalyptic nor a political revolutionary in the literal sense of either of these terms. But neither was he a conservative, either politically or religiously. Nor did he differ from historic apocalypticism in the modern reductive sense, as if there were no cosmic referents to the discussion. I believe that the statement recorded as made by Jesus in Luke 10:18, "I saw Satan fall like lightning from heaven," was a perception, metaphorically expressed, of a true cosmic reality, even though something of a parallel may be found in I Enoch 86:1. It is in this context of understanding that I would discuss briefly Jesus' teaching on the Kingdom of God and at the same time take with the utmost seriousness the challenges to praxis that Käsemann so eloquently makes. The issue is how to carry out the praxis, for the great practical need of our time, in both understanding and execution, is how to appropriate and apply "the fundamentally rejuvenating deed of the Christ" in the context of the hindrance and opposition of adverse powers that have continued their activity, even though in some significant measure they are divinely restricted (cf. Col. 2:15; Heb. 2:8), until the present.

According to the accounts of the synoptic gospels, both John the Baptizer and Jesus of Nazareth began their public ministry with the proclamation of a call to repent, for "The time is fulfilled and the kingdom of God has come near" (Mk. 1:4, 14-15; Mt. 3:2; 4:17; Lk. 3:3; 4:43; actually, only in Mt. [3:2] do we find the statement "the kingdom of heaven has come near" attributed to John as well as to Jesus). As we shall see, there were differences in nuance of understanding as well as of lifestyle between Jesus and his slightly older cousin John. At the same time, they shared many elements in common in their ministries. Indeed, Jesus' coming to John to be baptized by him would seem to indicate his option for John as the most authentic contemporary link with the prophetic past of Israel. And Jesus evidently perceived his own submission to the form of repentance taught and offered by John as the most "appropriate point of departure for his own prophetic mission."

In the case of both John and Jesus, the call to "repent" was probably to be understood in its traditional Hebrew

prophetic sense of "return" (*shubh*), return to a right relationship of obedience and love with Yahweh their Maker
and Lord. Something of the depths of Jesus' understanding
of this "return" is seen in his parable of the prodigal son,
who belongs to the same family as the Father (he is a son,
though errant), comes to himself (Lk. 15:17—What depth
of meaning in this phrase! Cf. *The Gospel According to Thomas* 99:8), and returns to the accepting welcome and care
of his Father (Lk. 15:11-32). Nevertheless, the New Testament selection of the Greek word *metanoia* (to change one's
thinking) to render the Aramaic word that Jesus no doubt
used was also not mistaken. For as we shall see, interior
change—change in basic life orientation and goals, in attitudes and motives, in daily ways of thinking and feeling—
was also central to Jesus' teaching about the ethical content
involved in "return."[67]

One of the primary characteristics of Jesus' teaching of
the Kingdom of God from the very beginning of his public
ministry as recorded in the synoptic gospels is its association with good news (gospel).[68] This happy association is
seen, without essential difference of meaning, in each of the
synoptic gospels (Mk. 1:1, 15; Mt. 4:23-24; Lk. 4:16-19). That
is, instead of frightful destruction and carnage, the Kingdom of God is liberation from every bond—physical, mental, spiritual, societal—and restoration of *shalom*, which is
restoration primarily of right relationship with Yahweh
(with focus upon his graciously forgiving acceptance and
our gratefully loving response) and with our fellow human
beings (cf. Mt. 5:23-26).[69] It is also restoration of physical,
mental, and spiritual well-being and of the whole range of
societal (corporate as well as individual) meanings implicit
in these words. This fact of the teaching means that Jesus
was not an apocalyptic in the sense of expecting the prompt
destruction of the present order of things with concomitant
"wiping out" of the bulk of humankind, although we should

note that in some apocalyptic circles the pious of non-Israelite nations were seen as sharing in the divine salvation to come, along with the devout remnant of Israel.

We need, however, to be careful with our words at this point. There is good reason to believe that Jesus prophesied, in the specific sense of predictive prophecy, something akin to the destruction of Jerusalem that actually occurred in 70 C.E. We noted above that such predictive prophecy was an integral element of the larger clairvoyant pattern characteristic of the mainstream of Hebrew prophecy. It is only to be expected that Jesus had comparable, if not greater, prophetic powers. Indeed, we are told by the Jewish historian Josephus that another Jew with the name Jesus, son of Ananias, prophesied almost continuously for seven years and five months, beginning in autumn of 62 C.E., the downfall of the city of Jerusalem. The Roman siege of the city, we may recall, began in 66 C.E. and ended with its destruction in 70 (*The Jewish War VI*, 300-309). There are, some readers may recall, instances—very few, to be sure—of rather specific prophecies of events of both the First and the Second World Wars of this century that were made some years before their occurrence. Carl Gustav Jung relates in his autobiography, *Memories, Dreams, Reflections*, that he himself had experienced on several occasions in 1913 and early 1914 highly vivid visions of World War I, which was soon to burst upon the world. The distinction made, for example, in Mark 13 between "all these things," apparently descriptive of events prior to and including something like the destruction of Jerusalem, and "that day or hour," which "no one knows, neither the angels in heaven, nor the Son, but only the Father," suggests an important difference between an impending catastrophe of vital significance for the Jewish people and the end of history (Mk. 13:1-37, especially 30-32; cf. I Thess. 5:1-2).

The above would suggest that Jesus followed the mainstream of the Hebraic prophetic tradition in affirming a divinely guided progression in human history and a climax thereof. We may say that, on the one hand, the Kingdom of God in the teaching of Jesus is akin to the Buddha's perception of *Nirvāṇa* and its manifestation as *Dharma*. It is representative of Ultimate Reality; it is power unto righteousness available now to persons on earth who would receive it. On the other hand, perhaps differently from the Buddha's understanding of *Nirvāṇa-Dharma*, Jesus evidently perceived the Kingdom of God as destined to manifest in mightier and more extensive form even on this earth, as the writer of Revelation put it, in the form of "a new heaven and a new earth" (Rev. 21:1). There are, however, certain possible qualifications to these statements on the end of history which we do not have space here to consider in detail. I refer to the fact that the Greek of the New Testament frequently uses various terms, such as "end of the age" (no definite article in the Greek of Mt. 13:39) or the "age to come" (*ho aion*, e.g., Mk. 10:30; Mt. 12:32; 13:39-40, 49; 24:3; 28:20) as well as simply "the end" (*to telos*, e.g., Mk. 13:7, 13; Mt. 10:22; 24:6, 13-14; Lk. 21:9). "The end of history" is a modern phrase, and some of Jesus' statements may not have meant precisely that. We may be properly reminded also that the language concerning the return of Jesus ascribed to angels in the first chapter of Acts affirms a coming "in the same way as you saw him go into heaven" (Acts 1:6-11). The implication there is of a return that will be quiet, unspectacular, and witnessed only by those who follow him. We may also note that the Gospel of John seems to regard the coming of Jesus in Palestine as an "eschatological event" (of realized eschatology) denoting a change of the (astrological?) aeons (cf. Jn. 1:12-13; 20:22 with Gen. 2:7).

Only in the Marcan account are Jesus' proclamation of the nearness of the Kingdom of God and his call to repent prefaced by a statement that "the time is fulfilled" (Mk. 1:14-

15). Some such faith-concept of fulfillment, however, of a climax in God's ordered plan for humanity and the cosmos was apparently widely held in the early community of believers, especially with regard to the person and role of Jesus. The author of the Gospel of Matthew describes the—miraculous—birth of Jesus, the Savior of his people, as the fulfillment of God's promise made through the prophet Isaiah (Mt. 1:22-23). The apostle Paul affirms the gospel of God, which he sees as especially concerned with Jesus as Messiah, as Son of God and our Lord, to be the fulfillment of God's promises "through his prophets in the holy scriptures" (Rom. 1:1-4). As Dale Patrick has put it, "All that God has said and done in Israel's history is brought to completion in the kingdom of God." That is, that which is now being manifested before the eyes of Israel—and the world—is a synthesis "in one image" of all that God is, has done, and will do in and for humanity and the entire cosmos.[70]

The above discussion is intended as background material for better understanding of my central affirmation, viz., that Jesus in his teaching of the Kingdom of God laid primary emphasis upon its present availability, even if not in its totality, and the vital importance of present human response, appropriation and application of the Kingdom possibilities individually and corporately available in the current situations of human life. This is to say that Jesus in his person and in his ministry proclaimed the availability of the Kingdom of God as a universal reality, a reality that had always been available in all times and places—and in a sense he was "bringing to the remembrance" of his hearers that which they already inwardly knew.[71] The intimation of Jesus, however, and the witness of the New Testament as a whole is that through the life, through the cross, resurrection, and ascension of Jesus the Kingdom of God is brought to a new focus of expression in human history. Divine life and power have been made available in new measures of quality and quantity, singularly in the person of Jesus, and also for others through his instrumentation then and now. This is also to say that in Jesus of Nazareth the future of persons and of the cosmos in God was made manifest, and therefore our future is, as it were, proleptically working back upon us now. For through the Christ of God the present of every person and of all else has an open door to the future, which is the Kingdom of God in complete fulfillment both within and without.

Even though the term Kingdom of God is not found in the Hebrew Old Testament, the concept of the kingly rule or dominion of God emerged with increasing clarity and force over the centuries in the Old Testament, in both psalmists and writers of wisdom literature as well as in the prophets.[72] This affirmation of faith, however, included full recognition of the fact that the perfect rule of God was no longer a reality on earth. And yet no faithful Jew could in faith or theological discourse allow that recognition to become affirmation of a permanent condition of life, and the whole of late pre-Christian Judaism is made up of a variety of responses in understanding and practice that were designed to cope with that unacceptable—as a permanent reality—present fact of existence (cf. Heb. 2:8; 11:10). Pharisees, Sadducess, Essenes, Herodians, Zealots—all represented differing modes of attempts to cope with this intolerable present fact, although more quietistic forms of apocalyptic faith may have constituted what we could call withdrawals more than positive attempts to cope. My contention is that the older prophetic stream of Israel looked for an ultimate resolution of this dilemma by divine action which is best called eschatological, but laid its primary religious emphasis upon what was possible by divine action and human response in the present. Jesus of Nazareth clearly belonged to this stream.[73]

The presence of eschatological dimensions in Jesus'

teaching of the Kingdom of God is, therefore, not to be denied. But the question is, where was his primary focus? I
believe that while Jesus perceived and did not hesitate to
depict his perception of the larger framework of divine activity, his primary emphasis was upon the present power of
God at work in the world (cf. Mt. 12:28; Lk. 4:21; 11:20) and
present human response and change, both in life orientation and in lifestyle. There was, in Jesus' teaching, no need
to wait for external events of any kind as prior conditions
for this human commitment and change that he called for.
We note that the whole of the Sermon on the Mount in the
Gospel of Matthew presupposes the present difficulties and
obstacles of human life as precisely the context within
which Kingdom-oriented human life is to be lived out (Mt.
5:1-7:29; cf. 13:41). The Lord's Prayer equates the presence
of the Kingdom of God with the doing of God's will—both
on earth—and implies that those who follow Jesus will pray
for that presence and will work to do that will here and now
(Mt. 6:9-10; "Your will be done" is omitted, perhaps, in Lk.
11:2, but the textual evidence is ambiguous; in Luke, however, a close connection between the Kingdom and the Holy
Spirit is frequently affirmed; cf. Lk. 11:13; 12:32; Acts 1:4-8).
It is unthinkable that in Jesus' understanding the doing of
God's will is something to be left to the end time. In fact,
nowhere in all our extant literature is Jesus recorded as saying such a thing.

For Jesus the proper human response to the divine initiative of love—which latter phrase is one way of denoting
Jesus' proclamation that the Kingdom of God is near—involved faith in the sense of willing submission and obedience to the authority of the Creator as King. The story of the
healing of the centurion's slave seems to reveal that Jesus
warmly approved the cast of mind that is quick to acknowledge rightful authority and as a consequence is ready to act
with dispatch (Mt. 8:5-13; Lk. 7:1-10). The incident shows

how far Jesus' mind was from sentimentality and how Christian faith is properly that of a "person under authority." I am reminded that Martin Niemoeller said one time in my hearing (March 10, 1964), "The Kingdom of God is the reconstruction of the authority of God over human life." We may note that in the Marcan version of Jesus' promise to those who leave all "for my sake and for the sake of the good news," they will receive "a hundredfold now in this age: even with persecutions" (Mk. 10:28-31; cf. Mt. 19:29). And as the apostle Paul later put it, "See, now is the acceptable time; see, now is the day of salvation" (II Cor. 6:2).

We may say specifically, then, with reference to Jesus' proclamation of the Kingdom of God as having come near, that the larger context of the event impels us to state that Jesus' intent was to affirm the universal availability of the Kingdom, given the proper receptivity of persons anywhere. Notions that the Kingdom of God was mediated solely by the physical presence of Jesus during his earthly ministry or later solely through the transmission of the same message and/or sacramental instrument by his professed followers are more representative of Western cultural pride and ecclesiastical exclusivism than of the witness of the New Testament. Jesus as the manifestation of the universal Logos of God was neither then nor now confined to such limits. The same can be said *in similem partem* of the Kingdom of God. We note especially in Matthew that the presence of the Father in heaven is repeatedly equated with his presence "in secret," a phrase which in its context appears to mean that the Father is behind all, within all, and knows all (Mt. 6:1, 4, 6, 18).

At this point it may be in order to anticipate a bit and add in support of the above thesis the nature of the apostle Paul's understanding of the Kingdom of God. It is of no little significance that Paul as a figure of commanding stature in the first or apostolic generation of Christian faith should emphasize the interiority of the Kingdom of God. Paul's own Christian faith clearly included eschatological aspects, even though with regard to this theme there are some discernible differences of emphasis, perhaps of understanding, between his earlier and later letters, and he evidently expected the return of the Lord Jesus to occur in his own lifetime (I Thess. 4:13-5:11; II Thess. 2:1-12; Phil. 3:20-4:7). The association of these eschatological aspects with the Kingdom of God in Paul is normally limited, however, to statements that the Kingdom is something to be inherited (I Cor. 6:9; 15:50; Gal. 5:21—Christians, however, are cited as already "heirs of God and joint heirs with Christ," Rom. 8:17; cf. I Pet. 3:7; Eph. 3:6).

But in Paul the emphasis is normally upon present reality and opportunity: "the kingdom of God is not food and drink but righteousness and peace and joy in the Holy Spirit" (Rom. 14:17). "The kingdom of God depends not on talk but on power" (I Cor. 4:20; the context of discussion is that of present power, cf. I Cor. 2:1-5). Paul came to speak of the Kingdom of Christ ("the kingdom of his beloved Son") as the present form of God's rule and affirmed that since we are believers God had already "rescued us from the power of darkness and transferred us into the kingdom of his beloved Son, in whom we have redemption, the forgiveness of sins." Paul makes this affirmation of a highly significant present reality immediately following his statement that the ultimate inheritance is to be shared with "the saints in the light" (Col. 1:12-14; cf. I Thess. 2:9-12). Paul also, to be sure, elsewhere affirms that we have to do with a process of cosmic scope which is as yet by no means completed in large scale or in small (Rom. 8:18-25; Phil. 1:6; 2:12-13; 3:12-16). At the end of the present order of things, Christ "hands over the kingdom to God the Father, after he has destroyed every ruler and every authority and power ... When all things are subjected to him, then the Son himself will also be subjected to the one who put all things in subjection under him, so that God may be all in all" (I Cor. 15:20-28). This is affirmation of the present universal, even if invisible, not completely implemented and not fully accepted by all on the historical level, rule of the Christ as the vice-regent of God (cf. Col. 1:17). With reference again to the aspect of interiority, it is highly significant that in Colossians, which I regard as largely an authentic letter of Paul, he boldly affirms that the very mystery which has been throughout the ages, the word of God, but is now revealed to his saints is precisely Christ in you (*Christos en hymin*), the hope of glory (Col. 1:25-29; 2:2; cf. Rom. 8:9-17; II Cor. 13:5; Gal. 2:20).

The aspect then of the Kingdom of God that bore primary significance for human beings in Jesus' teaching was clearly relational and present. Jesus' aim was the restoration of right relationships between God and his creation, supremely between the Maker and those whom the Scriptures call his children, persons made in his own image, i.e., persons possessing similar self-awareness, similar self-consciousness. As we noted in Jesus' parable of the prodigal son, the son's return was to the person and "place" of the Father, his own original home. This parable is not, strictly speaking, a parable of the Kingdom, but if we interpret it in association with Jesus' teaching of the Kingdom of God—as the larger context in Luke allows us to do—we may understand its meaning in the unsentimental way that Jesus evidently intended. That is, however kindly and warmly forgiving was the Father's welcome of the errant son, the latter's return was to the authority of the Father. If we apply the language of the Kingdom to this parable, we may assume that the Father is King. But both sons are also royal, of the same lineage and family, yet lesser in authority. Jesus evidently wished a certain tension to remain in his hearers' minds with regard to the proper relationship of human beings to their Maker, tensions between the familial aspect of their relationship with God the Father and the authoritative aspect with God the King (Lk. 15:11-32).[74]

This is to say that we have to do not merely with a "preliminary manifestation of the sovereignty of God" in Jesus' person and ministry, but with an invitation to others to participate in a royal relationship in the present, even though Jesus himself no doubt well knew and subsequent history has abundantly demonstrated that this participation would in most cases be only partial and its fruits at best inadequate. Even, however, with this prospect of long continuing inadequacy, men, women and children may enter this Kingdom-relationship with full authenticity now (cf. Mt. 5:20; 18:3-4; 20:1-16). The New Testament presents us with an almost bewildering variety of facets of this central fact. On the one hand, we note what is apparently Jesus' own affirmation that his casting out of demons from possessed persons—he affirmed that this was "by the finger of God"— was a sign that the Kingdom of God had come *(ephthasen)* in the experience of persons (Lk. 11:20). On the other hand, likewise in Luke, we find Jesus' insistence that the coming of the Kingdom is not primarily a matter of externals but of interiority (Lk. 17:20-21).[75] The two elements together combine the dimensions of cosmic victory and human personal transformation-in-process.

Even in the Gospel of Mark the interiority of the Kingdom of God in present manifestation and working process finds a special emphasis. The Kingdom of God is a mysterious reality, perceptible to those who are open to the understanding given them, but however powerful it is in the slow might of its working, persons do not normally recognize it, until its full flowering and harvest, as the supreme bearer of power that it is (Mk. 4:11-12, 26-32). As Günther Bornkamm has put it, the Kingdom of God is portrayed in Jesus' parables as "the greatest of all, hidden in the least significant of all, but effective even in the smallest things."[76] This

Kingdom is equated with life, which may well in its larger Marcan context, as in John (Jn. 3:36; 5:24; 6:33), refer to present opportunity, as indeed the parables of the Kingdom in Mark 4 imply. Mark's account of Jesus' discussion with some members of the party of the Sadducees regarding the resurrection, a discussion reported in all the synoptic gospels, is also significant in this context. Jesus' affirmation that the God of Abraham, Isaac, and Jacob is the God of the living and not of the dead, that the patriarchs are living now, shows Jesus as having moved out of all limitations of eschatological dimensions of thought into awareness of the eternal present with God (Mk. 12:18-27; Mt. 22:23-33; Lk. 20:27-40).

As Raymond E. Brown has put it, confusion about eschatology may be said to have characterized early Christian thought, but in Jesus' own message a more appropriate term would be "a tension between realized and final eschatology." That this tension was kept in proper balance is at least in part indicated by the presence in various layers of the Gospel of John of a primary emphasis upon present divine gifts and opportunities (realized eschatology) even as apocalyptic expectations are in a measure retained (cf. Jn. 5:19-30).[77] Also in John, Jesus before Pilate emphasizes that his kingship *(he basileia he emē)* does not have its origin in this world, but that it is a present reality emerges clearly from his language in the interchange (Jn. 18:33-40).

Mark, however, gives us with special fullness of explanation Jesus' teaching of the prior importance of inner ethics (Mk. 7:14-23). It will not do to push aside the significance of this teaching as "characteristically Hellenistic" as if, indeed, such interior matters were not significant before God in the Hebraic tradition.[78] Perception of the central importance of the thoughts, feelings, and motives of persons is clearly an integral element of the teaching of Jesus, as of the entire New Testament; it is by no means absent in the Old Testa-

ment (cf. Joel 2:13; Ps. 34:18; 51:6,17; 147:3; etc.). We are reminded in particular of Jesus' "morality of intention,"
whereby to think adultery is the same as doing it. "For out of
the abundance of the heart the mouth speaks" (Mt. 12:34).[79]
And the initial impact of the saving power released through
the Christ event seems to have been the cleansing of human hearts (Acts 15:9).

                                  2

The second most significant aspect of the Kingdom of
God in the teaching of Jesus is the ethical, which refers, of
course, to the quality of the relational. It should be noted
again that for Jesus the ethical aspect is secondary only in
theological priority, never in temporal sequence. In his
teaching as recorded in the gospels of the New Testament,
the concept of the Kingdom of God is impregnated from
beginning to end with ethical qualities. This fact constitutes
further reason to conclude that Jesus was primarily concerned with the ethical response of human beings in the
present. An apocalyptic emphasis can easily shift into a relative disregard of the significance of ethical activity, except
possibly on the basis of a motivation of fear.

This present generation needs, I believe, a rethinking of
the principles and practice of ethics perhaps more than any
other single issue. For one thing, in considerable measure
as a justifiable reaction to the often hyper-individualism in
both faith and ethics of the older Protestant evangelicalism,
Christian theologians and ethicists sometimes betray a veritable fear of discussing issues of individual ethical response.[80] It is, of course, true that "no man is an island," and
twentieth-century depth psychology, especially that of Carl
Gustav Jung, has shown us that there is no absolute border-
line between and among the individual foci of consciousness that we call human beings. We shall discuss this point

further in comparison with the Buddha's teaching. But we are still individual foci of consciousness, in some measure distinct even if not totally separate, and the main thrust of biblical witness is to emphasize the fact of human freedom, within limits, and the consequences of individual as well as of corporate conduct-being.[81] Jesus clearly spoke to his hearers as persons who were both free to respond and individually responsible before God (even while they were also participants in community); Paul spoke in similar wise (cf. Mk. 4:1-9; I Cor. 3:10-17).

Another point of significance to be made with reference to the ethical issue in the teaching of Jesus has to do with what we may call process. As is well known, much confusion has been caused in the history of Protestant evangelicalism, especially in its popular forms, by varying forms of simplistic perfectionism. This concept-practice has at times understood Christian conversion as properly bringing instantaneous and total change of character as well as of life direction. While there have been many instances of dramatic conversion in the history of the Christian church, not a few cases manifesting remarkable evidences of sudden change in lifestyle, only the naive fail to recognize these changes as partial and inadequate. The apostle Paul's experience of Christian conversion on the road to Damascus was certainly one of the most dramatic of all (Acts 9:1-9; 22:1-21; 26:1-18). Yet Paul in one of his last letters, Paul at his most mature and mellow, wrote to the Christian community at Philippi in unforgettable language as to how he was as yet, then at the end of his life, still on the way, imperfect, inadequate in response and appropriation of the acceptance which Christ Jesus on the other hand had completely made of him (Phil. 1:6; 2:12-13; 3:8-16). This awareness of "unfinished business," I believe, has very wide significance for the comprehension of Christian faith needed in this day.

Jesus clearly called for utter committal of self in his appeals for renewal and restructuring of religious faith. His language on this theme, as recorded in Matthew, is particularly graphic as well as unmistakably lucid. Human beings are summoned to seek the Kingdom of God—and his righteousness—first above all things (Mt. 6:33). They are to "hunger and thirst" for that relationally rooted goodness, to yearn with all their strength of self in focus (Mt. 5:6; cf. 22:34-40). This point of human aspiration—as we shall see, the working out involves process—in the teaching of Jesus is precisely the area of creative divine-human encounter, the starting point, from the human side, of all religion and ethics. Anyone can desire or want, and hence no one is excluded for external reasons. We may note that here we have no theological game-playing as if the theological priority of divine grace could be allowed to weaken the vigor of human quest or effort. Jesus' appeal is for what, under God, any human being can do, that is, make a radical change of life-orientation, of life-goal or direction; it is a call for utter surrender, utter committal to the living God as One, as both our origin and our goal, as ideal and end. In Christian faith there can be only one such focus of human life-orientation; that is God (cf. Mt. 6:22-24; Lk. 10:41-42; Jn. 5:24).

But the New Testament records of Jesus' teaching make quite clear that the working out of this conscious Godward reorientation of life normally involves process, development, growth—including both time and space and patience. We have already noted that the Letter to the Hebrews speaks of Jesus himself as also participating in such process, "Although he was a Son, he learned obedience through what he suffered; and having been made perfect he became the source of eternal salvation for all who obey him" (Heb. 5:8-9; 2:10; cf. Lk. 2:52). A careful reading of the gospels shows that Jesus called his disciples to participate in a developmental process comparable to his own (cf. Lk. 9:23).

We shall see later that this could also be a call to participate in redemptive suffering as well as final glory. Jesus' parables of growth, which are usually also parables of the Kingdom of God, are especially notable exponents of the theme of process-development. This theme is a central characteristic of the parable of the sower and the soils, of the parable of growth by means unknown, of the parable of the mustard seed (Mk. 4:1-34), as of the parable of the wheat and weeds, the parable of leaven, possibly even the parable of the scribe "who brings out of his treasure what is new and what is old" (Mt. 13:1-52; cf. I Pet. 2:2).[82]

This theme of process-development in Jesus' teaching of the Kingdom of God is also related to certain hints in the teaching which suggest an open-endedness that has often been missed in the course of especially the Protestant theological tradition. These are hints of punishment/discipline with a time limit, as of fire seen as more purgative than purely penal. These themes emerge in Matthew with the indication that there can be an end to the "payment" for wrong-being (Mt. 5:26; 18:34), in the witness of John the Baptizer that Jesus will baptize "with the Holy Spirit and fire" (Mt. 3:11—the Greek does not have a definite article before Holy Spirit), in the suggestion that there are degrees of punishment assigned even "on the day of judgment" (Mt. 10:15; again, in the Greek there is no definite article; this means that the phrase can be translated "a day of judgment"; cf. the Greek also of Mt. 11:24; Lk. 10:12). In the Lukan parallel it becomes clear from the immediate context that the burning of the chaff with "unquenchable fire" is remedial purgation rather than eternal punishment (Lk. 3:15-17). Later in Luke we find Jesus himself expounding in clearest fashion the principle of proportionate judgment (12:47-48). Imagery of fire as more disciplinary than purely penal is also used by Paul (I Cor. 3:10-15), as by James (5:1-11). The teaching of Jesus as recorded in the eighteenth chapter of Matthew clearly points to open-ended forgiveness of others—"seventy times seven" can mean no other than unlimited forgiveness—as the proper expression of human solidarity and community, indeed of love, even as it is characteristic of the mind and practice of God (Mt. 18:10-14, 21-22; cf. Lk. 17:4).

We may say, therefore, that there are remarkable similarities in Jesus' teaching of the Kingdom of God with Gautama's teaching of *Nirvāṇa*, as with its focus in *Dharma*. Jesus proclaimed the Kingdom as having both present and future aspects, as Gautama did with reference to *Nirvāṇa*. And like the latter, he emphasized in his teaching present opportunities and responsibilities in the context of the present reality of the Kingdom. Furthermore, like the Buddha's focus of aspiration upon *Nirvāṇa* as the "One" rather than upon the "many," the Christ taught men and women to seek first the Kingdom of God and his righteousness and only secondarily—in theological priority—to relate to all other things or persons in this world (Mt. 6:33; 5:6). This is also to love God and one's neighbor as oneself (Mk. 12:28-34). In both there is an utterly consistent suffusing of the whole teaching with ethical qualities. We do not seem to see, however, in the Buddha's teaching of *Nirvāṇa* the full clarity of presentation of the "personal" element that looms so large in the Christ's proclamation of the Kingdom.

3

An aspect of Jesus' teaching which is not specifically associated with the Kingdom of God but which gives us particular insight into the character and activity of the King—as Father and Owner—is seen in Jesus' parables of the divine quest of the lost (cf. Lk. 19:10). This teaching, however, while given especially graphic form in these parables, is actually a central theme of the entire New Testament. We have already noted in the Gospel of John the significance of the Father's sending of Jesus—and Jesus' sending of his disciples—as expressive of a primary aspect of the Father's will (cf. Jn. 4:23; 5:14; 9:35 for other indications of God's and Jesus' quest-activity). But we also find Jesus' parable of the husbandmen in Mark (and in the other synoptic gospels) the same principle, focused in Jesus but extended to the entire prophetic past of Israel and possibly to the whole range of human history. This latter parable, which is by implication a tale of the primary meaning and purpose of human life as stewardship of trust, tells the story of an owner of a vineyard who had built and equipped it and let it out to tenants. The owner "went to another country" and "when the season came" sent a servant to get from them "his share of the produce of the vineyard." This servant and a series of others were variously mistreated by the tenants, and finally, when the owner sent another, "a beloved son," they killed him, hoping to take over the property (Mk. 12:1-12; Mt. 21:33-46; Lk. 20:9-19; cf. Isa. 5:1-7; Jer. 7:25). The immediate context of this parable of "Murder in the Vineyard" in the synoptic gospels suggests a kind of "negative polemic," but it also gives us corroborative insight into Jesus'—there is no convincing evidence that this parable, at least in its basic structure, is merely the product of the early church in the context of tensions with the synagogue—perception of the Father, not only of his long-suffering patience but also of his continued "sending."[83] The parable, as it stands, suggests some ontological difference between the servants sent and the son, but their function is the same. All were sent, all were obedient, all were variously mistreated—in faithfulness to the Father's purposes.

The Father-Owner's quest of the lost is especially seen in the parables of the lost sheep and the lost coin (Lk. 15:1-10; Mt. 18:10-14). The parable of the lost son (the prodigal son) is included by Luke—the parables of the lost son and the lost coin are found only in Luke (cf. Mt. 18:10-24)—in the same passage, but its imagery is of a Father who quietly waits, although with warmly loving patience and anticipation, for the return of his errant son (Lk. 15:11-32). The imagery of the first two, however, is of the Father-Owner who seeks, who takes the initiative to "go after the one that is lost until he finds it." Luke records Jesus as concluding each of these two parables with the statement, "Just so, I tell you, there will be more joy in heaven [or "in the presence of the angels of God"] over one sinner who repents than over ninety-nine righteous persons who need no repentance" (Lk. 15:7, 10). The statement is of sweeping joy, not only in the Father's heart, but also in the whole realm of the heavenly hosts, over the repentant return of one of God's errant ones.

We took note in the previous chapter that this thesis of the Father—imagery expressive of the quality of both the character and activity of Ultimate Reality—as taking initiative, as "moving out," to seek and to save that which is lost is an aspect of Jesus' teaching which we do not find comparably in Gautama's. This point, then, prompts us to move to consideration of an element of the Christ's teaching which plays an almost comparable role in the Buddha's. This is what we have noted as *karma* in the latter's teaching and is found in Jesus—and in the whole range of apostolic teaching—as a form of the law of compensation. The apostle Paul preferred to denote the theme with the imagery of sowing and reaping (Gal. 6:7-9).[84]

This principle of sowing and reaping is an exceedingly important part of the teaching of Jesus that has been either largely neglected in recent years or grossly distorted into savagely vengeful final judgments on proximate issues by, respectively, the left or right wings of the Protestant tradition. One consequence has been, I believe, to contribute to the general inability on the part of the religious and cultural pundits of our society to understand the nature of the historical process. We shall consider later the more general implications of Jesus'—and the apostolic generation's—teaching of this principle. Let us first turn to the biblical witnesses to it.

A key passage in the synoptic gospels is the one in Matthew's Sermon on the Mount where Jesus is recorded as saying, "Do not judge, so that you may not be judged. For with the judgment you make you will be judged, and the measure you give will be the measure you get" (Mt. 7:1-2; cf. Mk. 4:24; Luke transfers the language into positive form, but allows the negative significance to remain as implicit; Lk. 6:37-38). There is an almost unquestioned consensus among biblical scholars that the Sermon on the Mount in Matthew is a collection of teachings and sayings given on a variety of occasions, and, therefore, the immediate context may not in all cases be significantly helpful for interpretation.[85] But we have teaching here that at first appears to be quite contrary to the open-ended, generous, forgiving compassion that Jesus consistently posited of the Father-King, as I have tried to depict in the preceding pages. The fact is, however, that this stern teaching is not contrary to the other but the opposite side of the same coin, a side as necessary to the whole as the other, an indispensable part of the Father's working. We find the same principle enunciated in Jesus' words when in the garden of Gethsemane one of his disciples (identified as Peter in Jn. 18:10) cut off the ear of a slave of the high priest: "Put your sword back into its place; for all who take the sword will perish by the sword" (Mt. 26:52; cf. Gen. 9:6; Rev. 13:10; Mt. 26:47-56; Mk. 14:43-50; Lk. 22:47-53—Luke alone reports that Jesus touched the slave's ear and healed him—Jn. 18:1-11).

Logically, the two sides of this coin of understanding are at times difficult to reconcile, but the apostle Paul emphasizes the inseparable combination of the two sides with his famous, "Note then the kindness and the severity (*apotomian*) of God" (Rom. 11:22). Paul himself, however, in the sentences immediately following this affirmation makes a preliminary attempt to reconcile the apparent paradox, "severity toward those who have fallen, but God's kindness toward you, provided you continue in his kindness; otherwise you also will be cut off. And even those of Israel, if they do not persist in unbelief, will be grafted in, for God has the power to graft them in again" (Rom. 11:22-23).

Actually, the whole of chapter seven in Matthew represents attempts on Jesus' part to communicate this sterner side of God's working, a severity which expresses itself in an ordering of consequences so as to follow prior actions more closely (more closely in causal sequence than necessarily in temporal) than human beings would commonly allow. And yet at the same time this movement of causal sequence is not held to be rigid, unbreakable, irrevocable. We have to do with a process of ethical causality which is both corporately—indeed, cosmically—and personally significant, yet breachable.

This seventh chapter of Matthew also contains what is the sole criterion given us by Jesus, as reported in the synoptic gospels, for discerning the authenticity of religious teachers. This is the ethical test: "Thus you will know them by their fruits" (Mt. 7:20). The passage as a whole, when considered in connection with the parables of judgment given in the twenty-fifth chapter of Matthew, emphasizes that the vital issues of life are not matters of names, labels, or other external forms but ethical. This is, of course, ethics in the sense not merely of external deeds, but even more of the interiority of human life, the basic orientation of the whole self of persons (Mt. 7:1-27; 25:1-46; cf. Mk. 7:14-23). But Jesus clearly and strongly emphasizes that this basic ethical orientation—the result, as we may distinctly infer from the whole spectrum of Jesus' teaching as recorded in the New Testament, of a series of religio-ethical choices of free persons—brings consequences of enormous import for human life both on this earthly plane and on others.[86]

Jesus also makes clear, as is recorded in other passages, that human beings should not interpret this principle of sowing and reaping in a judgmental or rigid way, at least in part because they do not know the details of the process involved. In the Gospel of Luke we find mention of an incident when some persons gave a report to Jesus of Pilate's bloody destruction of a number of Galileans at the very time that they were offering their religious sacrifices. This incident is not known to us from any other source, nor is the other incident known, which is mentioned by Jesus in the same context, that of the eighteen persons killed when the tower of Siloam in Jerusalem fell upon them. The recording of this discussion in Luke follows immediately after Jesus' warning to his fellow Jews that they could and ought to discern the signs of the frightful storm impending upon the nation. His questioners may have tried to turn Jesus' warning back upon him by suggesting that his fellow Galileans— who were perhaps involved in a kind of nationalistic, pseudo-messianic movement—had received an appropriate punishment for their own *hubris* and that Jesus was overreacting with warnings of disaster that could affect the whole nation (Lk. 12:35-13:7). The discourse was, of course, in the context of the Jewish popular notion that special sins bring special punishments.[87]

Jesus' response on this occasion is particularly significant. His first point was apparently that the persons who suffered these spectacular calamities were not to be identified as sinners (or "debtors" before God) beyond others simply because of the externally hideous nature of their death. There would appear also to be implied in his language the further point that there are factors or elements in the human situation beyond what are commonly known and that it behooves all to refrain from premature evaluations of the human guilt involved. But at the same time he strongly emphasized that this need to refrain from hasty judgmentalism does not mean that there is no compensatory process in which the ethical activity-being of persons in God's cosmos participates. Twice we find repeated in this passage Jesus' words, "but unless you repent you will all perish just as they did" (Lk. 13:3, 5). It is, of course, not without reason that Luke places immediately following this teaching Jesus' parable of the fig tree that after three years' tending bears no fruit. The point of the parable is the willingness of God to wait, not only to give another chance, but to give special care to the needs of the unfruitful. At the same time the parable warns against presuming upon God's patience (Lk. 13:6-9; cf. Jn. 5:14; 8:11).

In the incident of the healing of the man born blind as recorded in the Gospel of John we find a similar case of Jesus' refusal to assign particular blame and at the same time an emphasis in the entire passage that the process of moral judgment continues, although in ways different from the quick and superficial judgments of popular religion (Jn. 9:1-41; cf. 8:11). The corrections even of the Jewish written law, of the Torah itself, that we find in the early part of the Sermon on the Mount ("You have heard that it was said to those of ancient times... But I say to you") are by no means denials of the ethical principle of compensatory judgment but recastings of the whole issue of ethical conduct in the direction of emphasis upon the prior significance of interiority and the reconciliation of persons (Mt. 5:17-48). In particular, human beings are not to assume the divine role of executors of the compensatory process with regard to other persons or themselves (Mt. 5:38-48).

As we have noted, the principle of ethical compensation is described by Paul with the imagery of sowing and reaping. The context, however, within which Paul enunciates the principle and uses the imagery is particularly significant.

The context is the Letter to the Galatians, the main theme of which is to emphasize the liberating power of the work of Jesus Christ, "who gave himself for our sins to set us free from the present evil age, according to the will of our God and Father" (Gal. 1:4-5; cf. II Cor. 4:4; Eph. 6:12; I Jn. 5:19; Rev. 2:13). This affirmation of the liberating work of Jesus Christ under God the Father clearly refers to its power to free human beings—who are open—from the constricting bondage of their participation in "the present evil age," not to take them out of it (cf. Gal. 4:8-9; I Pet. 2:16). Paul stresses that this work is of God, an expression of his gracious love, and that the proper human response is not the ritualistic works of formal religion, but "faith working through love" (Gal. 2:16; 5:6, 13-14). But at the end of this "Manifesto of Christian Freedom," Paul warns his readers not to misunderstand the divine working of liberation, as if one could misuse with impunity God's gracious gift of freedom from past bondage. For the divinely ordered compensatory process continues to work even in the case of those who have been once set free from the bondage of their past. "Do not be deceived; God is not mocked, for you reap whatever you sow. For if you sow to your own flesh [in Paul "flesh" is regularly used in the sense of the human self in self-centered alienation from God, immoral in mind as well as in body; cf. Gal. 5:19-24], you will reap corruption from the flesh; but if you sow to the Spirit, you will reap eternal life from the Spirit. So let us not grow weary in doing what is right, for we will reap at harvest-time, if we do not give up. So then, whenever we have an opportunity, let us work for the good of all, and especially for those of the family of faith" (Gal. 6:7-10).

We have here a magnificent affirmation with particularly graphic imagery of Paul's above-mentioned kindness and severity of God as constituting two sides of the same coin (Rom. 11:22), a principle far from the semi-magical notions of grace and faith with which the history of the Christian church in every major tradition abounds. But I wish to stress that this passage in Galatians is not an isolated one, either with reference to the other letters of Paul or to the New Testament as a whole. I urge my readers to consult the many references which I adduce in the endnote at this point.[88]

The principle of sowing and reaping, I aver, is essentially akin to the understanding of *karma* in the teaching of the Buddha. It is not in itself the gospel, that is, it is not the proclamation of the possibility of liberation from the bondage of the human past. It is rather the divinely ordered causal structure within which the grace of God, especially as focused in the person and work of Jesus the Christ, may work. As in the case of the Buddha, the possibility-opportunity of liberation is the prior religious reality, a reality which the Christ served in a unique way to make possible, but which the Buddha, however proleptically, rightly perceived as possible in some way in his own time and place. To use traditional Christian terminology, the grace of God supersedes and transcends the principle of compensation, or *karma*, for those who will let it, but not so as to eliminate the ongoing working of the principle. We may infer from the teaching of Jesus and, indeed, of the mainstream of biblical witness that the nature of the causal process itself is so structured that, however firm, it is yet sufficiently open-ended and internally flexible as to allow the effective working of the liberating, healing, transforming power of God that we call grace. We use the term *grace* (*charis*) because it indicates the gracious goodness of God (cf. Mk. 10:18), his active, questing initiative in working for the salvation, the restoration to right relationship, the complete qualitative transformation, of the whole of the cosmos. The grace of God, however, does not destroy the causal process; it fulfills or, we may say, restores it to its proper equilibrium—and thus makes restoration and change possible for all, in the context of retention of the ongoing significance of the consequences of moral conduct.

A final point on this theme may be in order here. The principle of compensation may be properly viewed theologically as an element of the larger area of what traditionally has been called the providence of God. This latter is an exceedingly difficult and complex matter, and I have space here only to delineate certain basic issues. The issue in the present context is, of course, what is the teaching of Jesus and secondarily that of the apostolic figures of the New Testament. I shall refer to the complex variety of Old Testament positions only incidentally.

Briefly stated, the recorded teaching of Jesus on the theme of divine providence, fragmentary at best as we have it, stresses the prior fact of the loving care of God the Father for the whole of his creation. The Gospel of Matthew is perhaps the most fulsome in its account of this fact. One aspect of God's loving care that Jesus stressed is concern for the physical needs of creatures. God the Father provides food for the birds of the air and is responsible for the growth and the beauty of the flowers of the field (Mt. 6:26-29). This is the aspect of divine providence that Barnabas and Paul are recorded as stressing in their attempts to explain the past relationship of God to the pagans of Lystra, in Lycaonia of Asia Minor, and to their ancestors (Acts 14:8-18). But Jesus seems to imply that these gracious acts of God are not determinative of all external events, but rather constitute the provision of what is necessary to the sustenance of human (as well as other) physical life on earth and at the same time give the structure of opportunity, within limits, for what is necessary for human moral and spiritual transformation-growth.

In Matthew 10:29 we read in the NRSV translation words of Jesus spoken regarding the existence of sparrows, "not one of them will fall to the ground apart from your Father."

That is, the event does not take place apart from the Father's knowledge and structuring supervision-control *(aneu tou Patros hymon)*, but it is quite gratuitous, textually as well as theologically, to conclude that such events necessarily occur in accordance with the Father's will as may be implied from the older RSV translation. The new translation is a more faithful rendition of the original Greek.

In the same passage in Matthew 10 we find the famous statement of Jesus indicative of the close and eminently knowing as well as caring watch that God exercises over his human creation, "even the hairs of your head are all counted." Then follows the affirmation of what posture of faith ought to follow from this understanding: "So do not be afraid." This admonition, in turn, is followed by the statement, in agreement with the mainstream of biblical teaching, of what is a high anthropology, the high position of human beings in a cosmos of hierarchically arranged levels of value, "you are of more value than many sparrows" (Mt. 10:29-31; cf. 12:12, "How much more valuable is a human being than a sheep!").

The teaching of Jesus that I have already denoted in other contexts as the principle of proportionate judgment involves not only just proportions of punishment and appropriate time limits (Lk. 12:47-48, 59). Also involved is the positive principle of stewardship, whereby, as in the parable of talents, largeness of endowment is no reason for sloth and smallness of endowment no reason for despair. As we have seen with the possibilities of some form of human pre-existence, there may be no arbitrariness at all in the divine allocation of human talents and situations in any one time period. But equally implied in this parable is the possibility of human freedom of action, within limits divinely ordered, toward good or evil (Mt. 25:14-30; cf. Lk. 19:11-27). Indeed, the whole range of Jesus' teaching as recorded in the synoptic gospels—in a special way the parables of growth (Mt.

13:1-52)—implies the fact of human freedom, within limits, as human opportunity that is the expression of providentially ordered divine graciousness. Any interpretation of human life that turns this understanding into either denial of limited human freedom-opportunity or affirmation of unlimited (and thus unstructured) human freedom-potential misses the essence of what Jesus was about.[89]

A brief word may be added at this point regarding Paul's handling of this theme. As is well known, some of his most seminal thoughts on the theme are found in the eighth chapter of Romans. Paul seems to include the whole of humanity (with consequences for the whole creation) as having become, presumably as a result of their "ungodliness and wickedness" (Rom. 1:18-23), futile in their thinking, with minds darkened and desires frustrated. But this subjection is in hope, to the end that all the rest of creation may experience with the children of God liberation from bondage to decay (the destructive effects of disobedience) and participate in the glorious liberty planned for all. There is now at work a process that Paul describes with the imagery of birth pangs, summing up the universal experience of suffering with the words, "We know that the whole creation has been groaning in labor pains until now; and not only the creation, but we ourselves, who have the first fruits of the Spirit, groan inwardly while we wait for adoption, the redemption of our bodies" (Rom. 8:18-25). As we noted earlier, for Paul the process of divine salvation-restoration is by no means finished (cf. I Cor. 1:18; Phil. 1:6; 2:12-13; 3:11-16).

But Paul insists that in the entire process everything works together for good for those who love God, who are also persons who have been called into this response-relationship according to the purposes of God. Then follows language which some have interpreted as indicating Paul's belief in a totally determined divine predestination of human destinies, but which in the Greek, as illumined by the

larger context, reveals simply the structure of God's plan
under the aegis of his sovereignty (Rom. 8:28-30). We have
already noted that the conclusion of Paul's thought on this
theme in Romans is found in the eleventh chapter, where
he expresses his hope for the salvation of all Israel, including those who have rejected Jesus as the Messiah, and indeed of all humankind.

Actually, the closer detail of Paul's thought on this theme
is revealed in his pastorally oriented First Letter to the
Corinthians. Here he writes of the structure of moral consequence and freedom-opportunity which God provides for
all and which, to those who believe and understand, gives
both encouragement and freedom from anxiety, "No testing has overtaken you that is not common to everyone. God
is faithful and he will not let you be tested beyond your
strength, but with the testing he will also provide the way
out so that you may be able to endure it" (I Cor. 10:13; cf.
Phil. 4:11-13; I Thess. 3:4). The teaching of Jesus and the
chief tenor of the entire New Testament make it clear that
the phrase "the way out" is not to be understood merely in a
negative way, but in the positive sense of giving human beings the opportunity for coping with or correcting the situation that from one point of view may be considered as a
temptation, from another as a trial or as a disappointment.
The basic fact of human life implicit in Christian faith is that
God constantly gives opportunities "again and again—and
yet again." Jesus taught that as human beings we have the
right, by invitation, to ask of God, to petition, as our part in
this open-ended situation. And his promise is that our
prayers will be heard—even if not answered on our own
terms. For he says, "Ask, and it will be given you; search, and
you will find; knock, and the door will be opened for you.
For everyone who asks receives, and everyone who searches
finds, and for everyone who knocks, the door will be
opened" (Mt. 7:7-8; cf. Lk. 11:9-10).

To sum up then, as best we can, the New Testament teaching on divine providence, there seems to be, in spite of differing nuances of understanding, a remarkable basic unity of perception. This is that the present structures of human life—not primarily the institutions of society, but the particular concatenations of activities and situations that constitute the time-to-time context of personal and corporate being—are divinely ordained. They are ordained not in the sense that the activities and situations that lead up to the "present" focus or concatenation are totally of God; many, if not most, of these events are the result of previous human being and doing. They are ordained in the sense that the fact of any focus or concatenation (instead of chaos) is in accordance with the working of divine law, the law of sowing and reaping, of causal relationship.

This fact of divine law, however, being the basis for ordered concatenations of events or meaningful linkage as in a chain is never to be understood as if human beings are "boxed in" in any total way, even when their own contribution to negatively perceived aspects of the "present" situation may be substantial. Quite the contrary, the New Testament affirmation of faith is that the particular concatenation of activities, situations, and being that constitutes the inner and outer situation of persons at any time and place is precisely the divinely ordained arena of "present" human opportunity. It is properly seen as more mobile than static. The "present" is the time and place where we may meet God; hence, "now is the acceptable time . . . now is the day of salvation" (II Cor. 6:2)! The New Testament affirmation is further that the life and death, the resurrection and ascension of Jesus the Christ play a decisive role in making cosmically possible this meeting of human beings with their Maker (reconciliation—II Cor. 5:17-20; Col. 1:19-20—first in theological priority with God, then with other human beings, then with all else) as also their liberation from the constrictive aspects of any "present" situation into a process of spiritual and moral growth in continuing friendship with God and his Christ (cf. Jn. 15:12-15).

This "present," to be sure, is also the arena where we contend, perhaps more with ourselves than with others, but also "against the rulers, against the authorities, against the cosmic powers of this present darkness, against the spiritual forces of evil in the heavenly places" (Eph. 6:12; cf. II Cor. 10:36). It is, however, the place where by the grace of God significant victory may be won and owned, victory that causes no other to lose (*pace,* I Cor. 9:24). Furthermore, this "present" concatenation of activities, events, and being forms precisely the context for our own responsible participation—under and with our God, in his Spirit and through his Christ—in activity-being that may lead toward significant change, the transformation of our very selves and of all else according to the will of God.

From our customarily limited human perspective, the opportunities for change of ourselves or others may appear at any one time to be of slight consequence and the results of our efforts trifling. But that there is truly significant and potentially fruitful opportunity in even the apparently most hopeless and limited of human situations is a consistent theme of New Testament teaching. One can always serve, and "they also serve who only stand and wait." For this reason we may rightly speak of "history," of the divinely ordained significance not only of large-scale events in human life, but also of the importance before God of the "little things" that we are inclined to dismiss as trivial. These latter, we believe, also contribute—"line upon line, line upon line, here a little, there a little" (Isa. 28:10)—with their own rich significance and power to the fulfillment of the final purposes of our God.

4

A final word on the teaching of Jesus should focus on what in fact is perhaps its central theme and the heart of the gospel. This is Jesus' response to the question put him as to what is the first of all commandments. Jesus answered, "The first is, 'Hear, O Israel: The Lord our God, the Lord is one; you shall love the Lord your God with all your heart, and with all your soul, and with all your mind, and with all your strength.' The second is this, 'You shall love your neighbor as yourself.' There is no other commandment greater than these" (Mk. 12:28-31; cf. Deut. 6:4; Lev. 19:18). We may note that when the scribe who had been the original questioner responded in wisely understanding agreement, Jesus said to him, "You are not far from the kingdom of God" (Mk. 12: 32-34).[90]

Scholastically minded Protestants may object to my identifying this teaching as central and of the heart of the gospel. But the oneness of God was clearly central to Jesus' perception and teaching, and all christology and trinitarianism within the New Testament find their place subordinately under the rubric of prior divine unity. Jesus' call for human response to God as properly in the form of love for both God and neighbor (the widely inclusive range of what is meant by neighbor is clarified in the parable of the good Samaritan, Lk. 10:25-37) actually presupposes both the priority and the graciousness of the love of God for his entire creation which, as we have seen, is basic to the other recorded expressions of Jesus' teaching. No human response of faith, however, according to Jesus' teaching and that of the apostolic generation, can properly be separated from obedience-response of the whole person, both inner and outer, which is best expressed by the term *love*. Jesus' "rule of ethics" was simply, "In everything do to others as you would have them do to you; for this is the law and the prophets" and "just as you did it to one of the least of these who are members of my family, you did it to me" (Mt. 7:12; 25:40). Given Jesus' emphasis upon the priority of the interior dimensions of human life, upon their motivational as well as intellective aspects, which we have already noted, nothing else than the other-directed orientation of life that the New Testament denotes with the term *love (agapē)* would do to identify this teaching of God's primary will, which is also his nature (cf. I Jn. 4:7-12). We should also note that what is called the Great Commission (Mt. 28:16-20) and is witnessed to in the other gospels as the risen Christ's summons of the church to missionary activity of the widest range, that is, to the widest personal, corporate, and cultural as well as geographical extent, is properly to be regarded as the expression of reaching out in love in accord with the Great Commandment (cf. Mk. 16:14-18; Lk. 24:45-49; Jn. 20:19-23).

It is singularly appropriate that the apostle Paul in his great hymn to love should identify it as the crown of all ethics and elsewhere cite it as the summation and fulfillment of the moral law of the entire tradition of Israel (I Cor. 12:31-13:13; Rom. 13:8-10; Gal. 5:14; cf. Phil. 2:1-11). But for Paul as for Jesus, the human response of love for God and fellow beings is not to be dissociated from faith as if it were some kind of self-contained ethical posture. Faith in turn is not primarily intellectual acquiescence to the truth of propositional statements, but fundamentally expressive of relationship: trustful, worshipful, grateful, committed, other-oriented, gracious. For Paul it is of the essence of this relationship that one be "known" by God, but to be known by God is unthinkable apart from loving him. Indeed, to love God is a sign that one is known by him ("anyone who loves God is known by him," I Cor. 8:3; 13:12). In the Johannine literature, as we have seen, love is the basic quality of the character of God and is expressed notably in his work of "sending," supremely in the sending of his Son (Jn. 3:16; I Jn. 4:7-21). But quite in the line of both Jesus and Paul, the disciples are also "sent," and the essence of their role as sent ones is to love—their neighbor as well as God (Jn. 17:18, 23; I Jn. 4:7-21). We may note that to love God, self, and neighbor is more of a unitary activity than is commonly thought. If God's Son is life (Jn. 14:6), to love God is to love life.

Related to this teaching of love as descriptive of the proper relationship of persons, both divine and human, is Jesus' imagery of the nature of the human self in this relationship. This is the imagery of discipleship wherein "those who lose their life for my sake, and for the sake of the gospel, will save it" (Mk. 8:35; cf. Mt. 10:39; 16:25; Lk. 17:33; Jn. 12:25). This language, however, is more than metaphorical. It is denotative of radical change in human life-orientation, relationships, and character.[91] We shall discuss later how close this language brings us to the teaching of the Buddha on the self.

The author of the Revelation has also given us helpful imagery in order better to understand the nature of this change. The imagery is well given in the sentence bearing words as of the risen Lord to the angel of the church in Laodicea, "Behold, I stand at the door and knock; if any one hears my voice and opens the door, I will come in to him and eat with him, and he with me" (Rev. 3: 20). The imagery here is of the empirical human self as akin to a house with a shut door, separate, alienated, self-contained. As in the teaching of Jesus himself, the Lord takes the initiative to knock and to speak in order to initiate (renew) the relationship. If the person opens the door of self, the Lord of life crosses the threshold and enters into a relationship of intimacy denoted by the imagery of eating and drinking. But the old self of the closed door—separate, alienated, self-contained—no longer exists. The language implies radical change in life orientation and in basic personal relationships.

Paul uses his own kind of distinctive imagery to portray
the change involved. This is imagery taken from the cardinal events of the life of Jesus, the crucifixion and resurrection of Jesus applied to the life-changes properly wrought
by faith-committal to God through Jesus Christ as mediator: "We know that our old self was crucified with him so
that the body of sin might be destroyed, and we might no
longer be enslaved to sin . . . But if we have died with Christ,
we believe that we will also live with him" (Rom. 6:6-8). In
Paul's Letter to the Galatians, one of his earlier writings, he
writes in similar wise, "I have been crucified with Christ; and
it is no longer I who live, but it is Christ who lives in me. And
the life I now live in the flesh I live by faith in the Son of God,
who loved me and gave himself for me" (Gal. 2:20).

Paul does not hesitate to use other images for the anticipated change even in Galatians. One image is that of liberation from slavery, another is coming into adulthood and its
attendant freedom and responsibility (Gal. 3:23-26; 4:1-7).
Furthermore, he makes clear in various passages that the
change, which he also denotes as a new creation and as reconciliation with God (II Cor. 5:17-20), is not to be understood as totally completed. As we have noted above, there is
still much to do and to become (Phil. 1:6; 2:12-13; 3:10-16).
In Colossians he specifically identifies the Christian recipi-
ents of his letter as persons who "have stripped off the old
self with its practices and have clothed yourselves with the
new self, which is being renewed (anakainoumenon) in
knowledge according to the image of its creator" (Col. 3:9-
10). This use of the present tense to denote the ongoing "renewing" (liberating, healing, transforming) work of God in
persons who are already committed believers is found in
many passages in Paul's letters (e.g., I Cor. 1:18; II Cor. 4:16:
"So we do not lose heart. Even though our outer nature is
wasting away, our inner nature is being renewed day by
day"; cf. II Cor. 5:1-10). A surprisingly large element of the

hortatory language directed to Christian believers to strive and to do is found in the Pauline corpus often immediately following statements of what at first appear to be completed conditions (e.g., II Cor. 5:17-20; the hortatory subjunctive is probably the better textual reading even for Rom. 5:1; cf. 6:13). The reason is that the final purpose of God through Jesus Christ is "to reconcile to himself all things, whether on earth or in heaven, by making peace through the blood of his cross" (Col. 1:20; cf. I Cor. 15:28).

5

What, then, of the church in the teaching of Jesus? The New Testament word for church (*ecclesia*), used to denote the universal fellowship of Christian believers, or the local congregation seen as manifesting that fellowship, had been previously used in classical Greek as a technical term for a regularly summoned legislative assembly. It was employed in the Septuagint to denote the congregation of the Israelites, especially when gathered for religious purposes (Deut. 31:30; Judg. 20:2; I Km. 17:47 = I Sam. 17:47; III Km. 8:14 = I Kg. 8:14). In spite of the important place, however, that the word has in the rest of the New Testament, it is found in the gospels only in Matthew (16:18; 18:17). The result is that many biblical scholars have concluded that "Jesus cannot have spoken often of the church, if he did so at all."[92]

As we have seen, Jesus' use of the term Kingdom of God reveals, among other things, the universal ranges of his ultimate concerns. He was ultimately concerned not only for Israel, not even only for all of Israel, not only for his own disciples, but for all of humanity, indeed the whole of creation. And yet he gave special attention to the training of those who would follow him more closely, particularly to the twelve (Mk. 3:7-19; Mt. 5:1 ff.; Lk. 6:12-16; cf. also the seventy of Lk. 10:1-24). These texts also reveal Jesus' ministry, like Gautama's, as including an alternation of both attention and somewhat of methodology with reference to the training of closer disciples and the "manyfolk" (cf. Mk. 4:10-34). Like the Buddha, the Christ evidently envisaged some mode of universal mission from the beginning, and his very appeal to the whole of Israel was probably that Israel might take up and fulfill as a whole the priestly-missionary role to which it owed its very constitution and best self-awareness as a people (Gen. 12:1-3; I Kings 8:41-43; II Chron. 6:32-33; Amos 9:11-12; Isa. 49:6; 56:8; Jonah 4:1-11).

There is no evidence of Jesus' employing the term *body* *(soma)* to denote the group constituted by his disciples. There is no evidence that he drew a fixed or permanent line of division between his disciples and others. Indeed, the whole of his ministry points to an abiding intent to extend what was only a provisional line (cf. Jn. 10:16; 17:20-22). As the Sri Lankan theologian S. Wesley Ariarajah has well said, the Christian community is not the final form of the community that God intends but "is the provisional, the sign-community, the leaven, the salt, the light, the servant." As is well known, the image of "the body of Christ" was particularly beloved of the apostle Paul with intent to denote the intimacy of relationship between the Lord Jesus and the fellowship of his believers. It was intended to indicate something of the spiritual participation of believers in the risen Christ, even as the particular image of the Christ as the head of the body was used to affirm his ongoing authority as Lord (Rom. 12:4-5; I Cor. 12:12-13, 27; Col. 1:18; Eph. 1:22-23).

Actually, we seem to find a progression in Paul's thought from a concept of the church as constituting interrelated parts of a body, imagery suggestive of an organic spiritual reality that forms a cooperating unity from its several parts in Romans and I Corinthians to the Christ as head both of this body and of all things in the cosmos in Colossians (and in the Deutero-Pauline Ephesians). This is affirmation of the

Christ as *pancrator*, "the head of every ruler and authority" in the universe (Col. 2:10; Eph. 1:22). As I have tried to indicate previously with various kinds of supportive evidence, apparently few if any in the apostolic generation thought of the church as a static body with permanently fixed boundaries. It was also, as we have seen, not a part of the original apostolic *kerygma* to speak with finality of the ultimate destiny of those who did not hear that *kerygma* or even of those who did not heed it (Rom. 9-11; I Tim. 4:10). The younger Paul's strong language in Second Thessalonians is, of course, eschatological, referring to judgment at the end of history (1:5-11); we see even here, however, that the issue is one of faith or unbelief, each correlated with ethical consequence (1:8; 2:12). And the best textual reading in II Thessalonians 2:13 is *aparchen*, the church as the "first fruits" of those to be saved "through sanctification by the Spirit [of spirit?] and through belief in the truth."

This is to say that the New Testament evidence all points to Jesus' having had an instrumental perception of the role and status of his followers, as the tradition of Israel at its best had of its own role and status. Their election was for service, not for privilege. The church of Jesus Christ can be seen in a sense, therefore, as the picked troops of the Lord, picked for special functions and training, even for special modes of relationship. They are not, however, all of the body to be, nor are they all of the troops presently under command and in service. This means then that the composition of Jesus' followers, neither then nor now, was fixed in any final sense, either in the direction of income or of outgo (cf. I Tim. 2:4; 4:10; I Cor. 10:12; I Thess. 3:5), regardless of the variety of ways the historic church has handled this issue. As Paul has rightly said, even if he begins somewhat scholastically, "God has imprisoned all in disobedience so that he may be merciful to all. O the depth of the riches and wisdom and knowledge of God! . . . For from him and

through him and to him are all things. To him be the glory
forever. Amen" (Rom. 11:32-36). To be a member of the
church of Jesus Christ is both high opportunity and consequent duty, but it does not bespeak the totality of "the riches
and wisdom and knowledge of God."

A further aspect of the church, according to the witness
of the New Testament, is that of the fellowship *(koinonia)* of
the followers of Jesus. The emphasis here, however, is upon
the quality of life of the fellowship, not upon its exclusivity.
The New Testament gospels show us the disciples as a mediating group between Jesus and others. The fellowship is
to be supremely marked by the unselfish love that its participants have for each another, and for others (Mt. 5:43-48;
Mk. 12:28-34; Lk. 10:25-37; Jn. 15:12, 17; I Jn. 3:11, 16-18, 23;
4:20-21; II Jn. 5-6; Rom. 13:8-10; I Cor. 13; Gal. 5:2; I Thess.
4:9-10; Jas. 2:8; I Pet. 1:22; 2:17). The best theological thought
of our day sees the Christian church as a sign, an effective
sign to be sure, but a sign of God's saving love for all, a sign
of universal salvation (by divine intent), a mystery, a sacrament of the unity of the whole of creation in God's plan for
all, as also a herald and servant of the purposes of God. Nowhere in the entire New Testament is there a passage that
posits formal membership in the Christian church as a condition of salvation.

The Work of Jesus the Christ

1

As indicated above, the purpose of this chapter is not to attempt a new "Life of Christ," but to focus on primary meanings of the event of Jesus the Christ. The "historical" basis of this last section lies in the events of the last week of Jesus' life as recorded in the New Testament, supremely the events of the cross, the resurrection, and the ascension. This is not the place to discuss details of these events. I would say only that I accept the event of Jesus' resurrection from the dead as "historical" even as I accept his death on the cross as historical. I put quotation marks around the word "historical" in the first instance, because it is clear from the New Testament accounts that there were transhistorical as

well as historical aspects in the event of the resurrection.
We are presented not only with an empty tomb (Mk. 16:6),
not only with a series of verbal communications (Mt. 28:9-
20; Mk. 16:9-19; Lk. 24:13-53; Jn. 20:11-23; Acts 1:1-8). There
are also stories, along with those of Jesus' eating food and
being tangible (Lk. 24:41-43; Jn. 20:24-29; Acts 10:41), of
Jesus' being able to appear suddenly inside different places
where the doors were closed (Lk. 24:36-43; Jn. 20:19, 26). As
we noted earlier, there are various accounts of bilocation or
out-of-the-body events that have been witnessed by others
as well as testified to by the subjects in this and in previous
centuries. I myself, however, know of no case that combines
all of the factors that are described in the New Testament as
involved in Jesus' resurrection, especially the combination
of bilocation with tangibility and the eating of food.
Whether certain aspects of the event, then, are better described as transhistorical or multidimensional, it is difficult
to say, but I personally wish to affirm my faith in the event
as one that "happened."[93]

The primary question for us, however, in this consideration of the crucifixion, resurrection, and ascension of Jesus
will be one of meanings. I should like to explore the possibility that we have in the case of Jesus of Nazareth what we
do not perceive in either Gautama, Zarathustra, or Muhammad;
that is, a consciously chosen vicarious-redemptive role. We
see in Jesus as in the others a comparable prophetic-critical
role, a comparable sense of relationship with Ultimate Reality. But there appears to be in Jesus a distinct self-awareness of being called and acting as an instrument of the Most
High to perform a service of cosmic import for others that
they could not perform for themselves, one that we do not
appear to find comparably in the other great figures of the
human religious pilgrimage here cited.

The problem of the self-consciousness or self-awareness
of Jesus has long been a critical issue among biblical

scholars, with interpretations ranging from total skepticism to uncritical acceptance of every intimation to be found in all four gospels. I shall give my own view with primary attention to the above-mentioned vicariously redemptive role.

We have already noted the importance for perceiving the self-awareness of Jesus in the parable of the wicked husbandmen (Mk. 12:1-12; Mt. 21:33-46; Lk. 20:9-19). There are, to be sure, problems about accepting the parable in its present form, with its allegorizing tendencies, as authentically of Jesus. It has internal inconsistencies and fits ill with certain aspects of the known legal and social situation of Palestine during Jesus' lifetime.[94] But as we have seen, no objection need be made merely because the parable as it stands implies on Jesus' part predictive knowledge—either of his own death or of the destruction of Jerusalem in 70 C.E. There is simply no reason, if we are willing to take in wider ranges of human experience, to doubt the structural possibility of such knowledge. We may also properly note a form of this parable in the Gospel of Thomas (Logion 65), particularly in the context of recent suggestions that this gospel may date from the mid-first century of our era.[95]

As we have also seen, the commonality of participating in divine sending by both servants and son in the parable comports well with a basic theme of the Gospel of John. The scriptural reference in the parable (Ps. 118:22-23) to the stone that once rejected becomes the very cornerstone, even if added by Mark and followed by Matthew and Luke, was clearly a significant element of the *loci communes* of the faith of the early Christian communities (Mk. 12:10-11; cf. Acts 4:11; I Pet. 2:6-7). These communities certainly thought that during his public ministry Jesus had such self-awareness of being sent by the Father and that for the purpose of dying a sacrificial death for others. Significant elements of the parable of the wicked husbandmen can, therefore, I believe, be retained as indicative of the self-awareness of Jesus.

We find in Matthew and Luke accounts of requests made of Jesus for a "sign from heaven" with materials that go beyond that of Mark and add a distinct christological note. They may also give us further indications of Jesus' self-awareness (Mt. 12:38-42; Lk. 11:29-32; cf. Mk. 8:11-12). These accounts cite a statement of Jesus that makes an implicit comparison of his own ministry with that of Jonah; viz., "something greater than Jonah is here!" Then there is a further statement made in connection with mention of the queen of the South's coming from afar to hear the wisdom of Solomon; viz., "something greater than Solomon is here!" Statements of this kind may appear to comport ill with the modesty and reserve of Jesus that we have already noted. But the fact that the neuter form of the adjective is used *(pleion)* may be Jesus' way of saying that a greater action of God is occurring than in the former instances. The emphasis could thus be upon the greater glory of God and Jesus' work as the Father's agent rather than upon his own person. We may note that a number of scholars believe the shorter form of the incident as given in Mark is an abbreviation of the original rather than the other way around.[96]

Another account of significance for Jesus' self-awareness is a Matthean passage, where, in a consistently Semitic context and mode of thought, we find the following statements:

> I thank you, Father, Lord of heaven and earth, because you have hidden these things from the wise and the intelligent and have revealed them to infants; yes, Father, for such was your gracious will. All things have been handed over to me by my Father; and no one knows the Son except the Father, and no one knows the Father except the Son and anyone to whom the Son chooses to reveal him. Come to me, all you that

are weary and are carrying heavy burdens, and I will give you rest. Take my yoke upon you, and learn from me; for I am gentle and humble in heart, and you will find rest for your souls. For my yoke is easy, and my burden is light (Mt. 11:25-30; cf. Lk. 6:47; 10:21-22; Sir. 24:19; 51:23-27).

This passage has been the occasion of much debate for various important reasons. If we consider these reasons as a whole, it would seem that while "some of the phrases may reflect ideas and sayings of Jesus," the present format of the passage undoubtedly represents language of the early Palestinian church, possibly the utterance of a Christian prophet who spoke under the inspiration of the Spirit (cf. I Cor. 2:10-11; 14:26-33; Rev. 1:1-20; Ignatius' *To the Philadelphians* 7:1). A particularly difficult statement in the passage, for example, is the affirmation that "no one knows the Father except the Son and anyone to whom the Son chooses to reveal him" (Mt. 11:27). Almost everywhere else in Matthew and in the other synoptic gospels Jesus assumes that his hearers know God either in some direct way or from the Scriptures or from his providential care of all creation (cf. Mt. 5:1-12, 17-18; 6:25-33; 10:19-20). The statement would appear, therefore, to be expressive of some mode of post-resurrection understanding within the church—possibly given by the risen Christ—of Jesus' identification with the Logos of God as the agent of all divine revelation throughout the world.[97]

The point, however, that the deepest truths have been hidden from the "wise and intelligent," that is, from the official custodians of the wisdom of Israel, and revealed to the "infants" of that society is in keeping with Jesus' prophetic, nontechnical teaching of the "weightier matters of the law: justice and mercy and faith" (Mt. 23:23; Luke has "justice and the love of God," 11:42). The statement that "All things have been handed over to me by my Father" (Mt. 11:27) is also clearly akin to the affirmation ascribed to Jesus after his resurrection (Mt. 28:18; cf. Jn. 3:35; 13:3) that became a cardinal theme of apostolic faith (I Cor. 15:27-28; Phil. 2:9; Eph. 1:22; I Pet. 3:22). As I have intimated, the possibility is real that Jesus could have made the statement after his resurrection on the basis of his own awareness of a full and indissoluble union with the Father achieved as a result of his redemptive work. But the mode of Jesus' affirmations of authority and status made during his public ministry seems to emphasize that which he would share with his followers. It is significant also that this passage (Mt. 11:25-30) begins with the prayer-address of Jesus, "Father, Lord of heaven and earth." This is the first time in the course of the Gospel of Matthew that Jesus' otherwise relatively familiar term for addressing God as "Father" (Aramaic *Abba*) is specifically followed by the identification of the Father as the almighty Creator and Lord of all the worlds (cf. Gen. 1:1).

We learn earlier in Matthew that Jesus "summoned his twelve disciples and gave them authority over unclean spirits, to cast them out, and to cure every disease and every sickness" (Mt. 10:1; cf. Mk. 3:13-19; 6:7; Lk. 9:1). In our present Matthean passage we note that Jesus asks "all you that are weary and are carrying heavy burdens" (a universal appeal) to take his yoke upon them and learn from him how to practice his ways (Mt. 11:28-29). This is to identify himself as a model of both knowledge of and relationship with the Father not only to depend upon but also to emulate. Jesus' ascription to himself of the qualities of gentleness and lowliness of heart, while odd as self-ascription, takes on a different light when the qualities are seen as aspects of a model to follow in conduct as well as to turn to for help.

The apostle Paul, too, evidently thought of "the meekness and gentleness of Christ" as model for emulation, as a paradigm of action-being that was in fact widely accepted in the church of the apostolic period (II Cor. 10:1; I Thess. 1:6; I Pet. 4:1). He also saw the divine authority and modes of operation of Christ Jesus as realities that Jesus did not wish to keep to himself but to share with as many as would receive and apply the same (Phil. 2:1-11; cf. Rev. 21:7).[98] Similarly, in the Gospel of John the act of foot washing is specifically cited by Jesus as an example *(hypodeigma)* for the disciples to follow (Jn. 13:12-15). The implication of the preceding discussion then is that the "uniqueness" of Jesus may be properly considered functionally as initiating an open-ended activity that others may follow rather than merely as an exclusive prerogative that none may attain. This thesis, I believe, also applies to Jesus' vicariously redemptive role, which I should now like to consider in more detail. I wish to begin by briefly discussing the Marcan verse "For the Son of Man came not to be served but to serve, and to give his life a ransom for many" (10:45; cf. Mk. 14:24; Mt. 20:28; Lk. 22:27).

C.K. Barrett has marshalled convincing evidence of the emergence in late pre-Christian Judaism of an understanding of *human* suffering as a means of atonement for sin. "Death in particular acts as an atonement, both for the individual who dies, and for others, if the man who dies is righteous." This theology of martyrdom, which had probably begun its development well before the second century B.C.E., was evidently the result of a deep need to understand religiously the meaning of the suffering, especially the persecution, of the Jewish people as a whole and later of individuals. Barrett contends that this understanding, which comes to a particular clarity of focus in the Maccabean period (cf. I Macc. 2:50-51; II Macc. 7:37-38; IV Macc. 6:27; 17:22; 18:4),[99] is in keeping with basic themes running throughout the earlier Hebrew Old Testament period. This is to say that the concept of representation, that an individual may represent his people, bear their punishment or suffering—as they may bear his—is a significant theme of the Hebrew Old Testament as well as of the later period of Jewish history (cf. Jn. 11:49-53). Barrett further sees the development within this later period as involving belief that a martyr's death could influence the destiny of the people as a whole. His conclusion is that "a creative mind working" upon this background of thought could produce a saying of the kind recorded in Mark 10:45.[100]

A number of scholars have subsequently indicated their essential agreement with Barrett's main thesis even as some differ from him in reaffirming the close ties frequently assumed to exist between Mark 10:45 on the one hand and both the servant figure of Isaiah 53 and the Son of man in Daniel 11 and 12 on the other (the theme of vicariously redemptive suffering is also present in the last, as Daniel 11:33, 35 make clear). W.J. Moulder, for example, concludes that "Jesus consciously united in his person the two central concepts of the Jewish faith, *barnasha* [Son of man] and *ebed Yahweh* [servant of Yahweh]" and stresses that Jesus' assumption of the servant's role and mien in his perception of his mission is to be understood from Mark 10:45 as the result of "an inward, voluntary humility" (cf. Mt. 8:20).[101] Karl Kertelge is largely in agreement with Moulder; he stresses the self-offering of Jesus "for many" as properly belonging to the larger role of the selfless spirit of service in his teaching as in the tradition of Israel (Mk. 10:42-45). This selfless spirit of service is indicative of a fundamental dimension of both the conduct and the self-understanding of Jesus and preserves it—in Jesus' mind—from any narrow range of soteriological interpretation.[102] I myself believe that at least roots of the later Maccabean development can be traced back to an earlier period in Israel, for I feel that it is not appropriate to consider Isaiah 51-53 as a theological "sport" or "erratic block" in its own time.

Martin Hengel, writing more recently, has brought together an abundance of material from the earlier Greek as well as later Hellenistic period, including the Roman, to show that for Greek-speaking Gentiles, the early Christian message of the soteriological meaning of the representatively atoning death of Jesus was quite understandable on the basis of their own religio-cultural background. In fact Hengel claims that the widespread Greek and Roman tradition of sacrificial dying, almost always with religious implications, for city-state, for friends and family—later even for philosophical truth or wider spiritual ends—expressed in both history and legend was the primary influence-factor in the later comparable developments in Maccabean Israel. Hengel is no doubt right in his affirmation of the essential cultural unity and cultural sharing that had come to prevail throughout the entire Middle East following the conquests of Alexander and the establishment of the kingdoms of his successors. But if one examines his evidence carefully, it appears that the Greek tradition from Homer and the heroic period to the Greek "enlightenment," which later we see focused in Euripides, passed through a development-process that was similar in kind and roughly contemporaneous with the Jewish developments. And these latter Jewish developments by no means need to be explained totally on the basis of cultural influence or borrowing on the historical plane. As in the case of development-changes in Mahāyāna Buddhism that occurred over a period largely contemporary with the beginnings of the Christian movement, there are historical events of great significance and yet mysterious origins which are not always to be explained totally on the basis of direct cultural influence on the historical plane. I believe that we possibly have to do with a certain evolution of human consciousness together with a divine working both within and without Israel that made the Christ event culturally comprehensible as well as religiously necessary for its larger environment and time.

In fact, we have to do with what appears to be a primal sense of the expiatory and propitiatory value of life willingly and freely offered for others, especially by a righteous person, as an almost universal phenomenon in all societies in their earlier histories. As is well known, this sense was widely if inchoately expressed in those early histories through the practice of human as well as animal sacrifice. It must have frequently become a dreadfully oppressive psychological burden upon persons and communities, particularly as connections between moral guilt and human destiny were evidently more often fearfully intimated than rightly understood, and the victims chosen were no doubt often unwilling as well as "unworthy." Greek tragedy was concerned to provide emotional catharsis from as well as to give dramatic expression to these profound mysteries of human life.[103] As Plutarch, who was a contemporary of the second Christian generation (ca. 46-120 C.E.), made clear in his *Pelopidas*, enlightened Greek religious thought in general had come to regard the requirement of human sacrifice as unworthy of Zeus, the father of gods and human beings. But perception of an abiding religious significance, as well as inherent moral nobility, in the voluntary sacrificial offering of human life for others continued in the Hellenistic tradition and, indeed, has remained an ineradicable part of the human experience in all cultures to the present day.[104]

There is, therefore, no inherent reason to doubt that the statement ascribed to Jesus in Mark 10:45—"the Son of Man came not to be served but to serve, and to give his life as a ransom for many"—was comprehensible as well as appropriate to the human need of Jesus' contemporaries within and without Palestine. Indeed, there are good reasons to believe that the tradition of the saying came out of the earliest Palestinian Jewish Christian community and, as an increasing number of scholars are coming to affirm, that the

saying was a logion or authentic statement of Jesus himself.[105] Let us briefly consider some of these reasons.

We must acknowledge, of course, that this Marcan affirmation as by Jesus himself of his serving, vicariously redemptive role under God does not as a formula play a
prominent role either in Mark or in the other synoptic gospels. Explicit language of this kind is found only at two foci
in the synoptic tradition: Mark 10:45 (Mt. 20:28) and the
accounts of the Last Supper (Mk. 14:24; Mt. 26:28).[106] The
reason is obviously that such statements did not occupy a
prominent place in the teaching of Jesus, as we have already
seen. But the dominant place given in all four gospels to the
events of the death, resurrection, and ascension of Jesus
makes quite clear that both the writers and the communities which they represented had come to believe that these
events—and specifically their effective power under God to
serve the deepest needs of others—constitute the highest
meaning of the life and ministry of Jesus. Such was the case
even though the apparent failure involved in Jesus' death
contradicted popular expectations with regard to the presumed externally victorious role of the Messiah. And the
apparently universal presence of this faith-understanding
in every segment of the earliest expressions of the Christian
movement is a powerful indication that Jesus himself,
whether from the beginning of his public ministry or as a
gradually emerging awareness during it, had come to perceive this vicariously redemptive role—service of others
through both his life and his death—as the primary and cli-
mactic reason for his being "sent." But it would have been
inappropriate to the modesty and reserve of Jesus for him
to have heralded this understanding-truth during his public ministry, as indeed was evidently the case with the "Messianic Secret." Some things in life are better left to be said by
others.

Let us note briefly, however, some of the evidence for

what I have called the apparently universal presence of this
faith-understanding in every segment of the early Christian
movement.[107] A key passage is, of course, I Corinthians 15,
where the apostle Paul recounts the essence of the gospel,
as he understood it and believed he received it from others.
This he had delivered to the Corinthians, "as of first importance," when he first founded the church, probably over the
year 49-50 C.E. The very first element of the account is that
"Christ died for our sins in accordance with the scriptures"
(I Cor. 15:3). The further references in this passage to Cephas
(Peter), the twelve apostles, James, and others make it clear
that the tradition that Paul had received went back to the
earliest days of the Palestinian Jewish Christian community,
that is, to the mother-church in Jerusalem. And this tradition, which Paul claims he had personally appropriated in
one form through his Damascus road experience (Acts 9:1-
19) and in other ways during the manifold experiences of
his missionary career, appears throughout his writings as
we have them in the New Testament.[108]

As Martin Hengel has pointed out, the expressions found
in Paul regarding the atoning death of Jesus, often in stereo-
typed forms indicative of an already firm tradition, are primarily of two classes. One class consists of statements that
indicate the "giving up" of Jesus for the salvation of others.
The second class of statements found in Paul is that which
denotes the Messiah as "dying" for us. We noted this mode
of expression already in I Corinthians 15:3, where the verb
"died" *(apethanen)* is in the aorist tense, indicative of single
or pointed action that is effective once for both one time
and the future. The same is true of Rom. 5:6, 8; 14:9; I Cor.
8:11; Gal. 2:21; I Thess. 5:10 (aorist participle). But when Paul
moves beyond the bare statement of fact to describe the
larger significance of the event of Jesus' death ("for us"), as
we have already noted in the case of Philippians 2:1-13, he
at once begins to emphasize its paraenetic meaning; that is,

its role as a model of life-being and action for all disciples of Jesus. This mode of thought and expression is also true of I Peter, the author of which follows his similarly formulaic statement of Jesus having "suffered" (some manuscripts, including papyri, have "died") with exhortation for his Christian readers to arm themselves with the same thought—of suffering consecrated to the will of God—that they might live "no longer by human desires but by the will of God" (I Pet. 3:18-4:2). In an earlier passage Peter (perhaps Peter, but at least Petrine) describes even more succinctly how Christians should take suffering patiently as their divine calling "because Christ also suffered for you, leaving you an example, so that you should follow in his steps" (I Pet. 2:20-21).[109]

We thus see in this discussion of Jesus' vicarious service, even to the extent of suffering and dying, that there is in the New Testament witness a continuum of activity and meaning affirmed as the proper role of all the reconciled, a continuum from Father to Son to all his brothers and sisters (Rom. 8:17; cf. Rom. 8:29; Heb. 2:9, 17-18; 5:8-9; 7:25, 27; 9:22; 10:12).[110] This continuum of activity is akin to the continuum of ontology that we noted earlier, especially in the Gospel of John. However human beings may now be empirically estranged from the Father in relationship and in conduct, when reconciled (restored)—even if imperfectly—they are to participate in the divine oneness through both relationship-being and service, a service that is working toward the restoration of the whole cosmos (cf. I Cor. 15:28). We can in this way understand the otherwise mysterious words of Paul, "I am now rejoicing in my sufferings for your sake *(hyper hymon)*, and in my flesh I am completing what is lacking in Christ's afflictions for the sake of his body, that is, the church" (Col. 1:24; cf. 2:1). Also in Romans, Paul seems to be saying that the very status of believers as "heirs of God and joint heirs with Christ," indeed their subsequent

glorification with Christ, are dependent upon their suffering with him now (Rom. 8:16-17). This principle of the efficacy before God in some profound sense of human suffering
for others appears to have been important for Paul, as is
clear from Philippians 2:17, 30; 3:10-11; 4:14 (cf. Rom. 12:1-
2; Gal. 6:17; I Thess. 1:6).[111] That this principle was also a
part of the wider apostolic faith seems clear from II Timo-
thy 2:10-12 (cf. Ignatius, *To the Romans* 2:2, 4:2). There is
nothing lacking in what is needed of divine resources for
any person at any moment of existential need, but the Father uses the lesser brothers and sisters as well as the Son in
his work, which, as we have seen, is an ongoing work (cf. Jn.
5:17-21; 9:4; 14:12). We may recall that in the synoptic tradition also Jesus shares his authority and power to do comparable works with those whom he sends out (Mk. 6:7; Mt.
10:1; Lk. 9:1; cf. Acts 3:1-10; Rom. 15:19; Gal. 3:5; Heb. 2:4). It
is clear that the author of Luke-Acts understands Jesus'
death as at least a "martyrdom which is a model for his disciples" (cf. Acts 22:20; Lk. 11:50; 22:20—continuity in the
Greek word for "blood poured out"). Luke also, however,
according to a preferred textual reading, in his account of
the Last Supper uses the expression "for you" *(hyper hymon)*
twice to indicate that in some way the event of Jesus' self-
offering is efficacious or beneficial for others (Lk. 22:19-
20).[112]

The above, I trust, has been of some help in enabling us
to intimate what may have characterized Jesus' self-awareness with regard to his own person and role. The language
of Mark in 8:31, as we have noted, also strongly suggests that
Jesus "perceived" his suffering to be a divine necessity, as
the will of God for him. I would suggest that this precogni-
tive perception needs to be read as an activity working at a
higher level than that ordinarily understood as of a "religious genius." We are dealing here with a personage possessing at least the spiritual endowments of an older

Hebrew prophet (cf. II Kings 6:15-19), and I would suggest that Jesus not only "thought about" the coming event, he "perceived" it as an event to come and also as a call from God that would be cosmically significant for others. We may recall that Luke records Jesus as saying "I *saw* Satan fall like lightning from heaven" (Lk. 10:18). The real question, of course, is whether Jesus was correct in his perception; that is, was his call in fact a revelation from the living God and cosmically significant? The nature of both the language and the context of the passage (Mk. 10:45) uniformly suggests, as we have seen, a primitive Palestinian Jewish source; all in all, we have weighty reasons to believe that it comes from Jesus himself. But was it a true perception? The testimony of the church of the apostolic generation was virtually unanimous in affirming that it was a true perception. Can we also affirm it? I believe we can. Let us consider further why and how.

I believe that the suffering of Jesus was indeed cosmically meaningful for "many"; that is, as many as would, from within Israel and from without Israel. This comprehensive meaning can surely be ascribed to Jesus even though an important stream of late Judaism allowed no redemption for the Gentile nations (cf. Acts 10:45, 11:18). As I have discussed in a previous book, another important stream did allow such.[113] We may initiate the discussion of rationale, however, with recognition of the fact that in the Roman Empire at the beginning of this era, the term *ransom* primarily meant the purchase price paid for the liberation of a slave. Notions that the suffering of Jesus constituted some kind of literal payment to the devil to compensate for his rights of possession over humankind bound in the service of sin represent calculations of a mental level below that, I believe, of the thinking of both Jesus and the apostolic church. But many in our own generation find it difficult to understand the seriousness of the issue on the cosmic level

as well as the personal largely because they do not see the
need for a "righting of wrong" on a cosmic scale. This is because, I believe, they do not understand the vitally important role, which we noted earlier in this chapter, in the
teaching of Jesus, of the apostolic church, as well as of the
mainstream of the Hebrew prophetic tradition that preceded them, of "sowing and reaping" as a basic principle
operative in the universe under God.

We are, of course, not in possession of final knowledge as
to why the kind of selfless service, even self-offering for others to the point of death which we see in Jesus' life and
death, should be the most effective means for the "righting
of wrong" that human beings on this earth evidently need.
What we have seen thus far is that such action-being seems
eminently fitting as a deed, singularly appropriate to the
need, as perceived by the great majority of human beings in
every society in all times and places. It was deemed appropriate by both the Hebraic and the Hellenistic traditions of
the Middle East and Mediterranean worlds preceding the
time of Jesus. It has spoken to the deepest perceptions of
human beings in all parts of the world since that time. The
emergence of the principle of graciously vicarious redemption as a major theme of Mahāyāna Buddhism shows, as
does the worldwide spread of Christian faith, that this understanding has been experienced by human beings everywhere as both fittingly germane and specifically helpful to
their deepest needs. Its emergence in various forms in Islamic history, in a scriptural and theological context that
appears at first to be inhospitable, constitutes, I believe,
further significant support to this affirmation of an almost
universal human perception of the appropriateness of vicariously redemptive activity to meet the deepest needs of
human beings.[114]

I believe, then, that Jesus perceived the central meaning
of his work on earth as redemptive for the many, as a sacri-

ficial service to liberate human beings from the bonds which they themselves had forged in their own past and which had become a part of the inner and outer structure of their lives, both as individuals and as groups. These were and are bonds that we human beings are not able to cut loose by and of ourselves. This redemptive work, I further affirm, was not confined to the event of the cross. Jesus had to suffer "many things." Moreover, Jesus' teaching of a radical rejection of self for the sake of the Kingdom of God or gospel (Mk. 8:34-35; Mt. 6:33; 10:38-39; 16:24-25) points to the fact of such suffering throughout his public ministry— and before. But this teaching is a paradigmatic rather than an exclusive activity; it is one in which others are called to share.

For Jesus the *climax* of this redemptive work was clearly the cross; the consummation of this life of service was "to give his life a ransom for many." It would be a mistake, of course, to see the chief significance of the cross in the enormity of the physical suffering. The crucifixion of criminals was a common punishment in the Roman Empire. The gospel accounts record the crucifixion of two such criminals together with Jesus (Mk. 15:27, etc.); and many men were crucified in Jewish Palestine in his time. There is no reason to believe that Jesus' physical pain was greater than that of the others. The issue is rather one of kind or quality of meaning, of both deed and person. The account of Jesus' experience in Gethsemane gives us particularly meaningful suggestions toward gaining some such understanding (Mk. 14:32-36). But with reference again to the question of whether Jesus' perception of the cosmic meaning of his role was true or not, the apostolic witness is consistently clear that the church believed not only that the perception of the cosmic meaning of his role was true, but that its truth had been demonstrated by Jesus' resurrection (Acts 5:31; Rom. 1:4-5; Col. 2:13-15; 1 Pet. 1:3).

This is, of course, not the place to debate the issue of the "historicity" of the alleged resurrection of Jesus. As I have already indicated, I personally consider part of the discussion misplaced at least because certain New Testament accounts themselves testify to aspects of the event that transcend the historical as the term is commonly used. And yet the event was experienced by men and women who were themselves in history; even the most skeptical of investigators would hesitate to deny the reality of that experience as human experience, whether the persons were deluded or not. But if we are entitled to take seriously at almost every level of human experience—as I believe we are—the principle that the fruit is significantly revelatory of the kind and quality of the tree, the testimony of the historical records is weighty that the first believers in the resurrection of Jesus did not act like deluded persons. To the contrary, they followed what was evidently the intent of Jesus himself, that his suffering and resurrection be not an exclusive activity, but a paradigm for others to follow, a paradigm of continuing atoning significance (cf. Col. 1:24; II Cor. 4:10-12, 16-17; 6:1-10; 11:16-33). The fruit in the church, although clearly not perfect, appears to have generally been "good." The apostolic generation also perceived the patient bearing of suffering to be a means of communion with the Lord and sharing in his victory (Phil. 3:10; I Pet. 4:13). The point always seemed to be that suffering according to the will of God is meaningful for both self and others. And yet the faith of the early church was that both the crucifixion and the resurrection of Jesus somehow constituted a unique redemptively atoning activity for others, for many, that was and remains of cosmic significance. In dependent relationship to him, it was believed the principle of sowing and reaping, the otherwise inexorable law of *karma*, can be overcome. Jesus' work was thus both unique and a model for others, a paradox to be understood more in the human experience of obedience than of reasoning.

2

One of the most suggestive books on this theme that I have read is the little volume *From Buddha to Christ* written by Hermann Beckh in 1925 and first published in book form in English in 1977. Beckh had studied jurisprudence at the University of Munich and served for a time as a judge. He then turned to in-depth study of Sanskrit, Tibetan, and other Asian languages and became professor of Oriental languages at the University of Berlin. Later, as a member of the communion known as the Christian Community, he turned his massive erudition and fine perceptions to the problem of the relative spiritual significance as well as historical stature of the Buddha and the Christ.

Like Romano Guardini, Beckh also saw the Buddha as a forerunner of the Christ, indeed as the last of the really great teachers of humanity before the Nazarene. He wrote most appreciatively of the compassion, of the "love, the kind friendliness towards all beings" that played so important a role in the life as well as in the teaching of the Buddha. He saw the latter as bringing a kind of religious and spiritual renewal to meet the needs of his time, as contributing a uniquely clear perception of the human ethico-spiritual dilemma, of both its cause and cure. Indeed, Beckh concluded that through the life and work of the Buddha "a first preparatory but most significant step had been taken ... towards the Christianizing of human consciousness."[115]

Beckh's strongest language, however, is reserved for the delineation of his convictions regarding the larger cosmic significance of the person and work of Jesus the Christ. He sees the Christ event "as the beginning of a new age and a new spirit, as the germ of a new humanity and a new world." "In the cross on Calvary the Tree of Death becomes again

the Tree of Life." Beckh sees "the spiritual sun-ray which
shone from the cross on Calvary" as penetrating the depths
of human consciousness so as to transform "the whole con-
figuration of the human soul." This is to give to everything
on earth the potential of "a new beginning, a revolution, a
crisis." Specifically, Beckh perceives that Jesus as the Christ
has taken upon himself the consequences of the deeds
which every person has wrought so as to restore both person and earth, in process of time, to a harmonious balance.
Beckh's view is that this work of the Christ, while completed
once for all in history, is in process of completion with regard to its appropriation and application in the lives of persons. The forgiveness of sin made possible through Jesus
the Christ marks the initiation of a process of human transformation. This means also that the present role of human
beings is to collaborate with the Christ in the divine work of
universal restoration and new creation.

Beckh furthermore insists that the objective influence of
the Christ event upon all humanity and upon the whole of
earth must be perceived as a reality at work in some ways
independent of conscious or explicit profession of Christian faith. "Quite independently of religious creeds, the
mystery of Golgotha exercises a universal influence." In the
context of discussion of the transformation of a significant
stream of Buddhism into what came to be called the
Mahāyāna, Beckh makes a statement remarkably reminiscent of a similar view suggested by as careful a scholar as
Edward Conze: "The great revaluation of all values brought
about by the deed of Christ affected also the spirit of Buddhism."[116]

It is only proper to add that Hermann Beckh came to
these conclusions not only from his own immense erudition and profound reflection, but also because of his openness to the clairvoyant perceptions of Rudolf Steiner. We
have already identified Steiner (1861-1925) as the Austrian

philosopher-scientist who made notable contributions in his time to pedagogical theory and praxis, especially in work for the mentally handicapped and disturbed, to drama, the arts and architecture, to biodynamic agriculture, to phar-maceutical as well as medical theory and practice. Steiner, who was one of the most learned people of his generation in both natural science and the humanities—he was invited to become at the age of twenty-nine the editor of the Weimar Edition of the writings of Goethe that were con-cerned with natural science—claimed to have direct spiri-tual or clairvoyant perception of events of the life of Jesus and of their cosmic significance which are otherwise known only through historical documents and traditions and rational reflection thereupon. Steiner's own description of this phenomenon was as a "spiritual activity which in clar-ity was fully comparable to mathematical thinking." This statement, I believe, was not the consequence of spiritual presumption but indicative of an activity that Steiner also consistently checked in the most rigorous way with both the data and the methodology of ordinary sensory percep-tion; that is, with the common procedures of historical and other scientific investigation.[117]

Very brief mention should be made at this point of other instances in the history of Christian spirituality of similar perception of events in the life of Jesus by direct spiritual or clairvoyant means. We may recall Anna Katherina Emmerich (1774-1824), a religious of the Order of St. Augustine in Münster, Germany. Another example is Therese Neumann (1898-1962), a person well known for her unusual gifts in our own time. Like Anna Katherina, Sr. Therese was noted for her experiences of stigmata, wounds akin to those of Jesus on the cross (seen also in the lives of Catherine of Siena and Francis of Assisi), for her experiences of levitation, of bilocation, for her extraordinary perception of the history of associations of material objects (psychometry). Therese also had remarkable visions of details of the life of Jesus. The case of Anna Katherina, however, is particularly significant because of the careful theological evaluations made of her life and visions by responsible leaders in the Roman Catholic Church in Germany and France both during and shortly after the end of her life.[118] We should also note an even greater abundance of such materials in the case of Edgar Cayce.[119]

The meaning of the above is to affirm that the Christ event is unique; it is also the pivotal, the single most important event of human history. Jesus the Christ is "the one whose deed has balanced the event symbolized in the Fall." From the deed of the Christ flows the power of redemption from the original sin of us all. I am speaking here not merely of the moral influence of the teaching or person of Jesus the Christ as transmitted on the historical plane but also as an impulse of actual power flowing from its Source in the "realms above." This is the power that is also at hand, "has come near," is available to those who would receive it on the terms that the Christian church has traditionally called the obedience of faith.

It is also the intent of the above to say that such an affirmation of Christian faith in no way means that only those who affirm it in the historic Christian context share in its effects and benefits. I am not proclaiming here a salvific universalism, in the sense of a guaranteed universal salvation. But the faith-obedience of those in other historic religious traditions has not come into existence nor developed apart from the ongoing influences of the Christ event or of its Person. They have all had and continue to have their opportunities to know divine truth, divine goodness, and saving power (cf. Rom. 1:19; 2:15). In ways perhaps beyond those envisaged by Albert Schweitzer, the man of Galilee continues to come to human beings all across the world in every age as "One unknown, without a name" and yet recognized, if not by name yet by character, as the one to whom we all rightly belong and by whom, under the Father and in the Spirit, we are saved.[120]

This is also to affirm the reality and the universal availability of the Kingdom of God, of which Jesus the Christ is the prime representative and now Lord. I would affirm that central to Jesus' meaning in proclaiming the Kingdom of God in his public ministry was reference to the "realm" other than the plane of human history in which the rule of God operates and the will of God is done without hindrance. This is, I believe, a perspective that emerged naturally out of the experience of historic Israel with its developing perceptions of the "I Am" (Yahweh), the Lord Most High, the Lord God of hosts. We may properly recall that the hosts are the heavenly hosts, the angels, archangels, cherubim, and seraphim which, whatever the extent of Iranian or Babylonian influence, became an integral part of the faith of post-exilic Judaism.

This view of a multitiered universe may also have extended to pre-exilic times in Israel; it is certainly the perspective that lies behind the account of Elisha's clairvoyant perceptions as recorded in II Kings 6:1-23. It was fashionable in the late nineteenth and early twentieth centuries to denote and essentially to dismiss as unreal this kind of a worldview as mythological, however sophisticated the varying definitions given the term *myth*. Christian theologians and biblical scholars of liberal persuasion were tempted to follow a widespread tendency in Western culture from the time of the Enlightenment to extrapolate from the otherwise legitimate methodological limitations adopted by early modern science. The limitations were to concentrate upon the data of sensory perception and the empirical method. In the process of extrapolation, however, many persons came to assume that such limitations mean that the data of sensory perception are the only data that exist.

We find, nevertheless, a number of perceptive thinkers in our own day who are trying, with the help of perspectives emerging from the new physics, to counteract this tendency of now several hundred years' duration and to affirm without apology a contemporarily acceptable form of a multi-tiered universe. Among these thinkers may be cited Huston Smith, Jacob Needleman, and a number of writers who have contributed to the English journal *Studies in Comparative Religion,* such as René Guenon, Frithjof Schuon, Marco Pallis, and others. It is not without significance that Krister Stendahl is said to have read Huston Smith's seminal work *Forgotten Truth* "with quiet awe."[121]

Jesus' proclamation that "the kingdom of God has come near" (Mk. 1:15) meant that this realm whose reality is ontologically prior and axiologically superior to the plane of history is about to take a "new turn" in its relationship to this plane. A shift in the ages is beginning. Jesus himself was and is God's primary agent of this new turn, which has been prepared on a cosmic scale and is in process of being effected on a like scale. The primary meaning of the new turn then and now, however, lies in the new opportunities for liberation from the human past and present and for reconciliation with the divine Lord and with one another which it presents.[122] The phrase "come near" is, therefore, not primarily a "threat." The meaning of the ontological priority and axiological superiority of the Kingdom is that the plane of human history is a realm ever under evaluation "from above." As such it is appropriate to recognition of the "spatial" as well as "temporal" nearness of the kingdom not only to believe the good news of the opportunities it offers, but also to work, with God through the Spirit of his supreme agent Jesus the Christ, at the changes in conduct and attitude that constitute the response (repentance) appropriate to recognition of the reality and claims of the Lord of the Kingdom.

Yet the reperceptions of the eschatological dimensions of the Kingdom of God that have emerged over the past century and more have not been entirely mistaken. As we have seen, the main intent of Jesus' proclamation of the Kingdom was to emphasize its present opportunities and even its inner aspects. Albert Schweitzer and others to the contrary notwithstanding, Jesus did not focus in his proclamation upon the imminent end of history. As Leon Morris has reminded us, it is not clear that conviction of the near return of the Christ dominated the thinking of the early Christians, at least after the apostolic generation.[123] Perhaps we can legitimately ask, was the thought of the end of the age based on astrological concepts?

And yet even the apocalyptic elements of the synoptic gospels and the apostolic literature are not to be totally dismissed. Perhaps we are to take seriously the possibilities of the near end of history. The New Testament is not one in its witness with regard either to the mode or the time of the return of the Lord. As we have noted, the testimony of the first chapter of Acts is that he "will come in the same way as you saw him go into heaven" (Acts 1:11; cf. Heb. 9:28). This word appears to refer to a mode of manifestation once again unassuming, perceptible only to those with faith, perhaps to be accompanied with cataclysms in the realm of nature but understood only by believers. Are we not able to interpret also with religious meanings the prognostications of professional geologists regarding certain possible, not to say probable, events of this kind within the North American continent? But whatever the mode and whenever the time, this is the return of the One both known and unknown, the supreme expression within human history of the heart of the universe that we believe is "most wonderfully kind."[124]

PART

The Buddha
and the Christ,
Issues Personal
and Cosmic

1

Views on the Nature of Humanity

1

A n initial question would surely be, what is the point of comparison between these two figures, however great, whose time and place in the course of human history were so widely different? And also the movements that they initiated, at least until recent years, have been largely divergent streams of human activity except for minor points of contact. One reason then for comparison that I should like to suggest comes from the insights of the Austrian philosopher and educator Rudolf Steiner. Readers may differ in their willingness to accept such insights, insofar as they clearly transcend at some points the ordinary parameters of the methodology of academic scholarship. But this is a religious study, a study of perhaps the two greatest figures of human religious history, and we ought not, I believe, to restrict the ranges of our inquiry by the norms of more common human experience.

Steiner saw profound meaning in the person and work of Gautama the Buddha as, among other things, elements in the divine work of preparation leading to what Christians call the Christ event. This is to say that the Buddha was a profoundly significant moral and spiritual teacher who had a role of cosmic import to fulfill as a part of what Roman Catholic theologians have long called *praeparatio evangelica.* Steiner also perceived the Buddha as one who at present "sends his forces down from the higher, supersensible worlds" as a spiritual figure "fully dedicated to the work of the Christ Impulse." The last phrase is a term used by Steiner to denote the spiritual and moral influences upon humankind that over the centuries have been offered through the divine activity in which the risen Christ plays the central role. Steiner is here making an extraordinary claim, namely that the Buddha in "sending down his influences from the spiritual worlds" has been a cooperator with the risen Christ and from the beginning of the Christian movement has contributed and continues to contribute to the activity that we call Christian. Steiner believed that this work of the Buddha *post mortem* has particularly inspired those individuals who had not yet been "permeated by the Christ Impulse."

Again, some of this kind of thought transcends the ordinary limits of the methods and perhaps even the concerns of academic scholarship. But if only a part of the Western world were to take Steiner's contentions with some seriousness, it would, I believe, work to change the attitudes of all Westerners not only toward the Buddha but also toward the whole of Asian history and culture, toward Asians as persons. It could create a new attitude of legitimized respect for Asians among Westerners, an attitude that has been largely lacking in our societies over long centuries. It could also expand the horizons of Christian faith and theology better to fit us for the global age that is already with us. Such, as I have contended earlier, is also to see something of the wider presence and work of God in the world.

Another reason that I may offer for the validity of comparison is one that has been made recently with great force by the Swiss Roman Catholic theologian Hans Küng. This is what he believes to be the significant connection between ecumenism and world peace. Küng, of course, understands ecumenism in this context as a wider ecumenism, including relationships not only among Christian churches, but also with and among other religions in the world. He contends that ecumenical dialogue, which, of course, requires the kind of informed participants that I hope to aid by the content of this book, for the first time in human history "has now taken on the character of an urgent consideration for world politics. It can help to make our earth more livable, by making it more peaceful and more reconciled."

At the conclusion of his massive collaborative work on *Christianity and the World Religions,* Küng writes as follows:

There will be no peace among the peoples of this world without peace among the world religions.

There will be no peace among the world religions without peace among the Christian churches.

The community of the Church is an integral part of the world community.

Ecumenism *ad intra,* concentrated on the Christian world, and ecumenism *ad extra,* oriented toward the whole inhabited earth, are interdependent.

Peace is indivisible: it begins within us.[1]

2

I should like to begin our comparison of the Buddha and the Christ with what may be a natural transition from Hans Küng's last sentence just quoted, that is, the anthropological understanding of the two. What do these two great figures of human history have to say about the human condition, about its empirical nature, about its potential?

The anthropological question is, as we have seen, one of the most controversial aspects of the Buddha's teaching both within and without historic Buddhism and one frequently seen as constituting a notable difference from the teaching of the Christ. Readers, however, will have noted that I do not comparably find such a difference. Indeed, I believe that the very word *anātman* (Pāli: *anatta*), which appears in the early texts in the sense of "not-self" or "nonself," is largely a term of Buddhist scholastic provenance insofar as it is understood as meaning "no-self." The Buddha, however, never denied the existence of the human self; he simply refused to identify it with any element of phenomenal existence. He refused to speak of it as in any sense "substantial," that is, as having ultimately independent or eternal reality in itself. In fact, the Buddha clearly did not wish to discuss the nature of the self as a philosophical problem. His concern was primarily pragmatic and, given his perception of the human empirical self, his focus came to be upon the transformation of the self-as-is, the self-centered or selfish self. This means that the Buddha's understanding of the human self was dynamic rather than static. He saw human beings as capable of transformation both morally and spiritually, and the essence of his message was that the proper goal of human life is not isolation but relationship. This is relationship supremely with *Dharma* as the focused force of *Nirvāṇa* or Ultimate Reality available and at work in the world and subsequent relationship with all else in the cosmos in a non-self-centered way.

This religious posture is, I believe, far closer to that of Jesus than has been commonly realized. Jesus, to be sure, as heir of the historic Hebrew tradition, saw human beings specifically as the creation of God the Father, the Maker and Sustainer of the whole universe. Gautama, in spite of his recognition of the creator-god Brahmā Sahampāti, refused to discuss the issue of creation, since he apparently saw it as of only subsidiary importance in coping with the human existential situation. But both Jesus and Gautama were one in calling for radical transformation of the spiritual direction and moral quality of human beings and of human life. Both had a similar view of the desperate need of human beings in their empirical condition of isolation or alienation from proper relationships in the cosmos and consequent evil-selfishness, a self-centeredness as harmful to self as to others. Both were one in seeing the solution of the human dilemma as the restoration of proper relationships and participation in a process of qualitative or ethical transformation of human character.

At this point it may be in order to identify and stress more than I did in previous chapters the nature of Jesus' call to change as recorded in all four gospels of the New Testament. An early form of this call is found in the Gospel of Mark, where we see Jesus addressing his disciples together with a larger crowd, "If any want to become my followers, let them deny themselves and take up their cross and follow me. For those who want to save their life will lose it, and those who lose their life for my sake, and for the sake of the gospel, will save it" (Mk. 8:34-35). Matthew gives us the same content—with the omission of the phrase "for the sake of the gospel"—but notably considers the teaching so important that he repeats it later in another context (Mt. 10:38-39; 16:24-25; it is, of course, not impossible that Jesus himself repeated the teaching on more than one occasion). Luke gives the same teaching with characteristically strong Lucan language (Lk. 14:24-27), but also repeats the central point in other contexts (Lk. 9:23-24; 17:33). The Gospel of John gives the same teaching in equally vigorous language: "Those who love their life lose it, and those who hate their life in this world will keep it for eternal life" (Jn. 12:25). It is significant that in this same passage in John we find the citation of Jesus himself using the imagery of death of self as the avenue to new life, "Very truly, I tell you, unless a grain of wheat falls into the ground and dies, it remains just a single grain; but if it dies, it bears much fruit" (Jn. 12:24).

When this teaching in the gospel accounts is compared with that of the apostle Paul, we are able, I believe, to identify what must have been held to be a central element of Jesus' teaching as of the Christian church of the apostolic period. This is to see the condition of the empirical or alienated human self as requiring such thoroughgoing, root change that the metaphor of physical death and resurrection came to be used. Sir James Frazer long ago revealed with many examples how this metaphor was not only widely used across the world but constituted the basis of a variety of ritualistic patterns, especially in rites of initiation, in many preliterate societies.[2] In fact, this imagery is close to being universal in human experience. In Jesus and Paul, and in the case of not a few others in the early church, the imagery was used not only as metaphor, but allowed to lead to physical death itself. Yet physical death was clearly not the intent. Radical transformation was the true goal, and that was to the end of new life, indeed of eternal life.

Thus Paul could say, "I die every day" (I Cor. 15:31) as an existential explanation of his earlier claim, "I have been crucified with Christ; it is no longer I who live, but Christ who lives in me" (Gal. 2:20). In his later letter to the Corinthian church Paul continues to use this metaphor of death and resurrection, sometimes with physical death in the offing as a possibility, but never losing sight of the central faith-affirmation of new life with its new and better qualities. Hence he could write, "So we do not lose heart. Even though our outer nature is wasting away, our inner nature is being renewed day by day" (II Cor. 4:16; cf. 4:11; 6:9; 7:3).[3] We see in this quotation an emphasis that Paul makes elsewhere, that the root *locus* of transformation is the inner self of persons, their thoughts and feelings, their prevailing attitudes and desires, their motivations and reasons for action. In his letter to the Christian community in Rome, he appealed to the believers, "Do not be conformed to this world, but be transformed by the renewing of your minds, so that you may discern [Paul no doubt also implied "and do"] what is the will of God—what is good and acceptable and perfect" (Rom. 12:2). In the preceding verse Paul makes clear that this process of transformation is fundamentally relational in that it is the proper consequence of the offering of self (selves) to God "as a living sacrifice, holy and acceptable to God, which is your spiritual worship" (Rom. 12:1). The whole of life thus becomes worship, even as the whole of life is to be transformed.

This is the kind of emphasis upon the interiority of persons that we have noted as characteristic in a primary way of the teaching—and life-practice—of both the Buddha and the Christ. The transformation of persons that they envisaged and taught was so radical and thoroughgoing as to include every aspect of the human self, both inner and outer, indeed the whole of human life and praxis.

We have also seen that both Jesus and Gautama perceived this anticipated transformation as leading to some kind of eternal life, as participation in new modes of life that begin in this world and continue beyond physical death. Rather than death of self meaning annihilation of the self, this is death of an inadequate self unto a new self. In terms of both quality and time, new life is seen as not only transcending the limits of the empirical self, but even as moving quite beyond the limits of time and space. Both historic Buddhism and historic Christianity have in many cases done well in their portrayals of the glories of the new life in this world and in a special way in the next.[4]

3

Another aspect of the views of humanity of both the Buddha and the Christ that is particularly significant for discerning the central thrust of their persons and teaching—and life practice—is the range of their inclusiveness toward persons. This inclusiveness was, and is, not only highly significant as characteristic of their own persons; it distinguishes them in the whole course of human religious history. We have noted that the Buddha at a relatively early period after his experience of enlightenment and the beginning of the gathering of disciples gave his initial direction to the monastic disciples to enter upon what was in principle a universal mission. That is, there was never a geographical limit set nor envisaged, except for the practicalities of what was possible for that time and place. The later expansion of Buddhist faith and practice throughout Asia was a natural development of this early intent and direction. The monastic emphasis of the Buddha was clearly related to the training of persons who could move out in missionary activity with the expeditiousness of meditating mendicants.

But the Buddha was inclusive in other ways beyond the geographical. The work of the monastic missionaries was to be "for the blessing of the manyfolk, for the happiness of the manyfolk, out of compassion for the world, for the welfare, the blessing, the happiness of *devas* and men."[5] It is interesting that a part of the early tradition suggests that the teaching on earth of the *Dharma,* which is "lovely at the beginning, lovely in the middle, lovely at the ending," may redound to the benefit of supernal spirits as well of persons on earth. In the passage from which I have just quoted, the account also indicates that there are beings "with little dust in their eyes," who because they are not hearing the *Dharma* are retrogressing spiritually, but who on hearing it would learn and grow. This saying, we should note, is properly not to be understood as direction to go only to the "best prospects," but as reason for hope on the part of the missioners. It indicates that there are those who are spiritually prepared to receive the truth, as if the fields were "ripe for harvesting" (cf. Jn. 4:35). But the missioners are also to go to the "manyfolk."

We noted that in contrast to the harsh and evidently at times repulsive appearance and manners of certain of the ascetics of his time, the lifestyle practiced and taught by the Buddha, as of the monks of the order, was refined and generally pleasing to persons of every social class. This aspect of the man and the movement was clearly a factor in the winning of many followers both monastic and lay. In the early texts there is also consistent socio-economic ethical teaching reminiscent of the later "Protestant ethic" denoted by Max Weber. Merchants and craftsmen are warned against covetousness or attachment to material things. Their methods of gaining wealth must be honest and hurt no one, but wealth rightly gained and bountifully used for others is seen to bring blessings abundant, praise on earth and delight in heaven. It may also be enjoyed in moderation.[6] In other words, economic activity as such is praised, and a high value is assigned to property. In fact there is apparently no instance in the early texts of praise of poverty in itself, apart from the monastics who have left the world. This positive understanding and appreciation of the value, both spiritual and practical, of the life of lay persons in the world goes far to explain the wide and continuing acceptance of Buddhism in early centuries both in India and in the lands beyond.

It is equally necessary to emphasize the Buddha's acceptance of men—and women—of other classes than the
wealthy and the powerful. His framework of understanding
enabled him to affirm and even give high religious value to
the newly emerging world of mercantile activity of the larger
Ganges River valley. But unjust economic methods were
severely reproved, with the specific warning that they bring
the perpetrator to punishment (potentially for a limited
period of time) in Niraya (hell); all persons were enjoined to
practice love and mercy.

The texts indicate that even slaves could enter the monastic order provided their masters freed them; we note later
rules which state, however, that a runaway slave should not
be received.[7] These qualifications are without doubt an integral part of the larger picture, but the otherwise universal
concern and openness of the Buddha and the order constitute the predominating motif. A moving instance of this
openness is seen in the account of the conversion of the
streetsweeper Sunita. One of the poems of the *Thera-gāthā*
records the scene wherein the scavenger, poor and of
humble birth, "one for whom no man cared, despised,
abused," accustomed to bend his head before others, saw
the Buddha accompanied by a number of monks enter the
city of Rajagriha (the present Rajgir, south of the Ganges
River in the state of Bihar) near his place of working:

> I laid aside my baskets and my yoke,
> And came where I might due obeisance make
> And of his loving kindness just for me,
> The Chief of men halted upon his way.
> Low at his feet I bent, then standing by,
> I begged the Master's leave to join the Rule
> And follow him, of every creature Chief.
> Then he whose tender mercy watcheth all
> The world, the Master pitiful and kind,

Gave me my answer: come, Bhikku! he said.
Thereby to me was ordination given.

The poem—its polished form clearly representing a later recension of the tradition—goes on to describe Sunita's experience of enlightenment as a result of his faithful observance of the Master's teaching. The concluding verses relate the Buddha's smiling in approval as he states that supreme holiness is gained (not by birth or anything else external but) "by discipline of holy life, restraint and mastery of self."[8]

One consequence of this transcendence of the distinctions of caste and social status was that a member of the Brāhman caste who entered the order might be in the position of receiving instruction in the emerging doctrine and rules from a member of a lower caste who had preceded him in ordination. He would, of course, have to respect him and call him friend or brother. It was evidently the practice of the order during the lifetime of the Buddha to address each other as "friend" (avuso; cf. Jn. 15:12-15). We read in one of the primary accounts of the death of the Buddha that he advised his cousin Ānanda to have the order change this practice, but it is highly doubtful that this injunction goes back to the Buddha himself.[9] It seems rather to reflect later practice, when monasteries, like their counterparts in Europe, tended to reflect in their organization and style the class distinctions of secular society.

A final word in this context should be given on the question of whether Gautama shared the fairly common Indian view of women as inferior.[10] The texts give clear indication, with critical nuances evidently heightened as time passed by the increasingly monastic mentalities emerging, that women were regarded as among the monks' chief obstacles to progress in the spiritual life. Among the sayings recorded on the eve of the Buddha's death are his alleged instructions in answer to Ānanda's questions:

"How are we to conduct ourselves, Lord, with regard to womankind?"

"As not seeing them, Ānanda."

"But if we should see them, what are we to do?"

"No talking, Ānanda."

"But if they should speak to us, Lord, what are we to do?"

"Keep wide awake, Ānanda."[11]

This direction to keep alert was, to be sure, one of those most widely used by the Buddha with reference to all the exigencies of human life. Neither the above, however, nor any other passage in the early texts gives any indication other than that he himself treated women with grave respect. It is certain that he boldly proclaimed his message to both men and women with apparently full confidence that both, within the context of family life as much as in the monastic orders, could attain to the highest, to *Nirvāṇa*. Some of the language in the texts may derive from the Buddha's concern to develop an order of itinerant missionary monks for whom, in their celibate and mobile lifestyle, women could be both moral temptation and physical hindrance.

We learn that when in response to the Buddha's positive affirmations of the spiritual and moral potential of women, some women wished to have an order of nuns created, the Buddha was initially opposed to the request. We may well consider some possible reasons for this hesitancy. In the very earliest period the monks did not live in buildings but in forests, caves, or in groves of trees. The Buddha may have feared that women were not suited for this kind of homeless life; they could be exposed to personal danger. It was perhaps considered unseemly for them to beg, as the male monastics regularly did—although the texts indicate that they did beg when permission was granted to form an order of nuns, with somewhat stricter rules than for men. The deference to male monks that came to be a part of the rules for nuns—a nun was expected to be ordained in both orders—may probably be best understood in the context of the contemporary structure of families in India, in which the householder was always male. But with respect to women as such, the texts give us consistent reason to believe that the Buddha entertained high respect and had the highest expectations of their spiritual potential. The Buddha is recorded as saying to King Prasenajit of Kośala (the largest of the then four chief kingdoms of northern India), in response to his unhappiness over the birth of a daughter, that there are some women who are superior to men. Some women, he continued, are notable for their knowledge, morality, respect of their mothers-in-law, and faithfulness to their husbands.[12]

In this context and also in comparison with the Christ, it is in order to mention the incident recorded of the Buddha's meeting with the courtesan Ambapāli of Vaisāli, the capital city of Videha, a smaller kingdom north of the Ganges River. The position of certain courtesans of Indian society of the time was apparently similar to that of the *hetairai* of the classical period in Greece, in that they possessed considerable culture, social status, and wealth. Ambapāli had learned that the Buddha was staying—no doubt out of doors—at her mango grove and went out to meet him there with her retinue of servants in fine carriages that she evidently owned or could afford to order. The Buddha received her, "instructed, aroused, incited, and gladdened her with religious discourse." She thereupon invited him with the brethren to dine at her house the following day. The Buddha accepted the invitation with the then customary silence indicative of assent.

Later the same day a number of Licchavis of Vaisāli, men of high social position and wealth, we learn, hearing of the Buddha's arrival, also rode out to the mango grove to meet him. They were received and instructed in the same manner as Ambapāli. When they likewise invited the Buddha and the monastic brethren to dine with them the following day, he refused because of his prior promise to dine with the courtesan.

When on the next day the preparations had been completed, Ambapāli sent word that the meal was ready. We read that the Buddha, "who had dressed himself early in the morning, took his bowl and his robe, and went with the brethren" to the residence of Ambapāli. Here she served them sweet rice and cakes "and waited upon them until they refused any more."

After the meal, when the Buddha had washed his bowl and hands, Ambapāli came to sit by his side on a low stool. She then offered to the order of mendicants the property where they were. The Buddha accepted the gift and after further religious discourse rose from his seat and departed with the monks.[13]

The implication of the account is clearly that Ambapāli accepted the Buddha's teaching and was converted to the way of life consonant therewith. The passage, however, nowhere states specifically that she changed her profession. In the *Psalms of the Sisters*, largely poetic material issuing from the order of nuns, there is a poem ascribed to one Ambapāli that is the product of reflection on the transitoriness of physical beauty by an elderly woman. The introduction, of later origin than the poem itself, states that the woman strove for enlightenment in her old age.[14] We ourselves, given our own traditions, may wish for more clarity of ethical direction in the account, but there is, on the other hand, no word from the Buddha in any of the texts either approving or condoning the profession. If in the account as we have it, there is no clearly spoken, "Go your way, and from now on do not sin again," there is as warm and unambiguous acceptance of the person as we find in Jesus' treatment of the woman taken in adultery.[15] We may also note how the *Psalms of the Sisters* reveal clearly the high spiritual quality of life of these women. The testimony to joy and to a higher alertness of mind is as frequent as to peace and calm. One of the sisters is bold enough to compare herself in spiritual attainment with the great Kaśyapa, the first leader of the order after the Buddha's death.[16]

We cannot deny a certain antifeminism in early Buddhist monasticism, and as a result even in the more lay oriented Mahāyāna developments with their reformist efforts to capture the true spirit of the Buddha and his teachings, there were no women to be found in the Western Paradise depicted in the earliest versions of the Pure Land teaching in India and China. The assumption was that women had to be reborn as males in order to attain enlightenment, a view that was long to plague historic Buddhism in spite of its being specifically contrary to the teaching and practice of the Buddha himself. To be sure, most ordinary believers over subsequent centuries did not have easy access to the content of these teachings, and the weight of traditional cultural views and practices was heavy in every country into which the faith was introduced. But the feminine principle, if we may use the term, became increasingly strong within the Mahāyāna, as is evidenced by the obvious femininity of many of its images in painting and sculpture. Indeed, appreciation of the feminine element in the cosmos was evidently a part of the Mahāyāna from the beginning. Not a few contemporary Buddhists are showing increasing sensitivity in this area and are trying to recapture the open-ended and compassionate posture of the Buddha himself in this centrally important area of human relationships.[17]

4

Gautama the Buddha has historically often been designated—rightly so, we may agree—as the Compassionate
One. The same term may be applied to Jesus the Christ, with
at least comparable appropriateness. Much of his teaching
emphasizes the compassion at the heart of Ultimate Reality in the cosmos, the compassion of God the Father. This is
not only mercy and forgiveness that make possible the restoration of personal relationships with all creation; it means
also the granting of the chance to begin life again here on
earth, even daily, and the continuous offering of new opportunities in this life. There is a generosity, even a lavish
generosity, a graciousness in the compassion of God as depicted in the teaching of Jesus.

This divine generosity is portrayed by Jesus through his
parables, also in the poetic imagery drawn from nature that
we find especially in the Sermon on the Mount. His injunction—with special emphasis directed to his disciples in the
midst of larger crowds (cf. Mt. 5:1; Lk. 6:20)—"Love your
enemies and pray for those who persecute you" was to the
end that they "may be children of your Father in heaven." A
sign of this quality of the Father is that "he makes his sun
rise on the evil and on the good, and sends rain on the righteous and the unrighteous" (Mt. 5:44-45). Jesus saw the, in
fact, astonishingly abundant and consistent availability of
sources of food to the birds of the air as the result of the
Father's generous provision. The beauty of the "lilies of the
field" as of the grass, beauty that is an apparent "extra" beyond physical or other natural needs, he perceived as comparable evidence of divine graciousness and generosity (Mt.
6:26-30).

The parables of Jesus are again and again like facets of a
precious gem in their portrayal of this same divine graciousness. We have already noted, with some emphasis of expli-

cation, his parables of the lost who are found, indeed sought and found—the parables of the lost sheep, the lost coin, the lost (prodigal) son (Lk. 15:3-32). Another aspect of divine generosity is given in the parable of the landowner who hired workers to labor in his vineyard. Even though, as a result of the varying availability of workers, the landowner hired them at different hours of the day, he insisted on giving a full day's wage to every worker, to those who had served the shortest time as to those who had worked the longest (Mt. 20:1-16). Work is here depicted as a privilege rather than as a hateful task to be compensated for in a manner appropriate to its pain. But the real point of the parable is, of course, the generosity of God, the style of the Kingdom of God—the parable is one of Jesus' many similitudes of the Kingdom.

In Jesus' teaching this gracious generosity of God when applied to the human condition means that an open door of opportunity stands before every human being. His practical conclusion was, therefore, to say, "Ask, and it will be given you; search, and you will find; knock, and the door will be opened for you. For everyone who asks receives and everyone who searches finds, and for everyone who knocks, the door will be opened" (Mt. 7:7-8; Lk. 11:9-10).

We find, moreover, this teaching of Jesus regarding the nature and work of God the Father to be singularly exemplified in his own person and life. This aspect of Jesus' person is particularly seen in his own inclusive, generous acceptance of persons. The above-mentioned parables of the lost and found, as given us by Luke, are set in the narrative as Jesus' explanation of the public criticism—Luke notes the Pharisees and scribes of the day as particularly critical—made of his eating with "tax collectors and sinners" (Lk. 15: 1-2).

Marcus J. Borg, whose work on the life of Jesus I have cited before with no little appreciation, has seen these meals that Jesus shared with "tax collectors and sinners" as "one of the most striking features of Jesus' ministry."[18] It is, of course, important to note that "sinners," like "tax collectors," was a term not primarily of ethical—or theological—analysis, as we might think on the basis of our centuries-long Western anthropological tradition, but one used to designate a particular class of society according to the conventional understanding or distastes of the ruling elite. However ill these perceptions and ascriptions accorded with the prophetic tradition of Israel at its best, they were evidently a vital reality within the Jewish society of Jesus' time, and they denoted the marginal persons or social outcasts of that society.

These marginal persons were outcasts from the "best society" even though, as in the case of the tax collectors—Jewish entrepreneurs who contracted to collect taxes for Rome and were allowed, against a fixed amount to be paid into the imperial coffers, to levy whatever they could get from fellow Jews—they may have been financially wealthy. The story of the Jewish tax collector Zacchaeus, who was accepted as a disciple of Jesus after a past of unjust misuse of his office and personal accumulation of wealth over the years, is a case in point (Lk. 19:1-10). To the Jewish establishment, both religious and political, these outcasts were beyond the pale, hardly to be considered as fellow Jews, even as fellow human beings, and certainly not to be received into one's home to share in the table fellowship that had traditionally rich religious as well as social meanings.

Not a few, however, of these marginal persons were poor. Many were no doubt only partially observant of the Torah. Irritating to the establishment were those who failed to pay tithes or the temple tax that, in fact, constituted a kind of double taxation, for whatever taxes the Romans exacted were hardly to be avoided. We see that Jesus accepted these persons, however, not only as fellow human beings, but as equally valid sharers in the tradition of Israel (cf. Lk. 13:16; 19:9—the first instance in Luke being that of a crippled woman whom Jesus healed and the second being Jesus' affirmation of who Zacchaeus really was, a son of Abraham, even as the woman was called a daughter of Abraham). Above all, Jesus accepted them as persons already welcomed by God and as potentially able to receive and act constructively upon the best gifts that God the Father offers the human beings whom he has created.

Marcus Borg, as we have seen, identifies Jesus' acceptance of social outcasts as a major issue, perhaps *the* major critical issue, of his public ministry. This is because he believes it constituted a direct challenge to the primal religious self-identity and socio-economic place of the Jewish establishment in Palestine. To put the issue in other terms, Jesus' views and practices were seen as a veritable threat to the survival of the Jewish nation as the people of God in the context of the Roman Empire of the time. They were thus a major, perhaps *the* major factor leading to the establishment's rejection of Jesus as an authentic prophet of Israel and ultimately to his death by crucifixion. We shall discuss this issue in more detail later.

Borg's rationale for this conclusion—and he is by no means alone in the scholarly world with this view[19]—is that "the central ordering principle of the Jewish social world" was "the division between purity and impurity, holy and not-holy, righteous and wicked." Borg sees this "cultural dynamic of the society"—a dynamic controlled by the religio-political Jewish establishment—as leading directly to what he calls the "politics of holiness." This was a public posture and policy of separatism based on ethnic and ritual purity that without doubt constituted a major element of Hebraic history at least from the time of the Babylonian captivity (586-536 B.C.E.) and perhaps in some forms from earlier centuries as well. If, as Borg evidently believes, the central purpose of Jesus' ministry was to be an instrument of the living God to transform the people of Israel into "an inclusive community reflecting the compassion of God," Jesus' inclusive spirit and practices could indeed threaten in a radical way the identity and place of the Jewish establishment.[20] Let us try to analyze and reflect upon this thesis in the context of our own purposes.

The threat was in part such as to blur the lines of distinction between the ruling elite and the bulk of the Jewish people. The Gospel of John, which reveals perhaps more of this intra-Jewish class hostility than any other gospel, gives what may be an indication of the intense feelings involved by a statement allegedly made by Pharisees to the temple police on the occasion of one of the earlier of the several trips to Jerusalem during Jesus' public ministry that are identified in this gospel. This was a statement descriptive of "most" of the people, at least of those in Jerusalem at the time, "this crowd, which does not know the law—they are accursed" (Jn. 7:49). The particularities of this language admittedly may owe more to the feelings of the author of the gospel at the time of writing than to historical accuracy, but such feelings evidently did exist in Palestine in the first half of the century of the Common Era, as in the second half in Ephesus—or in Jamnia.

Another element of Jesus' possible threat to the self-identity of the Jewish establishment of his time was to blur the lines of distinction between the people of Israel and the Gentiles by which they were surrounded both within and without the Roman Empire. One aspect of this concern was allegedly fear that Jesus' popularity with the common people would lead to destruction of the distinctive identity of the Jewish people. The chief priests and Pharisees are reported in the Gospel of John to have said to one another, "This man is performing many signs. If we let him go on like this, everyone will believe in him, and the Romans will come and destroy both our holy place and our nation" (Jn. 11:47-48).[21]

This fear, however, probably represented a kind of deep unease rather than panic. In spite of various modern attempts, from the German socialist writer Karl Johann Kautsky (1854-1938) to certain contemporary Liberation theologians, to transform Jesus into a political revolutionary, there is actually no evidence at all within or without the gospel narratives to indicate that Jesus was a revolutionary in the sense of opting for social or political change through physical violence. I believe that the Gospel of John gives us an essentially probable if not documentarily accurate account of both the intent and practice of Jesus in its report of Jesus' appearance before the Roman governor Pontius Pilate. Jesus is here recorded as responding to Pilate's questions regarding his having been handed over to the Romans by "your own nation and the chief priests." Jesus is cited as answering, "My kingdom is not from this world. If my kingdom were from this world, my followers would be fighting to keep me from being handed over to the Jews [Johannine language to designate the Jewish establishment—Jesus and all the apostolic leadership were themselves Jews]. But as it is, my kingdom is not from here" (Jn. 18:36).

We have explored the gospel records regarding Jesus' use of the term Kingdom of God with sufficient fullness to recognize the essential accord of these words with the other gospel accounts. As Marcus Borg has put it, Jesus radically criticized the social world of first-century Palestine, of his own people, "warned it of the historical consequences of its present path [as he evidently perceived such with his prophetic insight], and sought its transformation in accord with an alternative vision." Borg holds that Jesus, as "a person of Spirit," had a vision of the role of the people of Israel at significant points different from that of the establishment and the conventional wisdom of the time. This latter was to carry on the spirit and practice of separatism, "the politics of holiness," vis-à-vis Hellenistic culture and the political rule of Rome.[22] Jesus, however, as we have seen, was primarily concerned with transformation of the interiority of persons and the application within the whole of life of the historic Hebrew prophetic ethical tradition. He would carry on the historic self-identity of the people of Israel as something other than absolute. Jesus' view of the role of Israel was instrumental. He looked toward an Israel that was open-ended and ultimately inclusive of other peoples, cultures, and even religions—even as he taught inclusiveness and acceptance of the persons of "the outsiders" within Jewish society.

The last sentence of the previous paragraph is actually a conclusion of my own thought as I have developed it on the basis of all that has gone before in this book. It will probably be necessary to cite further and more specific evidence for such conclusions as we go on. Let us, however, first take note of the historic fact that Jesus' contest with the so-called conventional wisdom of the society of his time, especially that of the Jewish religious and political establishment, was not a posture unique in the history of Israel.

A primary fact to note is that, even with some exceptions, the biblical witness in both the Old and New Testaments is remarkably open-ended and inclusive with reference to the universality of the presence and work of God in the world of his creation. This is with reference to aspects both revelatory and salvific. The book of Genesis begins with an account of the divine creation of the whole cosmos. This series of "events" has been called by some scholars the first of the universal or cosmic covenants to appear in Genesis (Gen. 1:1-31). The term *covenant* is defined in this context as the initiation (or restoration) of personal relationships between two or more parties, usually by the initiative of one party but with mutual responsibility on the side of all parties as the assumed basis for all accompanying agreements or promises. Creation itself is thus seen as constituting the establishment by the Creator of a relationship in love with the whole of his creation. The subsequent promises to Eve (Gen. 3:15) and Adam after their "fall" follow in the same context of universality, for the two are portrayed in the biblical account as the ancestors of all human beings.

This pattern of universal covenants, however, is given special clarity and focus in the Genesis account of the divine covenant made with Noah, his family, and descendants. Here the specific Hebrew term for covenant is used (*berith*). The inclusiveness of this covenant is seen not only in that the descendants of Noah are presumed to comprise the whole of subsequent humanity. The statement is made five times in the text that the covenant and the promises involved are not only between God and Noah, with his family and descendants, but also between God "and every living creature of all flesh that is on the earth" (Gen. 9:8-19). The repetition is certainly not without purpose, and a solid biblical basis is thus given for a worldview, comparable to that of historic Buddhism, that sees a certain interrelationship and spiritual value in the whole of phenomenal existence (or creation) and consequent human responsibility to respect and preserve it.

With respect to the biblical position, we may properly add that the later covenant with Abram (Abraham) that was designed to create the people of Israel—as a people with a divinely specified priestly mission—also belongs in its larger ranges of meaning to the category of universal covenants. Although apparently narrow in its intended specificity, its end is described in the text with language highly inclusive. For "in you [Abram] all the families of the earth shall be blessed" (Gen. 12:3; repeated in Gen. 18:18; 22:18; 24:4; 28:14). Here, too, the repetition would seem to mean that the biblical authors intended a universal or inclusive perspective to constitute the framework of all subsequent accounts, specifically those of the activities surrounding the creation of the people of Israel and the events of the Exodus and the Torah given on Mt. Sinai. The same perspective, we may note, is presumed in the whole of the New Testament as well.

The first eleven chapters of Genesis are commonly thought by biblical scholars to have been written as an introduction to the first canon of Scripture in the Hebrew tradition, the Pentateuch. The intent of the writers responsible for this work, generally held to be a product of the reign of King Solomon (961-922 B.C.E.), was evidently to set the liberation experience of the Hebrew people from Egypt under the prophetic leadership of Moses and the revelatory events connected with Mount Sinai in the context of the relation of the God of their faith with the whole world and all nations. As Millard Lind has put it, the major themes of the entire Bible, the themes of grace and rebellion, judgment and salvation, are universalized in these chapters "to show Yahweh's concern for the world behind his choice of Israel."[23]

The Bible, both the Old and New Testaments, is, of course, not a seamless robe of unvaried unanimity of content. The contention of some scholars is that even monotheism, the central element of the faith of Israel at least from the beginning of the period of the literary prophets, cannot be found in the earlier strata of the Bible.[24] But from this time of the formation of the first canon of Scripture, it is clear that the spiritual leadership of Israel had come to regard Yahweh as Creator and Lord of the universe and, therefore, Lord of the nations as well as of Israel. In spite of the narrow ferocity of passages like Deuteronomy 7:2, 5, 16 and Elijah's command to kill 450 prophets of Baal (I Kings 18:40), there is a basic assumption not only in the Genesis accounts of the divine creation of the entire cosmos and of the establishment of universal covenants, but also and consistently in the prophetic literature, in the psalms, and in the wisdom literature of the Old Testament. This is the assumption that not only Israel, but the nations, too, are enfolded within Yahweh's concern and care even as they are under Yahweh's lordship. This is also to say that the nations have some knowledge of Yahweh and of Yahweh's ethical character, of his love and care as of his promises.[25]

Readers whose theological nurture has been focused in assumptions of the History of Salvation School of Oscar Cullmann and others of the period before and after the Second World War or those who simply share in the common ethos of Western civilization, are not accustomed to understanding the primary faith-position of the Old Testament in the terms of the preceding paragraphs. They have largely tended to think that "God was speaking to Israel alone."

But such a narrow view, I contend, does not represent the main thrust—the structured background and assumptions—of the Hebrew Bible. We find, for example, that as early as the mid-eighth century B.C.E. the prophet Amos had come to a remarkably universal understanding of the providential lordship of Yahweh. This understanding is implicit throughout the oracles of Amos, but we find it expressed in particularly graphic mode when he asserts that Yahweh regards the movements of the Philistines from Caphtor (Crete?) and the Syrians from Kir (their previous location to the northeast?) as the result of Yahweh's providential guidance and of comparable religious as well as historical significance with the deliverance of Israel from Egypt. The very Israelites who regard themselves as the first of the nations (Amos 6:1—the age-old temptation to distort a perception of election for service to one of privilege!) are in fact the same to Yahweh as the Ethiopians, a people who, to Israel's view at the time, lived in the remotest part of the

world (Amos 9:7; cf. Isa. 14:16-27). Amos evidently believed
that Israel participated in a relationship with Yahweh in
some ways unique (Amos 3:2) and had gained its land with
divine help (2:9-10). But Amos gave it as the word of the Lord
that, to use the language of the German scholar Hans Walter
Wolff, "Israel should not draw from this the conclusion that
its God had guided only its history."[26]

In fact, one of the emerging theological *loci communes* of
our time is the contention, actually in accord with a mainstream of theological understanding of the first centuries of
the Christian church, that the presence and work of the living God in the history of Israel, as of the Christian church,
institutionally perceived, are not unique in the sense of
"confinement" therein. Rather they are representative.
Christian theologians especially from the so-called Two-
thirds World have been stressing this point in our day with
increasing boldness and force.

African theologians one after another are being drawn to
this understanding; one of the most incisive is the Roman
Catholic bishop, biblical scholar, and theologian from
Malawi, Patrick Kalilombe (b. 1933). He insists that "both
the Baptist (Mt. 3:9-10; Lk. 3:8) and Christ went out of their
way to stigmatize the misplaced confidence in mere belonging to an ethnic group, albeit a divinely chosen one"
(Mt. 3:11-12; Jn. 8:37-41). Kalilombe endeavors to demonstrate with solid biblical substance and theological rationale
that the main thrust of the teaching of the Bible is not exclusive but inclusive, that the beginning of all is the "cosmic
Covenant of love between God and mankind by the very
fact of creation." And with reference to the election-con-
sciousness of the people of Israel—or of the Christian
church—he contends that the special choices of God are "a
hopeful sign or proof of what in less evident ways he is doing all along with the whole of mankind, and they are meant
to serve this wider Covenant."[27]

Similarly in East Asia, the Taiwanese Old Testament scholar Choan-Seng Song (b. 1929) sees the story of God's redemptive work with the people of Israel as at the same time centrally meaningful for Israel and also symbolic of wider ranges of divine activity:

The people of Israel were singled out, under a divine providence inexplicable to us and even to them, not to present themselves to the rest of the world as the nation through which God's redeeming love would be mediated, *but* to be a symbol of how God would deal redemptively with other nations. In the light of the experience unique to Israel, other nations should learn how their histories can be interpreted redemptively. An Asian nation would have its own experience of exodus, captivity, rebellion against Heaven, the golden calf. It would have its own trek in the desert of poverty or dehumanization . . . An Asian nation will thus be enabled to find its place side by side with Israel in God's salvation.[28]

Choan-Seng Song insists in this way that the Old Testament is a religious document written at least in part to show how the historical experience of any people can be interpreted as an arena of divine presence and redemptive action. For this reason any "theology which regards Israel and the Christian church as the only bearers and dispensers of God's saving love must be called into question." Song summarizes his thought with the incisive words that a "very big theological blunder" was committed by those Western theologians who in the past tried to confine the redemptive work of God to the history of one nation and then the Christian church.

This understanding has come to mean for Song that we now may also, like Second Isaiah (Isa. 44:28; 45:1-4), like the

writer of the story of Melchizedek (Gen. 14:17-20), or like
Ezekiel (29:19-20), "begin to see those alien to our faith as
making a contribution to the development of human community, as agents of God." Specifically this understanding
has led Song to recognize that the lifelong unselfish toil of
the Buddha—from the age of thirty-five to his death at
eighty—for the liberation of others from self-centered and
ignorant suffering is not without divine redemptive significance even as Christians understand the term (cf. Col. 1:24).
Song holds that the teaching of the Buddha on the self
points to a transpersonal transformation of self that is actually "a fulfillment of personhood detached from historical
bondage and freed from the restrictions of the present life."
Therefore Song goes on to ask:

> Can we not say that Buddha's way is also a part of
> the drama of salvation which God has acted out fully
> in the person and work of Jesus Christ? The histories of
> nations and peoples that are not under the direct im-
> pact of Christianity are not just "natural histories" run-
> ning their course in complete separation from God's
> redemptive love and power . . . There are redemptive
> elements in all nations that condemn human cor-
> ruption and encourage what is noble and holy. Our
> evaluation of the history of a nation is not complete
> until such redemptive elements are properly recog-
> nized.[29]

The above may seem a somewhat lengthy excursus, but
the point of the complexity of the theological meaning, indeed the divine significance, of the people of Israel war-
rants, I believe, more than casual treatment in the context
of our consideration of the Buddha and the Christ.

Actually, we find two relatively distinct tendencies in Judaism prior to and during the lifetime of Jesus: one issuing

in the exclusive mentality and practices of Ezra and later Pharasaism, the other stressing more the inwardness of a denationalized religion and its relative independence of outer forms and expressing itself in love of God and all human beings.[30] We now know that Palestinian Judaism in the first half of the first century of our era manifested a wider range of religious options than was formerly thought. Pharisees, Sadducees, Essenes (given full, perhaps preferential, treatment in Josephus but not mentioned once in the New Testament), Herodians, Zealots, followers of John the Baptizer and of other charismatics—all contending for the allegiance of the people and constituting a kaleidoscopic scene of varying styles and tendencies of faith-understanding.

The Jews of the Dispersion, however, tended to stress the ethical and spiritual content of historic Judaism, its robust monotheism and noble ethical ideals. Even though they remained largely separate as a religio-ethnic group, for the sake of their own self-understanding and for missionary purposes they moved in the direction of mutual understanding and communications with their non-Jewish environment. The literary remains of Alexandrian Judaism, such as the Wisdom of Solomon, Sirach, II Enoch, and the works of Philo (20 B.C.E.?-42 C.E.?) show how Jews in the Diaspora could adapt and assimilate aspects of traditionally non-Jewish thought without sacrificing the essentials of their faith. To Philo, for example, the Greek philosopher Plato was, like the Hebrew lawgiver Moses, "holiest of the holy."[31]

The reason for this necessarily brief discussion of aspects of Israel's relationship with non-Jews is to bring to the fore what I believe to be implicit in the New Testament gospel accounts of the teaching and "intent" of Jesus. This is that Jesus' manifest focus in his public mission upon the people of Israel, upon his fellow Jews, was indeed open-ended, in-

tended essentially to prepare the people of Israel for fulfillment of the mission for which they themselves were originally elected, that "all the families of the earth shall be
blessed." Jesus' intent was surely not the "revitalization" of
the people of Israel as an end in itself, for their own good
alone—it did include, to be sure, the profoundest concern
for their own good, for their welfare: spiritual, moral, historical—but reached out in its ultimate concerns to the
ends of the earth and encompassed all peoples.[32] It is impossible otherwise to understand the astonishing vigor and
persistence, in spite of certain initial ambiguities in the earliest period of the history of the Christian church (cf. Acts
2:39; 10:1-43; 15:1-29), of the missionary expansion of the
church from Barnabas and Paul to the present day. All four
gospels of the New Testament cite as one aspect of the
conclusion of their story of Jesus his call to a universal missionary service (Mt. 28:16-20; Mk. 16:15—from the later addition—Lk. 24:47-49; Jn. 17:18; 20:21-22). Indeed, the New
Testament as a whole can properly be described as a missionary book, as a call to outreach to the ends of the earth in
consequence of the love of the Father and of the ongoing
presence of the Son whom he sent and then raised from the
dead.[33]

We may properly conclude this section then with brief
identification of the gospel witnesses to the wider perspectives and concerns of Jesus. However long and tortuous the
process may have been that led to their emergence, the literary prophets of the Old Testament, major and minor,
manifest a consistent understanding. This is that on the day
of the Lord—and before!—the nations are to be judged, like
Israel, in accordance with their ethical conduct and in pro-
portion to their knowledge (Amos 1:1-3:15; Jer. 7:3-4; Ezek.
16:44-58; Zech. 1:15; 7:8-9; Zeph. 1:3, 9, 18; Mal. 3:18). For
the nations have some knowledge of Yahweh and of his
will even as they also are the objects of his love and care (cf.

Lk. 12:47-48). In full accord with this tradition, the gospel writers of the New Testament agree in depicting Jesus as utterly free of nationalistic or ethnically based prejudice himself and as rejecting all notions of arbitrary divine retribution, eschatological or present, upon the nations (Mt. 19:30; 20:16 [Mk. 10:31; Lk. 13:30]; Mt. 11:21-24; 12:41-42; Lk. 9:51-56; Jn. 4:1-45). Among the synoptic gospels we find in Matthew alone specific criticism on Jesus' part of certain Gentile religious practices (Mt. 6:7, 32; but cf. Mt. 10:15; 11:21-24), but then in no other gospel is there found sharper criticism of common contemporary Jewish practices or more forthright affirmation of the sublime impartiality or fairness of God.

Special notice should be taken of Jesus' high appreciation of the faith and ethical conduct of certain Gentiles as recorded in the Gospel of Matthew (Mt. 8:5-13 [Lk. 7:1-12; Jn. 4:46-54]; cf. Lk. 10:30-37; 17:11-19).[34] In the context of the postures of contemporary religious parties and groups in Israel, Jesus emphasized the importance of quality of attitude or intent as compared with formal allegiances, and we note his insistence that his disciples not hinder others just because they are not of the "Jesus group." At this point Jesus proclaimed the principle that "whoever is not against us is for us" (Mk. 9:38-41).[35] In the Gospel of Matthew we find Jesus resolutely refusing to ascribe ultimate religious significance to formal acts or allegiances that are not expressive of deeper qualities of intent and faithfulness. That is, not those who proclaim the "name" or even perform miracles, but those who do the will of God shall enter the Kingdom (Mt. 7:21-23; 25:14-46; cf. Lk. 10:25-37; 13:22-30; I Cor. 13). Not a little theology of every major branch of the Christian church over long centuries is challenged by these words ascribed to the Master himself.

Also recorded in Matthew is the devastating statement of Jesus to his disciples made immediately after his warm

commendation of the faith of the Roman centurion whose
servant he was about to heal, "Truly I tell you, in no one in
Israel have I found such faith. I tell you, many will come
from east and west and will eat with Abraham and Isaac and
Jacob in the kingdom of heaven, while the heirs of the kingdom will be thrown into the outer darkness" (Mt. 8:10-12).
In Matthew is found the fullest statement of Jesus' "Great
Commission" to a universal mission (Mt. 28:16-20), but also
in Matthew is recorded Jesus' sharpest criticism of contemporary Jewish missionary practices whereby—by implication a criticism of concerns more for outer form than for
inner quality—converts were won to the faith of Israel only
to manifest ethical fruits of an even lower quality than their
mentors (Mt. 23:15). In Matthew's account of the eschatological parable of the sheep and the goats, final separation
of persons is made not on the basis of ethnic or cultural affiliation, not even on the basis of religious faith—the issue
of faith is not mentioned once in the parable—but as a consequence of the presence or lack of ethical, in particular of
compassionate, conduct (Mt. 25:31-46).

Statements like the above are, of course, properly to be
interpreted in the larger context of Jesus' recorded teaching—to be remembered also are the situation and purposes
of the author of the Gospel of Matthew—but they make
clear, I believe, the inclusive mentality of Jesus, his perception of the impartiality of God the Father, of God's generosity to all persons, not just to the people of Israel. The context,
for example, of Jesus' assertion to his disciples that the very
hairs of their head are all numbered before God (Mt. 10:30)
implies that the affirmation applies to all human beings.
Even in the case of sparrows, "not one of them is forgotten
in God's sight" (Lk. 12:6), nor will one of them fall to the
ground "apart from your Father" (Mt. 10:29). The high anthropology of Jesus is revealed in his teaching of a hierarchy
of values in the cosmos, whereby a human being is "of more

value than many sparrows" (Mt. 10:31; cf. "How much more valuable is a human being than a sheep!" Mt. 12:12). We are reminded here of Gautama the Buddha's statements of the high spiritual value and opportunities inherent in the human state.

Also of no little significance in perceiving Jesus' anthropological understanding is the confrontational colloquy recorded in the Gospel of John, which we considered in some detail earlier. Here we find Jesus replying to hearers who are critical of his own self-understanding that he had just expressed to them. He quotes to them Psalm 82:6, "Is it not written in your law, 'I said, you are gods?'" Jesus goes on in the exchange to affirm his agreement with the psalmist that "those to whom the word of God came were called 'gods'— and the scripture cannot be annulled" (Jn. 10:34-35). Elements of this language may be owed in part to the author, but the Gospel of John is clearly as noteworthy for its high anthropology as for its high christology.

A summation of Jesus' inclusive posture of faith and practice can be found in the famous passage in the fourth chapter of the Gospel of Luke, which gives a report of Jesus' first sermon in Nazareth, "where he had been brought up." The passage as a whole is a remarkable example of Jesus' selective use of Scripture to focus on the highest and best of the past of Israel.[36] The first part of the sermon stresses God's— and Jesus'—social inclusivism, indicating God's concern for every class of society. The second part emphasizes God's— and Jesus'—international inclusivism, indicating God's concern (not only currently, but also in the past) for those outside Israel. The reaction of violent anger on the part of Jesus' hearers on this occasion arose probably as much because of the first kind of inclusivism as from the second (Lk. 4:16-30). Perhaps correctly has it been said that the last human division to be overcome, more than that of race or education or culture, is class. The whole of the gospel tradition, however, combines to make clear Jesus' transcendence of every humanly created boundary. It is of no little significance that the primary content of Jesus' teaching, especially as recorded in the synoptic gospels, focuses on the Kingdom of God, not on the people of Israel nor any other narrower category.

2

Women and Children

1

We have already briefly mentioned something of Jesus' treatment of women in the context of discussion of Gautama's teaching and practices with regard to women. A few further words are in order to give some detail. We have noted the common Indian evaluation of women as inferior and the transcendence on Gautama's part of such views and his consequent respectful treatment of women. With some exceptions, Jewish attitudes and treatment of women from long before the time of Jesus differed little from those of the cultures surrounding Israel. As Marcus J. Borg has put it, a good wife was appreciated (cf. Prov. 31:10-31; Sir. 26:1-4, 13-18), but "women as a group were not well thought of."[37] As my friend and former colleague, Charles E. Carlston, has written in an exceptionally well-informed article, the picture drawn of women in the ancient world, within and without Israel, is grim. They are "basically ineducable and empty-headed; vengeful, dangerous, and responsible for men's sins; mendacious, treacherous, and unreliable; fickle"—and the list goes on! For our present purpose it is most significant to quote Carlston further to the effect that "this so-called wisdom is totally absent from the traditions about Jesus."[38] As we have seen, language of this kind can be found in the early Buddhist texts, but it is used as descriptive of humanity in its "natural" state, not of females as contrasted with males.

The gospel accounts are uniformly in agreement that Jesus, like Gautama, treated men and women with equal respect and as equally able to attain to the highest in spiritual understanding and moral achievement. Women were among the inner group of disciples who followed him about the country in his itinerant public ministry. Luke identifies these women as persons who "had been cured of evil spirits and infirmities" (= illnesses—we note that the gospel accounts do not identify the male members of the inner circle as having been "saved" from such publicly noticeable afflictions!). Luke names a few of the women, "Mary, called Magdalene, from whom seven demons had gone out, and Joanna, the wife of Herod's steward Chuza, and Susanna, and many others, who provided for them out of their resources" (Lk. 8:1-3).

The gospel records give us very little information about the logistics of Jesus' public ministry. In the light, however, of almost universal human experience of religious giving, it is not surprising that women should be singled out as those who were particularly responsible for the financial support of the new movement. Mark informs us that it was "Mary Magdalene, and Mary, the mother of James and Salome" who bought *(sic)* the spices that they—and perhaps other women also—might anoint the body of Jesus after his temporary burial (Mk. 16:1-2; cf. Mt. 28:1; Lk. 23:55-24:2; the author of John asserts that Nicodemus was the one who brought *[sic]* the spices to anoint Jesus' dead body, Jn. 19:38-20:10).

The parables of Jesus also give us hints as to how Jesus thought about women as persons and in their roles in society. Women appear as key figures in these parables with apparently equal frequency with men. In what we have seen as among the most significant of Jesus' parables, those portraying God the Father as seeking and finding the lost, we note that just as a man is the one who goes out to search for a lost sheep, the person who seeks and seeks until a lost coin is found is a woman (Lk. 15:1-10). Other parables in Matthew or Luke reveal comparable balancing of male and female figures (cf. Mt. 13:31-33; 25:1-30; Lk. 11:5-8; 18:1-8).

The gospel accounts of Jesus' healings show an apparently equal regard for women's needs as for men's. This pattern is revealed at the beginning of the Gospel of Mark, where we find toward the end of the first chapter how Jesus "cured many who were sick with various diseases, and cast out many demons." This larger work is preceded by narratives of more particular events, of Jesus' healing the mother-in-law of Simon Peter of a fever (Mk. 1:21-34). Similarly, Jesus is described as healing the daughter of Jairus, one of the leaders of the Capernaum synagogue, also the servant (identified as a slave in Luke 7:2) of a Roman military officer, a centurion. Significantly, the accounts of the first healing in both Matthew and Luke tell how Jesus graciously accepted the interruption of his move to help the centurion's boy in order to heal a woman who had been "suffering from hemorrhages for twelve years" (Mt. 8:5-13; 9:18-26; Mk. 5:21-43; Lk. 7:1-10; 8:40-56). We find Jesus willing to incur the anger of a synagogue leader—and many others of the establishment—by healing on the sabbath a woman who had been crippled with a bent back for eighteen years. Jesus proclaimed her to be a daughter of Abraham with the same ethnic—and sacred—status as any of his male hearers (Lk. 13:10-17).

We have already discussed certain aspects of the meeting of Jesus with a Samaritan woman, who, from common Jewish perspectives, suffered from the triple liability of foreignness, womanness, and a background of unseemly sexual conduct. Without condoning the last, Jesus took the initiative to address the woman courteously, frankly, and opened up for her, her family, and her community new avenues of access to the God of their faith—and his (Jn. 4:1-45). We read incidentally that Jesus' disciples, when they returned from their task of buying food in the town, "were astonished that he was speaking with a woman." Some biblical scholars have concerns over the historicity of this incident—largely because it is found only in the Gospel of John—but the account seems hardly that which the early church in any place would have invented.

A final word on this theme may properly begin with reference to the unanimous gospel records that Jesus appeared first to women disciples after his resurrection. Mark identifies these as "Mary Magdalene, and Mary the mother of James, and Salome" (Mk. 16:1; cf. Mt. 28:1; Lk. 24:10—Luke adds the name of Joanna). The later addition to the Gospel of Mark states specifically that Jesus "appeared first to Mary Magdalene" (Mk. 16:9). The Gospel of John gives us the fullest and most moving account of this meeting of Jesus with Mary Magdalene, also indicating that it was the very first of Jesus' meetings with disciples after he was raised from the dead (Jn. 20: 1-18).

The British scholar-writer A.N. Wilson makes an acute observation regarding the fact that all the New Testament gospel accounts agree in citing the first witnesses of Jesus' resurrection to be women. This fact, he avers, constitutes significant historical-sociological evidence for the larger truth of the accounts. Wilson notes that women were not permitted to give evidence in Jewish courts of law; the presumption was that their testimony would carry no weight. Hence no Jew in the first century of our era who wished to gain credence for the event of the resurrection of Jesus "would have chosen to concoct female false witnesses." The frank acknowledgment of the significant role of women disciples in the event reveals not only that the writers—and their communities of faith—had overcome to a certain extent traditional Mediterranean biases against women. It also tends to make the entire event more believable, at least as authentic human experience. As Wilson puts it, "If the Disciples had chosen to invent the story of the empty tomb, they would have said that the first witnesses were Peter, or James the brother of the Lord, or the rich men Nicodemus and Joseph of Arimathea."[39]

This is not the place to discuss in detail the process by which this extraordinary graciousness and openness of Jesus toward women as persons and as human beings gifted with possibilities, under the Father, of the highest and best of spiritual and moral attainments shifted into the "misogyny of the church Fathers." But we must acknowledge that even in the apostolic writings of the New Testament itself, this trend begins to emerge. Not a few in our day have pointed out that the apostle Paul in dealing with various problems in the church in Corinth admonishes the members that "As in all the churches of the saints, women should be silent in the churches. For they are not permitted to speak, but should be subordinate, as the law also says. If there is anything they desire to know, let them ask their husbands at home. For it is shameful for a woman to speak in church" (I Cor. 14:33-35).

Some scholars have speculated—without textual warrant—that this passage is an interpolation; indicative of the existence of these views is the fact that the passage is bracketed in the New Revised Standard Version of the Bible. To be sure, when Paul moves from practice to theology, he asserts that "in Christ Jesus," just as "there is no longer Jew or Greek, there is no longer slave or free, there is no longer male and female; for all of you are one in Christ Jesus." And we note that in the conclusions of some of his letters to churches, he includes not a few women as evidently among the most significant leader-workers of the church communities as much as they are his personal friends (cf. Rom. 16:1-16; I Cor. 16:19; Phil. 4:2-3; Col. 4:15—also see II Tim. 4:19-21). It is textually possible that Paul means by the *Iounian* of Romans 16:7 Junia, a female apostle as well as fellow Jewess. The New RSV so translates the verse.

But it is difficult to conclude that I Corinthians 14:33-35 is a later interpolation in light of Paul's rather extensive argument for a certain subordination of women to men in chapter eleven of the same letter (11:1-16). We note a more negative view of married life in Paul than in Jesus, although both held the single life to be most appropriate for their own apostolate (I Cor. 7:25-40; Mt. 19:10-12). Furthermore, we find similar negative views of women expressed in other apostolic writings of the New Testament (Eph. 5:22-24; I Tim. 2:11-15; Titus 2:5; I Pet. 3:1-7). We probably have no alternative but to accept the shift in faith-practice here described as a most regrettable downward drift from "the mind of Christ" that has remained in many ways to the present day, in both church and society. We find that Buddhist faith-practice over the centuries and in every country has manifested a similar "regrettable downward drift" from the teaching and practice of the Buddha.[40]

And yet, the above is not the whole story. As I have written elsewhere, wherever the Christian gospel has gone in the world, it has consistently brought with it, even if not perfectly or even adequately, something of the sweet savor of respect for the person as well as concern for the status and condition of both women and children that character-ized the Christ.[41] Similarly, in spite of the distortions of Bud-dhist monasticism and the failures of popular religion, much if not most of that which has been noble and good in Asian history may be attributed to the influence of the Bud-dha.[42]

2

With reference to children, there are, to my knowledge, no accounts in early Buddhist literature of Gautama's sin-gling out children for special consideration. That he did consider them, however, and that with understanding and compassion is indicated by the presence of innumerable references in the whole corpus of Buddhist literature to the Buddha's cultivation and manifestation of benevolence, of benevolent feelings toward all sentient beings of the cos-mos. Without doubt not a few of these references merge into the mythical and symbolic, but something of the tender-ness that Gautama manifested in his lifetime to human be-ings in need is revealed in an account from an early text. This story tells how Gautama once found a monk suffering from dysentery who lay physically helpless in his own filth. With the aid of his cousin Ananda, the Buddha washed the man with his own hands and laid him on a couch. On this occasion he is reported to have given the teaching, "Monks, you have not a mother, you have not a father who might tend you. If you, monks, do not tend one another, then who is there who will tend you? Whoever, monks, would tend me, he should tend the sick."[43]

This incident, affirmative of the solidarity proper to hu-man life—a concept greatly expanded in later Mahāyāna literature—brings to mind the saying attributed to Jesus in similar context of thought concerning the sick or otherwise needy. "Truly I tell you, just as you did it to one of the least of these who are members of my family, you did it to me" (Mt. 25:40).[44] The incident is reinforced by another account. A certain monk whose progress in the spiritual life was admittedly "sluggish and halt" was dismissed from the order by his (mentor) brother-monk. As he stood in inward misery at the gateway of the monastic park still longing to remain, we read in one of the poems of the *Thera-gāthā:*

> There he came to me, the Exalted One,
> And laid his hand upon my head; and took
> My arm, and to the garden led me back.
> To me the Master in his kindness gave
> A napkin for the feet . . . [45]

In the case of Jesus' relationships with children, there is no doubt that his loving and gracious acceptance of children is one of the most notable instances among all the great figures of human religious history. Without going into detailed consideration of the context, past and present, of the tradition of Israel in this matter, we may sense something of the tension between Jesus and his environment in the account given us in the Gospel of Mark. We read, "People were bringing little children to him in order that he might touch them; and the disciples spoke sternly to them. But when Jesus saw this, he was indignant and said to them, 'Let the little children come to me; do not stop them; for it is to such as these that the kingdom of God belongs. Truly I tell you, whoever does not receive the kingdom of God as a little child will never enter it.' And he took them up in his arms, laid his hands on them, and blessed them" (Mk. 10:13-16; cf. Mt. 19:13-15; Lk. 18:15-17).

Another account, also in Mark, gives us further insight into Jesus' perceptions of children:

Then they came to Capernaum; and when he was in the house [whose? Peter's mother-in-law's? Jesus' own?] he asked them, "What were you arguing about on the way?" But they were silent, for on the way they had argued with one another who was the greatest. He sat down, called the twelve, and said to them, "Whoever wants to be first must be last of all and servant of all." Then he took a little child and put it among them; and taking it in his arms, he said to them, "Whoever welcomes one such child in my name welcomes me, and whoever welcomes me welcomes not me but the one who sent me" (Mk. 9:33-37; Mt. 18:1-7 [in Matthean fashion the author adds a threat in vss. 6-7]; Lk. 9:46-48).

We have here another example of Jesus' affirmation of his own participation in larger human and cosmic solidarity, but the account is especially noteworthy in that Jesus particularly affirms his solidarity with the children of the world, even as his actions reveal his warm acceptance of their person and tender blessing of their being. Furthermore, the open, trusting, uncomplicated teachability generally characteristic of children is forthrightly given as a primary condition for "entering" the Kingdom of God. The Kingdom belongs to such.

3

The Order of Monks
and the Church

1

I previously identified the early Buddhist order of monks as meditative, mendicant, and missionary. This is to describe the order as a religiously disciplined, mobile missionary task-force, in some ways akin to the later mendicant missionary orders of the Roman Catholic Church. Perhaps the Franciscan order during the lifetime of Francis of Assisi (1182-1226) shows the closest kinship in style and spirit. We should note, however, that the monastic orders have been over the centuries the dominant, usually the only, organized form of Buddhist faith and life until the development of the Pure Land schools in Japan in the twelfth and thirteenth centuries and Buddhist lay societies within the past century. The monks clearly understood their commitment to the homeless life as properly involving lifelong mendicant poverty and celibacy. Differently, however, from Roman Catholic orders, the Buddha, whom the monks followed as the son of the Śākyans, was more their teacher and spiritual master than commander. So far as we know, he exacted no vow of obedience to himself, and except for the ultimate possibility of expulsion from the order, imposed no punishment. His authority, which was indeed regarded as unique within the order, he did not hesitate to use, however, especially when his judgment or decision was asked for.

If it was with the monks that Gautama shared the deeper levels of his understanding, it was to the end that they be the primary agents of missionary activity. The "manyfolk" remained the final object of concern on the human level. As we have seen, the monks were to teach the *Dharma,* which is "lovely at the beginning, lovely in the middle, lovely at the ending." They were to explain "with the spirit and the letter" the religious life appropriate to the laity, that of complete fulfillment and utter purity.[46] We note that an important purpose of the monastic rules of conduct was for the avoidance of conduct that does not serve "for the benefit of nonbelievers."

The Buddhist scholastic of Sri Lanka Buddhaghosa, writing in the fourth century of our era, has given an account of the daily life of the Buddha that may be faithful in its main outlines. The master's custom was to rise early in the morning and, after taking care of his personal needs by himself, he commonly sat in meditation until it was time to go begging for his food. He usually took only one meal a day, at noon. Sometimes he went out to beg alone; on other occasions he was accompanied by a number of monks. There were also frequent invitations in advance to dine at the home of a devout and generally prosperous layman who invited also all the attendant monks and whose wife and servants made the correspondingly strenuous preparations. The Buddha always accepted with the customary Indian silence that denoted consent.

On these occasions the Buddha taught the lay persons present. In other cases, as we have seen, crowds came out to meet him from a nearby town or village, and he taught them always "with due consideration for the different dispositions of their minds" and "as suited the time and occasion." He also often carried on discussions with Brāhmans and members of various religious sects of the time, usually impressing his hearers with his wise and apt answers to questions and Socratic leading of their train of thought.[47]

The point of the above is to make clear that while the Buddha commonly taught his monastic followers in greater fullness and depth, this was in large part to train them for missionary service to the wider world. This is also to say that spiritually there was no radical or fixed boundary between the monastic order and the world. The nature of the order was instrumental, its ethos pragmatic. The Buddha apparently had no secret doctrine and modified his teaching only as he sensed the extent of receptivity as well as needs of his hearers.[48] He offered his teaching freely to all, but recognized that not all were equally able to perceive and apply the truth as he understood it. A layman once questioned him on this matter, asking first whether he dwelt "in compassion for every living thing." The Buddha answered that he did. Then the layman, who was headman of his village, asked whether the Exalted One taught the *Dharma* in full to some and not in full to others. In place of a direct answer, the Buddha told a parable of three fields, "one excellent, one moderate, and one poor, hard, saltish, of bad soil" and asked whether the farmer would not sow them in that order.

The text goes on to say that so the Buddha preaches first

to monastics, both men and women, then to lay believers, and lastly to wandering recluses and Brāhmans (i.e., religious professionals) who hold views other than his own. The language and order of this conclusion may owe something to later Buddhist monastic recension, but one cannot help but feel that the lurking humor could go back to the Buddha himself. But whatever the order of teaching, this text and many others make clear that no one is to be left out of Buddhist concern, teaching, and help. In the same text a similar lesson is taught with a parable of three waterpots of varying quality. In each use the content of the waterpots, that is of the teaching, is the same. The Buddha is determined, however, not to neglect the third group—the critical professionals—"because if so be they understand but a single sentence of it, that would be to their profit and happiness for many a long day."[49] With reference to the second group, the "moderate soil"—householders, both female and male—the Buddha spent the bulk of his life, from age thirty-five to his death at eighty, in service to their needs, traveling nine months of each year, always with high respect for their condition and their spiritual and moral potential.

2

It may seem inappropriate for this section to be identified with the title "The Order of Monks and the Church," because the Christian church has always included lay persons within its membership, together with the clergy and other religious professionals, whose titles have varied somewhat over the centuries. The reason for this provisional alignment, however, has to do with the issues of exclusiveness and boundaries. We have seen that in the case of the Buddhist monastic order, its structure and rules were provisional at the time of the Buddha, and no fixed boundary was envisaged, in this world or any other, between the "saved" and the "damned" or any other distinction that implied a shut door with regard to human opportunities in the cosmos. The history of the Christian church has been more checkered on this point, to use the language of understatement, to be sure.

The issue of the church is indeed a delicate one. As we have noted, the word—*ecclesia* in Greek—is found in the gospels of the New Testament in only two passages, both in Matthew (16:18; 18:17). While the term appears frequently in the Acts of the Apostles and in almost every other book in the New Testament—as the product of obviously later usage—many scholars, as we have seen, believe that in all likelihood the term "church" in its later sense did not form part of the common vocabulary of Jesus' public ministry and teaching.[50]

We have already considered in some detail in the previous chapter the issue of the church in the teaching of Jesus. We need repeat here only the salient conclusions in order to indicate the absence of fixed boundaries in Jesus' understanding and intent, so far as we are able to discern these. As I have been suggesting also in our present context, Jesus' initial mission and appeal to his own people were at least twofold from the beginning. One was the call to repentance and return to fellowship with the living God, change of heart and life according to right understanding of the will of God. This change was indeed for the sake of the people of Israel themselves, not least to preserve them from the national disaster that Jesus seems to have perceived in the offing. His other purpose was surely to call Israel as a whole to fulfill their priestly-missionary role that "all the families of the earth shall be blessed" (Gen. 12:3; cf. Mk. 1:14-15; 6-12; Acts 13:44-47). This was the role to which, according to the record of Scripture, Israel owed "its very constitution and best self-awareness as a people" (cf. Amos 9:11-12; Isa. 49:6; 56:8; Jn. 4:1-11).[51]

One of the distinctive elements, however, of Jesus' public ministry that we do not find in Gautama's is the development of a growing opposition. There were not a few, especially among the religious professionals of his time, who criticized the Buddha, especially for his teaching. In his circle of close disciples, there was one monastic, Devadatta, a kind of Judas Iscariot, who is said even to have resorted to attempts at physical violence against Gautama's person.[52] But there is no evidence of opposition in the sense of a growing movement, nothing of the corporate ferocity that led to Jesus' crucifixion and death.

In the case of Jesus, as my friend and former colleague, Donald J. Goergen, O.P., has put it in his well-researched and perceptive book, "How gradual, pronounced, or widespread the opposition was it is difficult to determine." Goergen goes on to insist, moreover, in company with many scholars, that this opposition cannot be identified with Judaism as a whole. Indeed, from the beginning of his public ministry Jesus was warmly received and followed by many of his fellow Jews, with varied modes of "following." He was widely and generally respected, certainly revered by those whom he healed, seen by most as an authentic teacher, a sage in the tradition of Hebraic wisdom, heralded by some, it would seem, as a true prophet in the sense of the best of Israel's past, by others even as a messianic figure (cf. Lk. 24:13-21).[53]

We have already spoken some about the nature of the opposition to Jesus, finding it primarily in the religious and political establishment, to a certain extent from members of the Pharisees, although not from all in this party. To a larger and certainly more effective extent, opposition emerged from the ruling class in Judea, above all in Jerusalem, especially from the Sadducees, who constituted the true religious and political establishment as the party of the high priests and upper level of priests and scribes, and from

those of other groups willing to cooperate with the Sadducees. The reasons for the opposition can probably be
summed up in the words *fear* and *envy.* There was evidently
fear of the loss of personal and national identity, fear of the
loss of personal and group position, fear of the pain of
change, both personal and corporate. For above all, Jesus
did call for change, supremely change-of-life orientation
and change of character. We may properly also add the term
envy, I believe. The healing powers and winsome appeal of
Jesus in his early public ministry were clearly beyond what
the religious establishment individually or as a whole could
themselves manifest.

There is reason to believe, then, that the emergence of
this opposition, the nature of which with its increasing
depth and intensity Jesus was evidently able to perceive
with ever greater clarity as time passed, had a significant
connection with the emergence in Jesus' mind of the concept of a smaller community. This is the community of faith
and missionary service that his followers came to specify
with the Greek term *ecclesia.* As the opposition grew, Jesus,
it seems, began to perceive that his original intent under
God to call the whole of Israel to an effective repentance
and to the kind of missionary service that a whole nation
could fulfill in the midst of and through the multitudinous
variety of its actual occupations would not succeed. Taking
Mark as the earliest of the gospels and our best guide in this
matter, as I believe we can, we find various indications that
at first Jesus made serious efforts to avoid offending the formal structures of historic Israel as a community of faith (cf.
Mk. 1:43-44; 3:7-12; 5:18-19; 8:22). But opposition from religious professionals began from an early period of his public ministry (cf. Mk. 2:6-8, 13-17, 23-28; 3:1-6). Probably
Jesus himself and certainly the early Christian community
believed that this kind of opposition was endemic in Israel's
treatment of the prophets whom Yahweh had sent them in

the course of their history as a people (II Chron. 36:15-16; Mk. 6:4; 12:1-12; Mt. 5:12; 23:37; Acts 7:51-53; I Thess. 2:14-15; Jn. 5:10).

This consciousness of opposition with historic roots, we should note, is a phenomenon that we do not find ascribed to the Buddha in the early texts, even though, as we have seen, he did experience opposition from both within and without his followers during the course of his long public ministry. In his case the opposition never became connected with political interests. This is also to say that the opposition, which was largely confined to religious professionals, evidently had no organizational structure by which it could give teeth to its resentments.[54] We should add that over its long history India has seen relatively little large-scale religious persecution leading to physical violence. The events of 1947-'48 were indeed an aberration.

In Jesus' case in Israel, however, the opposition from religious professionals soon became lethal (Mk. 3:1-6) and began to include persons from the religious establishment, who, as we have seen, were also largely co-terminous with the political establishment of Israel (cf. Mk. 3:22; 7:1). That the atmosphere was charged with danger and could issue in ultimate reprisals against prophetic criticism became clear with the imprisonment and beheading of John the Baptizer (Mk. 6:14-29). In the Marcan account, from this time on, Jesus' response to criticism from religious professionals becomes more sharply critical in return (Mk. 7:1-23). And after this we find, in connection with the first indication in Mark that Jesus may have begun to think of his role as having messianic aspects, Jesus' first direct teaching that he would "be rejected by the elders, the chief priests, and the scribes, and be killed" (Mk. 8:27-33; cf. 9:30-32; 10:32-34). The text goes on to include Jesus' predictive word that his death would be followed by divine vindication of his person and work that the Christian community came to call resurrection from the dead. Not a few scholars question whether this prediction, if ever made by Jesus before his death, was made at this time or so precisely.[55] I myself believe that the precise timing is of only secondary significance. But we do have reason to believe that Jesus manifested instances of predictive prophecy in his public ministry, as we have seen in the relatively detailed treatment of the issue in Part II.

My own study of the gospel narratives, however, leads me to the conclusion that we have here depiction of what was probably a gradual shift in Jesus' perception of his role under God from that of a "hopeful" prophet in the historic tradition of Israel to one more like Jeremiah or the suffering servant of Deutero-Isaiah. This was an emerging consciousness that his service of God and his people would involve failure on the plane of historical experience.

Hence, the shift in emphasis from a call to the whole of Israel—although in an important sense Jesus never swerved from that intent and, even though he increasingly perceived that it would end in failure at the human level, his determination to go to Jerusalem to face the establishment directly was, in fact, the climax of his intent to address the whole nation (cf. Lk. 9:51-56)—to the calling and training of a smaller community of faith. Hence, also, the emergence of a "messianic consciousness" that somehow this suffering and defeat on the human level would redound to the benefit of many (Mk. 10:45).

I do not wish to focus undue attention upon the words "messianic consciousness"; certainly Jesus never manifests what is popularly known as a "messianic complex." I do believe, however, that we may appropriately use the term as descriptive of Jesus' emerging understanding in the context of likely failure of his mission at the human level. I make this affirmation, even though it is clear that Jesus "showed a marked reluctance to use the title himself"[56] until the end of his ministry and "sternly ordered" his disciples at the time of Peter's confession of Jesus as Messiah ("the Christ" in the Greek text) not to tell others of this insight (Mk. 12:35-37; 14:60-65; 8:27-30). The term *Messiah*, in Hebrew grammar an adjectival noun with the passive meaning of "anointed," was originally used, as we have seen, to designate the anointed king of Israel's early history and then in later centuries to designate (for many Jews) the Coming One of Israel's highest religious expectations. The extraordinary paradox of Mark and the other gospel texts is that this term denoting the royal Davidic figure of popular messianic expectation was first applied to Jesus by a leading disciple (Peter) and apparently accepted by him, even with reservations, at the time when Jesus had already perceived that his mission and ministry would end in his rejection and death. This means, of course, that Jesus' understanding of his own role and of the meaning of the term *Messiah* had come to differ radically from the victorious image of popular expectations.[57]

As we have seen, Jesus evidently aimed high from the beginning of his public ministry, at the whole of Israel and through Israel at the whole of humanity, but his methodology was not one of self-glorification. Self-aggrandizement was never his aim in any sense. Hence, his hesitancy to use language that could be misunderstood as denotative of self-glorification. The terminology of invitation—to come to his person—that we find in the Matthean account of Jesus' self-understanding is appropriately—however it may have been phrased by Jesus himself—associated with affirmation of Jesus' humility (Mt. 11:25-30; cf. Lk. 10:21-24; II Cor. 10:1).[58] Jesus, therefore, was able to accept the messianic terminology of Peter's confession only with the shocking proviso that it be not publicized and that it be understood primarily not as denoting glorious victory but humiliating failure. Yet this failure on the plane of human history, Jesus was evidently coming to see, could be associated with the term *Messiah*, because this was the suffering Messiah, whose suffering Yahweh—the God and Father of all peoples (cf. Mk. 11:17)—could and would turn into means for the liberation and blessing of many (Mk. 10:45).[59]

Some readers may object to my repeated use of the term *failure* with reference to Jesus' public ministry, but I use it advisedly. Firstly, the term *failure* is one way of perceiving Jesus' rejection by the religious and political leadership of Israel as specifically connected with his turning to the selection and training of a smaller community of faith and missionary service—a provisional substitute for the whole of Israel (cf. Acts 13:44-52; Rom. 11:1-36)—the *ecclesia* of God. The term *failure* is also one dimension of the suffering servant (cf. Isa. 53:1-12). It is the dimension that establishes commonality or solidarity with the whole of humanity. All of us who are human have experienced failure in some form—moral, social, professional, or other—and the Messiah of God who would touch us at our point of deepest need must also personally know and experience failure. But the most significant aspect of the failure of the suffering servant of biblical vision is that it is not only with others. It is supremely for others. The personal defeat of the Messiah of God (at the human level) leads to the victory of us "many." One of the most significant elements of biblical depictions of salvation is precisely deliverance from failure, failure whether physical, moral, or spiritual.[60] We may say further that the center and heart of the message of the four gospels, as of the whole New Testament, is Jesus' personal recovery from failure (his resurrection from the dead) and our own recovery from failure, including in our case moral failure (usually more than once, even daily—cf. I Cor. 15:31)—all by the power of the God and Father of us all (cf. II Cor. 13:4)—with implications both in this world and in all others.[61]

The apostle Paul, we may properly add, uses the term *weakness* to denote the "failure" of Jesus involved in his crucifixion by human beings and contrasts it with Jesus' present living by the power of God as the risen Christ (II Cor. 13:4). Paul even affirms this paradox as a cardinal principle of God's working in the cosmos, in that "power is made perfect in weakness" (II Cor. 12:9). He develops the theme in various ways to indicate that the, at times, apparent weaknesses in his own personal style as an apostle or in his life experiences may in fact be a surface appearance concealing true strength (II Cor. 12:10). Paul does not discount the fact that in his own case—or in the case of the Corinthian Christians to whom he was writing—the weaknesses may in fact be real weaknesses. But they are not the whole story—of himself or his life, or of any human being's—the final word is God's, and by the power of God our weakness may be turned into strength (II Cor. 12:9-10; 13:3-4; cf. Phil. 2:7-11).

Views of the World
and of the Cosmos

We have already considered certain aspects of the
worldviews of the Buddha and the Christ at the beginning of the previous section, as also in the first. These
aspects have to do with the Buddha's identification of the
"Object" of his worship as *Dharma*, with *Nirvāṇa* as the cosmic context of that focus, a context or realm structurally
akin to Jesus' teaching of the Kingdom of God as given us in
the gospels of the New Testament. I also tried to delineate
something of the tensions involved in these worldviews. I
refer to the tension created by the Buddha's understanding
of the operation of the process of *karma* in relationship with
his teaching of the universal possibility of liberation. We

noted a comparable tension between Jesus' proclamation of the Kingdom of God as good news, an open door of opportunity for every person, and his teaching of the operation of the process of ethical compensation in the universe ("sowing and reaping" in the metaphorical language of the apostle Paul). We were not able to work out these tensions in a fully satisfactory way at the level of philosophical or even theological thought. We were left, however, with the strongest of affirmations of a religious kind from both of these individuals to the effect that liberation or gospel or opportunity is the final word that they wish to offer the whole of humanity.

I should like at this point to identify with more precision what we may call the selective nature of the faith of the Buddha and of the Christ. In our previous discussion we noted the use by some scholars of terms like "Spirit," "the unseen world," or "supersensible realms." It is necessary to reiterate that in the case of both Gautama and Jesus their call to faith was to a more sharply delineated and "limited" focus or "Object." This is to say that the most important distinction of focus in human aspiration is not between the physical world and the unseen, but between qualitatively inferior modes of reality and the highest. Supremely, with reference to the focus of faith, the distinction of ultimate importance is between that which is good and qualitatively unchanging and utterly dependable and that which is not. For both the Buddha and the Christ elements of differing quality may be found at work in the supersensible realms as in the sensory.

We noted in Gautama's teaching, as in the whole of historic Buddhism, extension of *saṃsāra*, the realm(s) of change, impermanence, independability, to include *devas* (the gods of popular Indian religion), demons, and other beings of the unseen worlds, as well as human beings and animals in this world. In one sense, this is a hopeful worldview, in that it does not insist upon the fate of human beings as fixed for all eternity at the point of physical death on earth. In another sense, it implies that human life on earth is in some ways perilous, even as it is always replete with good possibilities. Not every influence that may work upon human beings, whether from realms seen or unseen, is necessarily benign. It is vital to discern that which is the Good, the "Lovely," and to limit the complete openness proper to authentic faith to a single "Object." This Gautama identified as *Dharma*.

In a similar way, Jesus asked for a sharp delineation and focus of the "Object" of faith. He, too, as we have seen, was aware of the perils of life in this world, spiritual, moral, and physical. He, too, knew well that not every influence issuing from either human culture or supernal powers is benign. Hence his sharp insistence that only God is good (Mk. 10:18). Hence that which we have seen as the central element of his teaching, the historic proclamation of Israel that God is one and that true faith is to "love the Lord your God with all your heart, and with all your soul, and with all your mind, and with all your strength . . . You shall love your neighbor as yourself" (Mk. 12:29-31; cf. Mt. 22:37-40; Lk. 10:27-28).

We must also recall, however, that neither the Buddha nor the Christ saw the totality of good to reside in their "Objects" of worship. That is, while naught else than *Dharma* for Gautama and God the Father of all for Jesus was worthy of the ultimate commitment of authentic faith, they both insisted that there is much good in beings in this world and in worlds beyond. Such must be affirmed even if the good in these beings is derivative and imperfect and they are hence not qualified to become objects of worship. As we have seen, the Buddha recognized not a little good in the persons and experiences of human life on earth, above all in the spiritual opportunities available to human beings in this context. He recognized as good and allowed to work in his own life influences from supernal beings, such as the *deva* of historic Indian faith, Brahmā Sahampāti, who among other things is said to have been a factor in the leading of the Buddha into his universal mission.[62]

In the case of Jesus, it is important to note again that, quite akin to the faith of historic Israel, his faith in and commitment to the unity of God did not prevent him from acknowledging the existence of angels, archangels, etc., and their benign, helpful role as ministering servants in the universe of God's creation, that is as instrumental workers in the Kingdom of the Most High. The Bible, both Old Testament and New, has numerous references to such beings, including those called cherubim and seraphim (cf. Gen. 3:24; Ezek. 10:1-22, etc.) The New Testament, especially the synoptic gospels and the Acts of the Apostles, is replete with references to the roles and works of angels. We note in particular the recorded references of Jesus to what have historically been called guardian (Mt. 18:10) or ministering angels (Mk. 1:13; Mt. 4:11; 26:53). The accounts of such in both Luke and Acts are particularly noteworthy for their beauty and appeal. In the worldviews of both the Buddha and the Christ the universe, seen and unseen, is perceived as richly peopled.

Nevertheless, both Gautama and Jesus were highly pragmatic, more pragmatic than theological, we may say. They were primarily concerned to be helpful to others, and they evidently perceived that human beings are in vital need of focus in their lives. In the midst of the varied and multitudinous "things" and events of human experience on earth, we evidently have an existential need to "pull it all together" in order to live our daily lives with any effectiveness at all. For such to be possible a focus is necessary. For Gautama this was *Dharma*, and he taught, as we have seen, that persons of right understanding in this world and beyond "live only under" *Dharma*. Among his last words to his disciples was the injunction to live with the *Dharma* "as your island, as your refuge, and no other."[63] This to live in the midst of the many with focus upon the One, as norm.

Like Gautama, Jesus, as we may discern from his recorded teachings, made little or no attempt to define the "Object" of his faith beyond that God is good—and one. What we primarily find in his parables and other teachings are intimations of the quality of the character of God, pointing to his impartial and generous love, his mercy, his initiatives to seek and to save the "lost" of human life. And, as we learn from Jesus' conversation with Mary and Martha recorded in the Gospel of Luke "there is need of only one thing" (Lk. 10:38-42).[64] We are to "strive first for the kingdom of God and his righteousness" (Mt. 6:33).[65] This is to say that human life is in need of a single focus, as "Object" of faith and as norm. And from this focus upon the One we may rightly cope with our tendency to be "worried and distracted by many things" (Lk. 10:41). Focus upon the One is not intended to downgrade the value of the many, nor to lessen the importance of relationship therewith. Focus upon the One is rather given us as the only way to deal rightly with the many.

Are we to say in conclusion that Gautama's perception-understanding of *Dharma* was totally identical with Jesus' awareness of the God of his faith-understanding? Not really. There are differences of some moment that we have noted in the course of our study, especially with reference to issues of personalism and initiatives of activity. But, as I suggested earlier, these differences may easily be overstated and historically have often been overstated. There are differences, we may recall, in the perceptions of the nature of the God of historic Hebrew faith, as between the preliterary prophets of the Bible, the literary prophets—including Jeremiah!—and the wisdom writers, on the one hand, and Jesus on the other. But we do not for that reason totally discount the religious value and meaning of the former group even if we believe the faith-understanding of Jesus to be truer, indeed Truth itself. It is part of the way of wisdom to be able to learn from others who, like ourselves, are imperfect and have inadequate perceptions of the Truth. For Truth in unmediated form is never available to us in the midst of the constraints of present life on the plane of history.

Another word may perhaps be properly added at this point. This is what I choose to call the way of sympathetic reading. It is very easy, for example, for Western persons, with our background of Cartesian philosophical distinctions between the self and all else in the cosmos, to read some of the texts of later Mahāyāna Buddhism and leap to the conclusion—with consequent rejection—that they are totally monistic in their worldview. Not a few passages in both philosophical and popular literature read as if no meaningful distinctions within the cosmos exist at all. But if one reads on, more perceptively and sympathetically, other images emerge, and important practical distinctions are found. "Mind only" is not the only thing to be said of that school of Mahāyāna thought. To know "things as they are" is the consequence of a profound spiritual breakthrough or reorientation of the self. As Joseph Kitagawa pointed out over a generation ago, while the Mahāyāna philosophically equated Nirvāṇa and the world of changing phenomena, religiously it "found an infinite distance between the two."[66]

A significant book was published in Japan in 1967 as one of the earlier contributions to Buddhist-Christian dialogue of the past generation. This was the record of an actual dialogue, between Reirin Yamada, then president of Kumazawa University, a major school of the Sōtō sect of Japanese Zen Buddhism, and Hidenobu Kuwada, longtime president of Tokyo Union Theological Seminary. We find here, too,

coming from Yamada, typical Mahāyāna language about
the All, the Great Universe, etc., that at first seems to suggest
a totally monistic worldview. But Yamada, even as he speaks
of the Great Universe *(Dai Uchū)* in a religious sense reminiscent of philosophical monism, moves on quickly to
speak of its fine qualities, its goodness, its graciousness
(megumi). He seems to point to an inner Reality not precisely identical with the whole realm of external phenomena. That is, there is a religious focus, a theological center,
of enormous practical importance in this faith and worldview. Hence worship becomes possible, hence the sense of
the Glorious in Buddhist experience, even the perception
that there is a final purpose for all living entities in the cosmos. There is an implied personalism in the "Object" of
faith, and most Buddhist texts speak of the "Other," even as
most Buddhists experience their faith in this way. There is a
focus.[67]

We may say, therefore, that the morphology of religious
experience, as of the understanding of the nature of human
life, is surprisingly similar in both traditions. Again and
again, even in the apparent formlessness of Zen language,
we find attempts to get at the heart of things, to find a focus.
Here, too, there is emphasis upon the death of the old self
and new life through the grace of the "Other" *(Nyorai)*. This
is to move from the isolated and selfish self into Great Harmony *(Dai Chōwa)*. We find affirmation of a real "other"
world and a determination to live by it, indeed to participate ("enter") therein. Zen meditation is directed to that
end, as is the whole of daily life. A central aspect of Zen perception of salvation is purification of the heart. And even if
this salvation is seen as also leading to what philosophically
may be regarded as transcendence of distinctions between
subject and object—religiously suggesting the absence of
fixed boundaries—distinctions of significance still remain.
There is a focus, a helping Life Power that enables the trans-

formation of human character. This is also the Power that enables human beings to express right thinking in action, to manifest a different world.

Much more could be offered from this splendid book, including what I would call finely perceptive appreciation of Jesus the Christ on the part of Yamada, the exponent of Zen. I should add also his astonishing insight into what he himself calls the suffering of God the Father in connection with the suffering and death of Jesus on the cross. The book, I believe, is assuredly an important example of the need for "sympathetic reading."[68]

5

The Spirit of Sacrifice and the Mystery of the Cross

The Buddha, as we have seen, taught that the way to liberation-transformation lies in aspiration toward *Nirvāṇa* and its ethical qualities and in dependent relationship with *Dharma*, the dynamic manifestation of *Nirvāṇa* in phenomenal existence. With few, if any, exceptions he did not draw attention to himself. There is no record in the early texts of his claiming that his person or life had in themselves—apart from their possible role as a model—any power to effect change in others or in the order of the cosmos. That is, he claimed no "vicariously redemptive" role for himself, no work of "substitutionary atonement."

We need to take, however, with the utmost seriousness

the sacrificial service to others involved in Gautama the Buddha's public ministry of forty-five years. The unselfish quality of this service is clearly manifested in his teaching on transcending the self-centered, selfish self to the end of friendliness and compassion for all beings. "It is good to help others." The powerful missionary thrust of both his life and his teaching reveals a person utterly dedicated to the welfare of others. It was perhaps only natural that the later Mahāyāna would strive to give this sacrificial spirit of the Master a more exalted and extensive role in the cosmos.

In various places in our study we have endeavored to come to terms with what, in the case of Jesus the Christ, may be called the mystery of the cross. Knowledgeable readers will have detected that, differently from some biblical scholars, I have not hesitated to acknowledge a "vicariously redemptive" role in the person and work of Jesus. With other biblical scholars, I have been willing to accept as literally the word of the historical Jesus the statement ascribed to him in the Gospel of Mark, "The Son of Man came not to be served but to serve, and to give his life a ransom for many" (Mk. 10:45).

In the context of historic Christian theology, the above might be viewed as the preamble for a lengthy disquisition, possibly a volume or more, on the meaning of the atonement. Quite to the contrary, this treatment will be brief. Similarly, readers should not expect a detailed Christology. I myself prefer to be brief with reference either to Buddhology or to Christology. My background of missionary service would seem to play a role here. I have found detailed theologies or lengthy confessions of faith to be counterproductive in the "universal mission" of our faith. It is significant that what may be the first short confession of faith in the history of the Presbyterian-Reformed tradition was adopted by the General Assembly of the Japanese church of that persuasion, the *Nihon Kirisuto Kyōkai*, in December

1890. This was a statement of faith that in five long sentences set forth simply and clearly what was then considered an adequate expression of Protestant evangelical faith.
It concluded with the Apostles' Creed.[69]

The meaning of the Marcan passage (10:45), as I endeavored to show previously and as almost the whole of the
Christian community of faith in the first apostolic generation and later believed, is that the suffering of Jesus, taken
together with his resurrection from the dead, had and has
had more than symbolic meaning as a model of life-activity
for others. It is also a model, to be sure, and has served as
such for long centuries. But the meaning of the word *ransom* in the passage, while clearly metaphorical because of
its common usage at the time as a term for "buying the freedom of a slave," was intended to indicate that activity in and
through Jesus, with vitally important consequences in human life and history, even in the cosmos, was about to occur. For the early Christian community this event "had
occurred" (cf. I Tim. 2:6), but it was also continuing as the
most important activity at work in their persons and in their
lives (cf. Gal. 2:19-20).[70]

This kind of faith-understanding, to be sure, takes us at
once beyond the limits of the empirical-historical methods
of historiography as a human science. I have already written earlier about problems associated with these limitations
and asked readers to note that even within them the writing
of history—historiography—largely employs data that in a
court of law are no more than testimonial, even anecdotal.
But, as we have seen, this is a religious study, and we have
the right to move beyond the methodologies of the human
or social sciences if we acknowledge what we are doing and
strive to be responsible within our broader parameters.

In this expanded context, then, I would like to draw once
again upon the insights of the Austrian philosopher-educa-
tor Rudolf Steiner. As one of the most broadly and deeply

educated persons in the central Europe of his day, Steiner possessed and faithfully practiced his own disciplines of thought and life. But he did not hesitate to exercise concerns for the wider picture, drawing upon his experiences of clairvoyant insight. In this context he forthrightly stated that "that which rayed forth spiritually from the Act on Golgotha spread through the spiritual atmosphere of the earth, permeated it, and is still there. Something new has thus been imparted to our earth."[71] Like theologians of the early church, such as Justin Martyr, Irenaeus, Clement of Alexandria, Origen, or even Augustine, Steiner believed that the Logos of God had been present and worked in all times and places throughout human history. It can, therefore, be said that "there was not so radical a difference between pre-Christian and post-Christian times" as orthodox theology has often maintained. Yet there is, according to Steiner, still a markedly great difference. The permeation of the spiritual atmosphere of the earth by the Christ-Impulse, as Steiner puts it, makes it possible for persons to "experience inwardly the Logos in its [his/her] complete original form."

For Rudolf Steiner the mystery of Golgotha, indeed the whole Christ-Event, was the Central Event of world history, and as this Reality is experienced through the universally available Christ-Impulse, there is found the criterion for "what is sound and what is unsound" in the course of human history. Even more, "the Christ is with us even until the end of the world . . . and abundant will be the forces of the soul, the strengthening of the soul which he will bear away who receives out of the depths of the spirit the direction of the Christ."[72]

Not all of us may wish to follow Rudolf Steiner into the farther ranges of his thought—he never asked or evidently wished such from others. But in our present context of a comparison of the Buddha and the Christ, Steiner's views are more than suggestive. With reference to issues relating to the concept of *karma*, Steiner held that human deeds constitute "objective cosmic facts." Thus the divine forgiveness of sins and the role therein of Jesus the Christ must of necessity involve work to deal with these objective facts. As Stewart C. Easton, one of the most knowledgeable of contemporary American writers on the contributions of Rudolf Steiner, puts it, in "the mystery of Golgotha" the Christ "actually took upon himself the consequences of human deeds insofar as they affect the earth and universe." Easton goes on to make it clear that with the use of such language Steiner does not mean there is no place for human participation in the process of compensation. But for Steiner the work of God in Christ is absolutely necessary to clear away certain "objective" obstacles within and without us that human beings are not able to remove themselves. This is the liberation from the effects of the past that enables human beings to have a new beginning, a fresh start in freedom, the liberation that leads to a new life in relationship and in cooperative orientation toward the purposes of the Most High. One may thus begin to cope constructively with the effects of one's own past and those of others, all with the help of the One who has continued to work on behalf of both humanity and the earth after his resurrection and ascension.[73]

These references to the insights of Rudolf Steiner do not, of course, constitute proof of any kind, certainly not at the level of empirical-historical studies. They may, however, constitute supportive data, along with the contributions of other responsible and tested figures in the history of Christian spirituality, for those who are open to consideration of such sources. In the present climate of opinion in the area of biblical studies in this country and abroad, we note not a few scholars who find it difficult to accept the New Testament—and traditionally orthodox theological—affirmation of faith that the work of God in Jesus the Christ has had in some literal, objective way consequences of cosmic significance for others. That is, consequences of liberation and betterment in the lives of other persons, in human history, in the earth itself. To my mind, it is at least suggestive that persons like Rudolf Steiner, Edgar Cayce, Therese Neumann, Sundar Singh, Anna Katherina Emmerich, Juliana of Norwich, and others give us testimony—using methodologies quite other than those of academic historiography but still meaningful, if tested in turn by the methodologies of other disciplines in the context of religious faith and practice, both within and without the Judeo-Christian tradition—that there is indeed reason to take seriously the historic positions of faith.

I refer to Rudolf Steiner also because he so sharply delineates the issues involved and in that context comes to his conviction that the Christ-Event has indeed dealt effectively with objective facts or conditions in human lives and in the cosmos and has had objectively helpful consequences in the same. Edgar Cayce is largely one with Rudolf Steiner in making these affirmations of faith. This is indeed that "He [Jesus] gave himself as a ransom for all" (5749-10).[74] This is to say that the passion of Jesus the Christ—with its climax in his suffering on the cross—was cosmically redemptive (liberating, restoring to right relationships, healing) in the widest and deepest sense of the word. In quite traditional language Cayce averred that "the blood as of the perfect man was shed, not by reason of himself but that there might be made an offering once for all" (1504-1). Another reading, in speaking of "the King on the cross," wonders who of all who were in the city of Jerusalem at that time "thought or felt that there would come the day when his words, even, 'My peace I give unto you,' would change the whole world, and that *time*, even, would be counted from that death, that birth" (262-71). In the Cayce materials we find repeated affirmation that the effects of the life and work—supremely in his cross, resurrection, and ascension, as in his abiding

presence—of the Christ "who took upon himself the burden of the world" (262-3) were and are universal in their
range and scope.

The above is sufficient to indicate that there are pointers
in the insights of these twentieth-century visionaries, functioning in part at levels other than the sensory-empirical,
yet not without critical reference to the latter, that may lead
us to consider with renewed seriousness the New Testament affirmations of the meaning of the death and resurrection of Jesus. One important qualification, however, must
needs be made, if we are to be faithful to the whole sweep of
the New Testament affirmations; that is, that if we may use
the word *atonement,* in the sense of vicarious atonement, a
work for others, we must also take account of the fact that
properly there is a reciprocal dimension. This is to say that,
on the one hand, the work of God through the Christ to the
end of the restoration of personal relationships—that which
we have seen to be the essence of salvation in biblical understanding—is a work that in a fundamental sense must
be done for us. On the other hand, the same term must become at-onement, in the sense of spiritual unity with our
Maker and our fellow creatures, a reality of relationship that
comprises the whole spectrum of ethical activity and for
which our conscious cooperation is necessary.

Endnotes

Preface

1. My friend and former colleague, Donald J. Goergen, O.P., offers a very helpful discussion of these issues in the introduction to his perceptive and richly documented work on the life and teaching of Jesus. In this section, entitled "A Reflection on Methodology," he identifies his agreements and disagreements with, for example, David Tracy, and insists that he himself uses but does not confine himself to "modern historical-critical exegesis." *A Theology of Jesus, I: The Mission and Ministry of Jesus,* Wilmington, DE: Michael Glazier, 1986, pp. 11-22.

2. Cf. Jeffrey Carlson's description of the "ongoing process of selective reconstruction" involved in the creation of the biblical canon(s). He further contends that every person's "religious identity is always/already a selective and syncretic product" of a similar process. "Syncretistic Religiosity: The Significance of This Tautology," *Journal of Ecumenical Studies,* Vol. 29, No. 1 (Winter 1992), pp. 23-34.

3. Paul D. Ingram, "Two Western Models of Interreligious Dialogue," *Journal of Ecumenical Studies,* Vol. 26, No. 1 (Winter 1989), p. 9.

4. Cf. Chrys Saldanha, *Divine Pedagogy, a Patristic View of Non-Christian Religions,* Roma: Libreria Ateneo Silesiano, 1984, *passim;* Richard H. Drummond, *Toward a New Age in Christian Theology,* Maryknoll, NY: Orbis Books, 1985, pp. 25-35.

5. John Dominic Crossan, *The Historical Jesus, the Life of a Mediterranean Jewish Peasant,* San Francisco: Harper Collins, 1991, pp. xxviii-xxxiv. It is of interest to note that Bruce J. Malina and Richard L. Rohrbaugh employ their social-scientific methodology almost totally on "a reading of the [gospel] document as it stands, to find out what that final author said and meant to say to the audience." *Social Science Commentary on the Synoptic Gospels,* Minneapolis: Augsburg Fortress, 1992, p. 15. Malina deals separately with the Gospel of John in his *The Gospel of John in Sociolinguistic Perspective,* Berkeley, CA: Center for Hermeneutical Studies in Hellenistic and Modern Culture, 1985, pp. 1-23.

6. Crossan, *op. cit.*, pp. 424-426; E.P. Sanders, *Jesus and Judaism*, Philadelphia: Fortress Press, 1985, pp. 1-58.

7. Helmut Koester, "History and Development of Mark's Gospel (From Mark to Secret Mark and 'Canonical Mark')," *Colloquy on New Testament Studies: A Time for Reappraisal and Fresh Approaches*, Bruce Corley, ed., Macon, GA: Mercer University Press, 1983, p. 77.

Part I

1. In China and Japan a date long traditional corresponds to 1067 B.C.E. Modern Buddhists in Burma, Sri Lanka, and India affirm 623 B.C.E. as the correct date, those in Thailand, Kampuchea, and Laos 624 B.C.E. For recent scholarly calculations see Edward J. Thomas, *The Life of the Buddha as Legend and History*, New York: Barnes & Noble, 1952, p. xix; Richard H. Robinson & Willard L. Johnson, *The Buddhist Religion*, 2nd ed., Encino, California: Dickenson Publishing Co., 1977, p. 20; Yutaka Iwamoto, *Bukkyō Nyūmon*, Tokyo: Chūōkōronsha, 1964, p. 38.

2. Karl Jaspers, *The Origin and Goal of History*, New Haven: Yale University Press, 1959, pp. 1-21. A.C. Bouquet prefers to extend the period to about 300 C.E. and, in order to include Egypt, to before 800 B.C.E. *The Christian Faith and Non-Christian Religions*, New York: Harper, 1958, pp. 47, 56, 405.

3. Richard H. Drummond, *Gautama the Buddha*, Grand Rapids, Michigan: Wm. B. Eerdmans, 1974, pp. 17-18.

4. Sir Mortimer Wheeler, *Early India and Pakistan*, New York: Frederick A. Praeger, 1959, pp. 94-98. Cf. E.O. James, *From Cave to Cathedral*, New York: Praeger, 1965, p. 202.

5. Gordon Childe, *What Happened in History?* Harmondsworth, Middlesex: Penguin Books, 1961, pp. 124-132.

6. The term *Aryan* has come to have distasteful associations in the West as a result of its abuse by German National Socialists under Adolf Hitler. In India, however, in addition to denoting a particular racial and linguistic group, it has long been used as an adjective to denote the moral qualities of "noble" and "good." Cf. K.M. Sen, *Hinduism*, Baltimore, Maryland: Penguin Books, 1961, p. 17.

7. Wheeler, *op. cit.*, pp. 113-117.

8. E.O. James, *The Cult of the Mother Goddess*, New York: Barnes & Noble, 1959, p. 101.

9. A. Berriedale Keith, "The Age of the Rigveda," *The Cambridge History of India, I*, Cambridge: Cambridge University Press, 1922, p. 85.

10. Stuart Piggott, *Prehistoric India*, Harmondsworth, Middlesex: Penguin Books, 1961, pp. 252-255.

11. The meaning of *Upaniṣad* has been much debated. Juan Mascaró perceives the etymology as from the Sanskrit verb *sad*, meaning "to sit," with *upa* and *ni* as prefixes respectively denoting "under" and "beneath," and understands the larger significance as denotative of sitting at the feet of a master. *The Upanishads*, Harmondsworth, Middlesex: Penguin Books, 1971, p. 7. Swami Nikhilananda prefers to interpret *sad* as meaning "loosen," *upa* as "nearness" and *ni* as "totality." The larger meaning would thus signify total loosening of the bondage of the world. *The Upanishads*, New York: Harper & Row, 1963, p. 23.

12. Cf. Arthur Berriedale Keith, *The Religion and Philosophy of the Veda and Upanishads*, Cambridge: Harvard University Press, 1923, I, pp. 257-312; *Satapatha-Brāhmana* 10: 4, 3 (quoted in Louis Renou, *Hinduism*, Washington Square Press, 1963, pp. 61-63).

13. In the *Śvetāśvatara Upaniṣad* (5:5-6) explanation is made that the *Upaniṣads* are the secret part of the *Vedas*. This statement is one way of acknowledging the fact that the teaching of the *Upaniṣads*, while related to and in part derived from the *Vedas*, is in fact significantly different from them.

14. Sen, *op. cit.*, p. 55. Denise Lardner Carmody sees little difference in the status or role of women as portrayed in the Vedic and Upanishadic literature, but affirms that both accorded women higher status and freedom than they received in the period from 500 B.C.E. onward. *Women and World Religions*, Nashville: Abingdon, 1979, pp. 43-45.

15. *Brihadāranyaka* 2:1, 15; 6:2, 7-8, 1:4, 11; *Chāndogya* 5:3, 7; 5:11, 4.

16. Cf. Sukumar Dutt, *The Buddha and Five After-Centuries*, London: Luzac, 1957, pp. 26-35.

17. This is, of course, not to say that animals and "lesser" life forms are not permeated and animated by the universal life-force or that they do not participate in meaningful evolutionary process. But we presumably cannot speak of reincarnation of animals, etc., in the sense of the continuity of human individualities experiencing repeated lives on earth. Rudolf Steiner suggests that the soul referents for animals may be "group-souls." Cf. his *Manifestations of Karma*, London: Rudolf Steiner Press, 1976, pp. 31-56.

18. Passages in Origen which give the clearest evidence for his views on reincarnation are: *Contra Celsum* VII, 50; *De Principiis* I, 7, 4; I, 8, 1; I, 8, 4; III, 3, 5; III, 5, 5. Cf. Henry Chadwick, *Early Christian Thought and the Classical Tradition*, London: Oxford University Press, 1966, pp. 88-89, 114-116. Ernst Benz has brought together a number of passages from Origen in the original Greek or in the extant Latin translation (where we do not have the Greek) which show Origen's rejection of the notion of transmigration. *Indische Einflüsse auf die frühchristliche Theologie*, Wiesbaden: Verlag der Akademie der Wissenschaften und der Literatur in Mainz, 1951, pp. 185-190. One is, however, somewhat puzzled by *de Principiis* I, 8, 4; cf. G.W. Butterworth, ed. *Origen on First Principles*, Gloucester, Mass.: Peter Smith, 1973, pp. 70-75. Henry Chadwick warns against admitted editorializing by Rufinus, Origen's Latin translator, to make the material palatable to the Latin-speaking orthodoxy of his time.

19. The traditional Hindu belief in the possibility of a series of incarnations of the divine (*avatāra*) stems from a comparable worldview. This concept is not found in the *Upaniṣads* and would no doubt have seemed alien to the authors of the *Vedas*. It appears, however, in the *Rāmāyana* and the *Mahābhārata*, in a classic way in the Bhagavad-Gītā. Cf. Sen, *op. cit.*, pp. 37-38.

20. Heinrich Zimmer, *Philosophies of India*, Cleveland: World Publishing Co., 1961, pp. 466-467.

21. Cf. André Bareau, *Die Religionen Indiens*, C.M. Schroeder, ed., Stuttgart: Kohlhammer Verlag, 1964, p. 11; Beatrice Lane Suzuki, *Mahayana Buddhism*, London: Allen & Unwin, 1959, p. 4.

22. *Anguttara-Nikāya* I, 145; *Buddhacarita* V, 1-23. Cf.

Hajime Nakamura, *Gōtama Budda,* Tokyo: Shunshūsha, 1978, pp. 63-73; Shōkō Watanabe, *Shin Shakuson Den,* Tokyo: Daihōrinkaku, 1967, pp. 63-68, 93.

23. *Dīgha-Nikāya* II, 157; *Majjhima-Nikāya* I, 163. That this goal was profoundly ethical—"that unrivalled goal of righteous living"—is strongly suggested by the later teaching described in *Sanyutta-Nikāya IV,* 38.

24. *Anguttara-Nikāya* I, 145.

25. Cf. Watanabe, *op. cit.,* pp. 82, 116.

26. *Majjhima-Nikāya* I, 163-166, 171; *Vinaya-Piṭaka, Mahā-vagga* I, 6, 8. Cf. Robinson and Johnson, *op. cit.,* pp. 24-26.

27. *Majjhima-Nikāya* I, 240-244.

28. *Majjhima-Nikāya* I, 245-247.

29. Christmas Humphreys, *Buddhism,* Harmondsworth, Middlesex: Penguin Books, 1958, p. 16. It is interesting that the apostle Paul in one passage of the New Testament uses the term *photismos* (illumination, enlightenment) to denote the experience of perceiving the gospel of the glory of Christ (II Cor. 4:4) and that Christian baptism later came to be often designated by the same term.

30. *Dīgha-Nikāya* II, 290-315.

31. *Sutta-Nipāta* 425-449. Māra is also known as Namuci. Cf. *DighaNikāya* III, 77.

32. *Majjhima-Nikāya* I, 4, 21-23. There are those who see "the Buddha beneath the Tree of Enlightenment (the Bo Tree) and Christ on Holy Rood (the Tree of Redemption)" as analogous figures, "incorporating an archetypal World Savior, World Tree motif." Cf. Joseph Campbell, *The Hero with a Thousand Faces,* Princeton: Princeton University Press, 1973, p. 33.

33. Cf. Fritjof Capra, "Ancient Buddhism in Modern Physics," *New Realities,* I, 1(1977), pp. 48-54.

34. Cf. Mircea Eliade, *The Quest, History and Meaning in Religion,* Chicago: University of Chicago Press, 1975, pp. 72-73.

35. Cf. Owen Barfield, *Saving the Appearances, a Study in Idolatry,* New York: Harcourt, Brace & World, n.d., pp. 140-141, 147; Saul Bellow, *Newsweek,* September 1, 1975, pp. 32-40; *Humboldt's Gift,* Harmondsworth, Middlesex: Penguin Books, 1977, pp. 427-431.

36. Cf. Richard H. Drummond, *Unto the Churches,* Virginia Beach: A.R.E. Press, 1978, pp. 30-35; Thomas Sugrue, *There Is a River,* New York: Dell, 1967, pp. 119-120, 126, 129, 144-145, 174-175; Harmon Hartzell Bro, *A Seer Out of Season, the Life of Edgar Cayce,* New York, NY: New American Library, 1989, pp. 23, 122-138.

37. Cf. Rudolf Steiner, *The Course of My Life,* New York: Anthroposophic Press, 1957, pp. 41-44, 75-78; A.P. Shepherd, *Scientist of the Invisible,* London: Hodder & Stoughton, 1975, pp. 113, 132; Sugrue, *op. cit.,* pp. 198-216.

38. *Vinaya-Piṭaka, Cullavagga* IX, 238. *Dhamma* is the Pāli form of the Sanskrit *Dharma.*

39. Majjhima-Nikāya I, 97-100. The Japanese Christian specialist in Buddhist Studies, Seiichi Yagi, identifies the young Gautama's perception of the root cause of human delusion as "the absolutization of the estranged ego." Such language is, of course, more contemporary terminology for the essential meaning of historic "idolatry." Seiichi Yagi, "Christ and Buddha," *Journal of Ecumenical Studies,* Vol. 27, No. 2 (Spring 1990), pp. 307-310. Yagi sees the historical Jesus as one with Gautama in understanding the primary problematic of human existence to lie in this absolutization of the relative, which in turn produces arrogance toward others. Marcus J. Borg defines selfishness in more common language as "preoccupation with our selves," *Meeting Jesus Again for the First Time,* San Francisco: Harper, 1994, p. 78.

40. *Sutta-Nipāta* 272, 592, 436-439, 585, 659; *Majjhima-Nikāya* I, 167, 173.

41. *Sutta-Nipāta* 718, 837, 501, 1119.

42. *Vinaya-Piṭaka, Mahāvagga* I, 6, 1-47.

43. Cf. *Chāndogya* VI, 1, 2.

44. Cf. Zimmer, *op. cit.,* p. 255.

45. *Vinaya-Piṭaka, Mahāvagga* I, 11, 1.

46. *Dīgha-Nikāya* II, 99-101, 156.

47. There are accounts in the canonical texts of miracles performed by the Buddha which can only be classed as legendary, as in *Vinaya-Piṭaka, Mahāvagga* I, 13-21; V, 4-8. Actually, a rationale for the Buddha's restraint in performing miracles is given in

Dīgha-Nikāya I, 211-223. For paranormal powers manifested in the Judeo-Christian tradition—apart from the many instances recorded of Jesus, and of the apostles, in the New Testament—an interesting example is the "reading of hearts" cited of Evan Roberts in the Welsh revival of 1904-1905. Cf. David Matthews, *I Saw the Welsh Revival*, Chicago: Moody Press, 1951, pp. 38-45. For the Buddha cf. *Anguttara-Nikāya* I, 169-172.

48. Cf. *Dhammapada* 321-323.

49. *Dīgha-Nikāya* I, 3; *Majjhima-Nikāya* I, 161.

50. Cf. *Vinaya-Piṭaka, Mahāvagga* VIII, 20, 1-3, *Theragāthā* 557-566.

51. There is evidence in the texts that the Buddha was not regarded by his disciples as utterly without fault. His cousin Ananda is recorded as reproving him on one occasion. Another account, which could hardly have been invented later, shows that the Buddha's ethical directions were resented by at least one of the monks. *Dīgha-Nikāya* II, 139, 162.

52. For example, Paul Hossfeld, following H.W. Schomerus, holds that in the case of Siddhārtha Gautama we have in no way to do with a *homo religiosus*, that in the proclamation and teaching which can with any likelihood be traced back to the Buddha there is not one intimation of authentic religion. Hossfeld's conclusion is that the Buddha was a sublime existential philosopher with primary emphasis upon practice rather than theory. "Jesus (der Christus) und Siddhārtha Gautama (der Buddha)," *Theologie und Glaube*, 64, 4-5 (1974), pp. 379-389. As Hossfeld himself makes clear in his survey of recent German literature on the subject, his view is by no means shared by all contemporary German scholars.

53. This is not to say that the gods *(devas)* are seen as having no supportive role at all. The early accounts portray the Buddha as significantly aided by them especially in his younger years. Cf. *Sutta-Nipāta* 407-408; Watanabe, *op. cit.*, pp. 158-174, 199-201; *Majjhima-Nikāya* II, 212-213.

54. The corpus of Buddhist literature called *Abhidharma* is largely devoted to psychological analysis and represents one of the first truly sophisticated systems of psychology in known human history. Cf. Robinson and Johnson, *op. cit.*, pp. 50-56. It

should be noted, however, that the analyses of human psychology in the *Sutta-Piṭaka* are much simpler than the elaborate system worked out in the later *Abhidharma* literature. As Fedor Stcherbatsky has pointed out, the primary concern of the early materials with regard to an understanding of human psychological processes was moral rather than scholastic: *Buddhist Logic,* New York: Dover, 1962, I, pp. 3-4. Cf. Lama Anagarika Govinda, *The Psychological Attitude of Early Buddhist Philosophy,* London: Rider, 1969, pp. 79-142.

55. *Dīgha-Nikāya* II, 313.

56. Winston L. King clarifies part of the issue with his statement that "Buddhism is no 'mere morality' since it aims at goals which completely transcend the ethical and always places its ethic in that transcendent context." He believes, however, that the self-development which was the aim of the Buddha "comes about only by one's own efforts." *In the Hope of Nibbana,* La Salle, Illinois: The Open Court Publishing Co., 1964, pp. 2-4. In an earlier work King suggests that the four elements of *Dharma, Nirvāṇa, karma,* and the Buddha constitute a "reality-complex" or "reality-structure" that provides a "God-substitute" and fulfills a "God-function" in Buddhism. *Buddhism and Christianity,* Philadelphia: Westminster Press, 1962, p. 38. These four elements are indeed integral to the worldview of especially early Buddhism and perform functions similar to those of God and his Christ according to Christian faith. In Buddhism, however, the four elements are not comparably the object of religious devotion, in early Buddhism not the Buddha, and in all Buddhist history not *karma.*

57. *Anguttara-Nikāya* I, 14-16; V, 26-27.

58. *Sanyutta-Nikāya* V, 2; 29-35; I, 87-88. Cf. Winston L. King, *Buddhism and Christianity, op. cit.,* p. 227; Robinson and Johnson, *op. cit.,* p. 57.

59. Mrs. Rhys Davids, *The Book of the Kindred Sayings, I,* London: Luzac, 1950, p. 112, ftn. 2.

60. *Majjhima-Nikāya* I, 426-432. Cf. *Sanyutta-Nikāya* V, 418.

61. *Sutta-Nipāta* 235; *Theri-gāthā* 116. Cf. *Sanyutta-Nikāya* I, 159.

62. *Sutta-Nipāta* 1109, 1131, 1094; *Anguttara-Nikāya* V, 65, 111.

63. *Sutta-Nipāta* 19, 739. There is also, however, an expression "mind-at-work" *(viññaṇassa)*, which is used in the pejorative sense of busy but pointless intellection *(Sutta-Nipāta* 734-735).

64. *Sutta-Nipāta* 593, 86; *Anguttara-Nikāya* III, 213, 297; IV, 14.

65. *Sanyutta-Nikāya* I, 210.

66. In addition to use of the term *ahimsā* (nonviolence, harmlessness) Buddhist ethics actually stressed positive giving, in the fullest sense of the word, as symbolic of the authentic moral life. Cf. Roy C. Amore, "Giving and Harming: Buddhist Symbols of Good and Evil," *Developments in Buddhist Thought: Canadian Contributions to Buddhist Studies,* Waterloo, Ontario: Canadian Corporation for Studies in Religion, 1979, pp. 93-100.

67. *Sutta-Nipāta* 514, 186, 228; *Anguttara-Nikāya* IV, 352, 358, 453.

68. *Anguttara-Nikāya* IV, 238; V, 9; *Majjhima-Nikāya* II, 98-105. Cf. Günter Lanczkowski, "Das Heilsziel des Nirvāṇa in der Lehre des Buddhas," *Asien Missioniert im Abendland,* Kurt Hutten und Siegfried von Kortzfleisch, eds., Stuttgart: Kreuz-Verlag, 1962, p. 148. Seiichi Yagi sees *Nirvāṇa* in the early texts as that to which disciples should awaken. "Christ and Buddha," *op. cit.,* p. 311.

69. *Majjhima-Nikāya* III, 4-6. Cf. *Milindapañha* 270-271.

70. *Udāna* VIII, 3.

71. *Visuddhi-Magga* 21.

72. Cf. Mrs. Rhys Davids, *The Book of the Gradual Sayings,* Vol. I, F.L. Woodward, tr., London: Luzac, 1970, p. viii.

73. Cf. *Mahābhārata* XII, 60.

74. In at least one passage in the early texts the Buddha is recorded as having identified the process of dependent origination, of moral cause and effect, with *Dharma,* but this was clearly not a common equation. Cf. *Majjhima-Nikāya* I, 190-191.

75. Mrs. Caroline Augusta Foley Rhys Davids, *The Book of the Gradual Sayings, op. cit.,* Vol. I, p. viii. A contemporary Burmese Christian insists that rightly understood, "Buddhism is profoundly theistic." Khin Maung Din, "Some Problems and Possibilities for Burmese Christian Technology Today," *Christian-*

ity and the Religions of the East, Richard W. Rousseau, ed., Montrose, PA: Ridge Row Press, 1982, p. 79.

76. Cf. *Sanyutta-Nikāya* I, 139. *Dharma* is used in this passage as a masculine noun, *Dhammo*. Cf. the comment of the translator, F.L. Woodward, *The Book of the Kindred Sayings*, Vol. I, London: Luzac, 1950, pp. 175-176, ftn. 4.

77. *Sanyutta-Nikāya* I, 139.

78. *Dīgha-Nikāya* III, 77.

79. It is historically significant that a *sola gratia* soteriology emerged later in the Mahāyāna, especially in the True Pure Land school in Japan (*Jōdo Shinshū*). The great Japanese Buddhist reformer Shinran (1173-1262) did teach a doctrine of salvation by grace alone, of which coin the obverse side was by faith alone, but he was no little discomfited by the fact that some of his followers went on, quite apart from his own intent, to belittle as well as to deny salvific value to all morality. Cf. Toshihide Akamatsu, *Shinran*, Tokyo: Yoshikawa Hirobumi Kan, 1965, pp. 242-252, 229, 284.

80. *Dīgha-Nikāya* III, 777.

81. *Dhammapada* 354. With reference to Wisdom cf. Ps. 37:30, 111:10; Prov. 4:11, 5:1-23; 7:4-5; 8:1-4, 11-12; 10:31; 14:33-34; 16:16; 17:24; 18:4; 23:24.

82. *Ibid.*, 368.

83. Cf. Prov. 2:6; 21:30.

84. *Wisdom of Solomon* 1: 6-7; 7:7-15; 8:17-18; 9:9.

85. A highly significant account is given in the Pāli texts of the Buddha's discussion with a number of persons from a tribal group called the Kālāmas, from Kesaputra of Kośala, who questioned him as to how to distinguish between true and false religious teachers. His answer was, in effect, to say that their criterion of judgment should be whether the teachings, when applied, produce the right ethical fruit. That is, do they lead to human moral and spiritual transformation-development? *Anguttara-Nikāya* I, 187-192. Cf. Mt. 7:15-20; 11:19; 12:33; Lk. 6:43-45; Rom. 12:2; Jam. 3:11-12.

86. *Sutta-Nipāta* 1054, 1064-1065; 81, 327, 344, 361, 374, 384-385, 453, 764-765, 934. Cf. I Cor. 2:4-5.

87. Heinrich Dumoulin gives it as his conviction that such

perception of transcendence was a part of the Buddha's own mind and notes that some early Buddhist art, such as certain sculptures of Bhārhut and Sānchi from the second century B.C.E., points in this direction. "Buddhism—A Religion of Liberation," *Buddhism and Christianity,* Claude Geffré & Mariasusai Dhavamony, eds., New York: Seabury Press, 1979, p. 27.

88. Buddhadāsa Indapañño, *Christianity and Buddhism,* Bangkok; Karn Pim Pranakorn, 1968, pp. 70-76. Cf. Marcello Zago, "L'équivalent de 'Dieu' dans le bouddhisme," *Église et Théologie* VI (1975), pp. 42-45. The Sri Lankan Roman Catholic scholar, Aloysius Pieris, S.J., does not hesitate to equate the Buddhist Dharma with the Christian Logos and sees both as *"an accessible dimension, a mediatory and revelatory self-expression"* of the Absolute [Pieris's italics], *Love Meets Wisdom, a Christian Experience of Buddhism,* Maryknoll, NY: Orbis Books, 1988, p. 132.

89. *Dhammapada* 118, 331-333.

90. In this awareness of the fundamental inadequacy of the empirical situation of human beings and in pointing to a way out of such which is helped by such awareness, the Buddha seems akin to most of the great religious teachers of human history. We may recall that William James declared the "common nucleus" of the intellectual formulation of all authentic religion to consist of two parts: an uneasiness and its solution. The former he described as "a sense that there is something wrong about us as we naturally stand." *The Varieties of Religious Experience,* New York: The New American Library, 1961, p. 383. In one suggestive passage the Buddha is recorded as likening the situation of the empirical human being who is under the dominion of Māra, the tempter, to "a fish taken from his watery home and thrown on the dry ground." *Dhammapada* 34.

91. *Majjhima-Nikāya* I, 171.

92. We may note that the New Testament term *epithymia,* which is sometimes translated as "passion" (as in Rom. 6:12, NRSV), is better rendered as "desire" and suggests misplaced desire with a wider emotive range than the merely sensual, as is true of "craving" in the early Buddhist texts.

93. *Vinaya-Piṭaka, Mahāvagga* I, 1. Cf. *Sanyutta-Nikāya* II, 1. Gerhard von Rad has identified perception of an all-embrac-

ing divinely established order of cause and effect at work in human life and involving an interpenetration of both moral and physical realms as a concept which Israel shared with other nations. He denotes this order as an act-consequence relationship *(Tun-Ergehen-Zusammenhang)*, one to be sure not without ambiguity in human experience but particularly stressed by the writers of the Wisdom school as well as basic to the thought of the prophets. *Wisdom in Israel,* Nashville: Abingdon, 1972, pp. 124-137.

94. Cf. Buddhadāsa Indapañño, *Buddha Dhamma for Students,* Bangkok: M.P., 1966, pp. 5-6, 19-20, 25, 50, 55, 63, 67.

95. *Digha-Nikāya* II, 290-304.

96. *Anguttara-Nikāya* I, 156-158.

97. A shorter, fourfold formula is also found and is repeated eight times in the *Mahā Parinibbāna Sutta.* This formulation, which may be earlier than the Eightfold Path, begins with observance of the rules of morality *(sila),* proceeds to concentration or the rapture of enlightenment *(samādhi),* whereby saving knowledge *(pañña)* is acquired, a state of mind or understanding that is liberation *(vimutti).* The ethical content, however, and mental-spiritual development envisaged in this formula are essentially no different from those of the eightfold version.

98. Cf. W. Norman Brown, *Man in the Universe, Some Cultural Continuities in India,* Berkeley: University of California Press, 1966, p. 10; Sarvapalli Radhakrishnan, *Eastern Religions and Western Thought,* New York: Oxford University Press, 1960, pp. 353-378.

99. *Sutta-Nipāta* 425-449. Cf. *Dhammapada* 106-108.

100. *Dhammapada* 1-2.

101. In one passage the Noble Eightfold Path is also termed lovely, that is, as expressing the qualities of *Dharma. Anguttara-Nikāya* I, 2-16; *Sanyutta-Nikāya,* 32-39. Cf. Buddhadāsa Indapañño, *Buddha Dhamma for Students, op. cit.,* pp. 21-22.

102. The Buddha apparently noted that there were human beings "with little dust in their eyes" who were presumably better prepared than others to receive the teaching, to learn and grow. But the missionaries were also to go to the "manyfolk." The early texts seem unanimous in that, while the Buddha felt impelled to adjust his teaching somewhat to the varying capacities

of his hearers, he excluded no one and considered no one's case hopeless. *Vinaya-Piṭaka, Mahāvagga* I, 11, 1. Aloysius Pieris, S.J., insists that "The idea of a *given* human potentiality for the transcendent is the most significant presupposition in Buddhist soteriology," *op. cit.,* p. 133.

103. There are elements in the teaching which point to a profound concern for others on the Buddha's part. He is recorded as having been asked by a Brāhman named Sangārava if his teaching were not inferior by being oriented to the welfare of the individual rather than the many. The Buddha's answer was that he had found *Dharma,* "that incomparable bliss which is steeped in the holy life," and teaches it to others. Because he teaches *Dharma,* "others too practice to attain that end," to the extent of "many hundreds, many thousands, many hundreds of thousands." *Anguttara-Nikāya* I, 167.

104. Cf. Karl Ludwig Reichelt, *Truth and Tradition in Chinese Buddhism,* Shanghai: The Commercial Press, 1927, pp. 38-39, 2, 31, 39, 132, 179, 195; Notto R. Thelle, "The Legacy of Karl Ludwig Reichelt," *International Bulletin of Missionary Research,* V, 2 (April 1981), pp. 65-70; Håkan Eilert, *Boundlessness, Studies in Karl Ludwig Reichelt's Missionary Thinking with Special Regard to the Buddhist-Christian Encounter,* Århus, Denmark: Forlaget Aros, 1974, *passim.*

105. *Dhammapada* 221, 173. Cf. *Anguttara-Nikāya* I, 62.

106. We may note the Buddha's response to the sufferings of the converted robber Angulimāla, now become a monastic follower. The Buddha urged the bloodied monk to endure with patience the abuse and physical mistreatment which he was receiving from his former victims. The Buddha gave as reason for his conviction that the monk was now experiencing an immediate ripening of *karma,* presumably a cosmic consequence of his conversion, and that this quick ripening constituted a shortening of the punishment which he would have had to endure for long years in Niraya (a hell-like abode). Angulimāla's perception of the overall experience was that, in spite of his present sufferings, his evilly wrought *karma* was essentially a closed account, "debtless, I enjoy an owner's estate." *Majjhima-Nikāya* II, 98-105.

107. For example, Walpola Rahula, *What the Buddha Taught,*

Bedford, England: Gordon Fraker, 1959, p. 51. For the great variety of interpretive views that have been held by Western scholars, see Raimundo Panikkar, *The Silence of God, the Answer of the Buddha*, Maryknoll, NY: Orbis Books, 1989, pp. 7-15.

108. Joseph Kitagawa has expressed this point by saying that while the Mahāyāna philosophically equated *Nirvāṇa* and *saṁsāra* (the phenomenal world), religiously it "found an infinite distance between them." *Religions of the East*, Philadelphia: Westminster Press, 1960, p. 186.

109. Cf. Heinrich Dumoulin, *A History of Zen Buddhism*, New York: Random House, 1963, pp. 38-45. Edward Conze describes the *Avatamsaka Sūtras* as affirming the one eternal principle of the universe, which is *serenity of Mind* and whose presence in the universe charges everything with spiritual significance. *Buddhism: Its Essence and Development*, New York: Harper, 1959, p. 164.

110. Santideva (ca. 600 C.E.), a follower of the great Mahāyāna philosopher Nāgārjuna, describes the blessing of enlightenment as a swelling joy which "sweeps in sweetness down the boundless waters of mankind." E.A. Burtt, *The Teachings of the Compassionate Buddha*, New York: The New American Library, 1960, p. 135. The need for ethical transformation as a part of spiritual reorientation is strongly emphasized by the classic figures of the Zen tradition in China. For Tao-sheng (360-434) illumination also meant change in human character. If the Buddha is not called, he does not appear. If the human heart is not a clear pond, the Buddha cannot appear there. Shen-hui (668-760) in the strongest language insisted upon human effort to follow the modes of ethical conduct taught by the Buddha. "Everybody must observe *śīla*—the Rules of Conduct." "If you do not observe the Rules of Conduct, you will not be incarnated in a scabby jackal, how much less in the *dharmakāya* [Dharma-Body, or undifferentiated Reality as taught in the early Mahāyāna philosophy] of a Tathāgata, the reward of his meritorious deeds." *Ibid.*, pp. 226, 232.

111. We find in early texts a certain identification of Buddhist disciples with *Dharma*, so that, just as Christians are in a sense Christ-persons, these followers of the Buddha were identified at times as *Dharma-persons*. In one passage we read that a number

of the Buddha's disciples agreed that he had become *Dharma* (*Dhamma-bhūta*). *Majjhima-Nikāya* I, 111; *Sanyutta-Nikāya* I, 33. In another passage which records his conversation with the elderly and grievously ill monk Vakkali, the Buddha is recorded as saying, "He who sees *Dharma*, Vakkali, he sees me; he who sees me, Vakkali, he sees *Dharma.*" The context of this statement, however, makes clear its meaning. Vakkali had just spoken of his previous longing to see the Buddha, but had been prevented by his physical weakness. The Buddha turned aside the implications of personal reverence in Vakkali's words and said to him, immediately preceding the above quotation, "Hush, Vakkali! What is there in seeing this vile body of mine?" The point of the account seems to be that the *Dharma* which the Buddha proclaims and, indeed, authentically manifests in his person and life is not primarily seen in the physical body nor is it confined in its manifestations to Siddhārtha Gautama. Thus to salute the body of his physical birth is not to render him the proper homage. *Sanyutta-Nikāya* III, 121.

112. Cf. *Majjhima-Nikāya* I, 4, 21-23.

113. Cf. James W. Boyd, "The Path of Liberation from Suffering in Buddhism," *Buddhism and Christianity,* Geffré & Dhavamony, eds., *op. cit.,* p. 20.

114. *Majjhima-Nikāya* I, 6, 17, 97-98, 283, 288.

115. *Sutta-Nipāta* 477.

116. *Sutta-Nipāta* 334, 514, 592, 626, 961-962.

117. *Sutta-Nipāta* 778, 912-913.

118. *Sutta-Nipāta* 501, 718, 837, 1119.

119. *Majjhima-Nikāya* I, 138. Cf. Mircea Eliade, *A History of Religious Ideas II,* Chicago: University of Chicago Press, 1982, p. 105.

120. Tathāgata was not an exclusive term and was employed in the early community also of other Buddhas. It probably denoted one who had attained to the indescribable state. Cf. Zimmer, *op. cit.,* p. 133.

121. *Majjhima-Nikāya* I, 484-488; *Anguttara-Nikāya* I, 248-249.

122. Paul Ramsey, *Reinhold Niebuhr,* Charles W. Kegley & Robert W. Bretal, eds., New York: Macmillan, 1956, pp. 85-86.

123. Edwin Arnold, *The Light of Asia*, Boston: Robert Brothers, 1891, p. 238. Cf. Dominique Dubarle, "Buddhist Spirituality and the Christian Understanding of God," *Buddhism and Christianity*, Geffré & Dhavamony, eds., *op. cit.*, pp. 66-67; Hans Wolfgang Schumann, *Buddhism*, Wheaton, Ill.: Theosophical Publishing House, 1974, pp. 80-83. See *Muṇḍaka Upaniṣad* III 2, 7-9.

124. *Sanyutta-Nikāya* III, 109-116. Continuity as "evolving consciousness" is repeatedly stated in *Majjhima-Nikāya* II, 263-266. Cf. *Anguttara-Nikāya* IV, 39.

125. *Anguttara-Nikāya* I, 138-141.

126. *Sanyutta-Nikāya* I, 93. The Ceylonese scholastic Buddhaghosa (fifth century C.E.) attempted to affirm continuity with the figure of a fruit that "is not the same nor something else. The fabricating power in seeds will show the meaning of the word." As sour cream arises from milk, neither an absolute sameness is obtained nor an absolute difference. *Visuddhi-Magga* XVII.

127. Cf. Keiji Nishitani, "The Personal and the Impersonal in Religion," *The Eastern Buddhist*, III, 2 (October 1970), pp. 80-88; Frits Vos, "The Discovery of the Special Nature of Buddha: Sudden Enlightenment in Zen," *Buddhism and Christianity*, Geffré & Dhavamony, eds., *op. cit.*, p. 33; Raimundo Panikkar, *The Silence of God*, *op. cit.*, pp. 28-29.

128. We find use of the neuter gender with reference to God as perceived in Christian faith among some theologians in the early church. For example, Gregory of Nyssa in his work "On the Soul and the Resurrection," composed in 380, wrote of *"to Theion*, which whatever it is in its own nature, our reason surmises to be engaged in supervising all things and distinguishing the good from the evil." J.P. Migne, *Patrologia Graeca*, XLVI, col. 57.

129. *Anguttara-Nikāya* I, 158; IV, 453.

130. Cf. Dumoulin, "Buddhism—A Religion of Liberation," *Buddhism and Christianity*, Geffré & Dhavamony, eds., *op. cit.*, p. 28; Peter Nemeshegyi, "Notions de Dieu et Expériences de Dieu en Asie," *Concilium*, 123 (1977), pp. 43-45. See Lama Anagarika Govinda, *The Psychological Attitude of Early Buddhist Philosophy*, *op. cit.*, pp. 141-142, 159; Panikkar, *The Silence of God*, *op. cit.*, pp. xv, xix, xxiv-xxv.

131. Hossfeld, *op. cit.*, p. 387. But cf. Dominique Dubarle,

"Buddhist Spirituality and the Christian Understanding of God," *Buddhism and Christianity,* Geffré & Dhavamony, eds., *op. cit.,* pp. 69-72; Hans Küng *et al., Christianity and the World Religions,* Garden City, NY: Doubleday and Co., 1986, pp. 306-328, 411-437.

132. We may also note in this context that in no place in the early texts is either *Dharma* or *Nirvāṇa* seen as responsible for the creation of the physical universe. Roger Corless reminds us that even Amitābha, the supreme Savior of Pure Land Buddhism, although regarded by his devotees as the most powerful of Buddhas and as the creator and sustainer of the Pure Land, "is not the sole Buddha, did not create the universe and cannot in any sense be regarded as a ground of being." "A Christian Perspective of Buddhist Liberation," *Buddhism and Christianity,* Geffré & Dhavamony, eds., *op. cit.,* p. 79.

133. Some of the language of the Chinese "Masses for the Dead," as of other Chinese Buddhist poetry, gives expression in the sublimest lyrical forms to this faith in the initiative-taking, concretely helpful compassion of the Ultimate as Amitābha. Cf. Reichelt, *op. cit.,* pp. 137-139; Burtt, *op. cit.,* pp. 128-129, 212. We find a distinctly personified *Dharma* in the tradition of Japanese Shingon *(Mikkyō), Dharma* who communicates (reveals) as well as creates, nurtures, and regulates all things. Cf. Minoru Kiyota, *Gedatsukai: Its Theory and Practice,* Los Angeles: Buddhist Books International, 1982, pp. 56-58.

134. Romano Guardini, *The Lord,* Chicago: Henry Regnery, 1954, p. 305.

Part II

1. We shall note later that extracanonical materials, that is, religious documents of Christian origin not included in the canonical scriptures of the New Testament, in some cases may be taken with considerable seriousness especially with reference to content of teaching. It is noteworthy how many extracanonical works John Dominic Crossan includes in the first stratum (30-60 C.E.) of his stratification of witnesses to the Jesus tradition. Cf. *The Historical Jesus,* San Francisco: HarperCollins, 1991, pp. 427-429.

2. Cf. John A. T. Robinson, *Redating the New Testament*, Philadelphia: Westminster Press, 1976, pp. 13-30; 86-117. Robinson follows the German scholar Bo Reicke in noting that it is really an example of uncritical dogmatism in New Testament studies to insist that the synoptic gospels (Matthew, Mark, and Luke) should all be dated after the Jewish-Roman War of 66-70 C.E. because they contain prophecies that "must" be regarded as *vaticinia ex eventu* (prophecies after the event).

3. Cf. Bruce Manning Metzger, *The Text of the New Testament, Its Transmission, Corruption and Restoration*, 2nd ed., New York: Oxford University Press, 1968, pp. 36-92.

4. Brooke Foss Westcott & Fenton John Anthony Hort, *The New Testament in the Original Greek*, New York: Macmillan, 1961, pp. 546, 564-565. Cf. Bruce Metzger, *The Text of the New Testament, op. cit.*, pp. 173, 185.

5. Bultmann was, however, quite firm in his insistence that Jesus really lived, "although that fact is not verifiable by historical science." *Faith and Understanding*, London: SCM Press, 1969, pp. 138, 174, 177, 181, 304. See also his *Kerygma and Myth, a Theological Debate*, London: S.P.C.K., 1953, p. 44. Bultmann perhaps did not take adequate account of the fact that all history, even "historical science," depends primarily on anecdotal sources.

6. Joachim Jeremias, *The Parables of Jesus*, rev. ed., New York: Charles Scribner's Sons, 1963, pp. 25-27, 115-230. See his *The Problem of the Historical Jesus*, Philadelphia: Fortress Press, 1964, pp. 12-21.

7. Nils Astrup Dahl, "The Problem of the Historical Jesus," in Carl E. Braaten and Roy A. Harrisville, *Kerygma and History*, New York: Abingdon Press, 1962, pp. 151, 157. Cf. James M. Robinson, *A New Quest of the Historical Jesus*, Philadelphia: Fortress Press, 1983, pp. 48-92, who argues for both the possibility and legitimacy of a new quest of the historical Jesus. We may note that the German biblical scholar Günther Bornkamm claims that the New Testament gospels bring the historical person of Jesus before our eyes "with the utmost vividness." *Jesus of Nazareth*, New York: Harper & Row, 1975, p. 24.

8. Suetonius, *Divus Claudius* XXV, 4. We have information, although from later sources, that there were anti-Jewish distur-

bances at an earlier period, during the reign of the emperor Caligula (37-41C.E.), in the cities of Antioch in Syria and in Alexandria. Cf. Martin Hengel, *Acts and the History of Earliest Christianity,* Philadelphia: Fortress Press, 1980, p. 103.

9. It is possible to infer from I Peter 4:16 that profession of Christian faith ("in the name") involved liability to criminal charges. Whether I Peter be regarded as Petrine or dated as late as 90 C.E. or later is immaterial here. The Book of Acts makes clear that from an early period public profession of "the name" could bring suffering in Palestine or in larger imperial context (Acts 5:41; 9:16; 21:13).

10. *The Letters of Pliny* X, 96-97.

11. Raimundo Panikkar, *The Silence of God, the Answer of the Buddha,* Maryknoll, NY: Orbis Books, 1989, pp. 129-147. Panikkar goes on to say that historic Buddhism as a whole may be designated as "a school of prayer—understanding prayer not in the sense of vocal prayer, but as interior contemplation." *Ibid.,* p. 155.

12. Edward Conze, "The Mahāyāna," *Concise Encyclopedia of Religious Faiths,* R.C. Zaehner, ed., New York: Hawthorn Books, 1959, pp. 317-318. The practice of yoga can be traced back, under that name, to the *Yogasutra* of Patanjali, a document that has been given dates of origin ranging from the second century B.C.E. to the fourth century C.E. In spite, however, of its provenance as probably much later than the time of the Buddha, the work clearly represents a summation of Indian practices stemming from earlier centuries.

13. Edward Conze, *Buddhist Thought in India,* Ann Arbor: The University of Michigan Press, 1967, pp. 17-30. Cf. Conze, *Buddhism: Its Essence and Development,* New York: Harper & Brothers, 1959, pp. 11-26. The Japan-based Belgian Roman Catholic scholar Jan van Bragt agrees with Conze's understanding at this point. He adds, however, that "Buddhism originally appeared not so much as a religion but as a counter-movement to the existing ritualistic religion." Van Bragt goes on to state that the same could probably be said of the activity (message) of the Chirst or of Socrates. "The Challenge to Christian Theology from Kyoto-school Buddhist Philosophy," *Studies in Interreligious Dialogue,* 1, 1(1991), pp. 46-47.

14. Marcus J. Borg, *Jesus, a New Vision, Spirit Culture, and the Life of Discipleship,* San Francisco: Harper & Row, 1987, pp. 15, 25-75. See also Borg's *Meeting Jesus Again for the First Time,* San Francisco: Harper, 1994, pp. 31-39; "The Historian, the Christian, and Jesus," *Theology Today,*Vol. 52, No. 1(April 1995), pp. 6-16.

15. *Ibid.,* p. 26. The terminology and concepts involved in the "primordial tradition" have been developed, following Aldous Huxley and Christopher Isherwood *et al.,* in almost classic form by Huston Smith in his *Forgotten Truth, the Primordial Tradition,* New York: Harper & Row, 1977, and in his *Beyond the Post-Modern Mind,* New York: Crossroad, 1982. Cf. Frithjof Schuon, *The Transcendent Unity of Religions,* New York: Harper & Row, 1975.

16. Perhaps a better known image to denote especially the accounts in the book of Genesis is that of an elliptical circle with heaven in the highest segment, sheol or hades at the lowest, the earth in the middle with waters "above the dome" and "under the dome" (Gen. 1:6-10). Cf. Colleen McDannell & Bernhard Lang, *Heaven—A History,* New Haven: Yale University Press, 1988, pp. 2-11.

17. The word in the Greek language that has come to be anglicized as "demon" originally had a positive meaning, akin to the Latin *numen.* What appears in the New Testament as *daimonion* was, in the dialogues of the fourth-century B.C.E. Greek philosopher Plato, the guardian Spirit who guided Socrates from his earliest years, particularly in keeping him from being or doing evil. Indeed, this was the attendant *genius* of every human being, the font of his good fortune (*Apology* 19, *Phaedo* 107e, 108b, 113d; *Laws* V, 732c). The meaning seems to have shifted in later Greek usage into that of an inferior divine being and then into evil spirit.

18. As may be expected, not every New Testament writer depicts the human existential situation in precisely the same way. The writer of the Letter of James, in language similar to that of the early Buddhist texts, insists that human beings are "tempted by one's own desire, being lured and enticed by it" (Jas. 2:13-14; cf. Paul's use of the same term—*epithymia*—in Rom. 7:8; Col. 3:5; I Thess. 4:5).

19. As we have seen, the Buddha and almost the whole of

subsequent Asian religious perception have assumed the possibility of repeated human lives on earth or reincarnation—with potentially positive as well as negative implications—as an important aspect of the functioning of the karmic process. The Hebrew Scriptures—we shall discuss New Testament themes later—do speak of a kind of genetically related extended time span. We note, for example, the proverbial expression, "The parents have eaten sour grapes, and the children's teeth are set on edge," a principle specifically rejected by Jeremiah (31:29-30) and in more detail by Ezekiel (18:1-20). Yet in the text of the Torah, in the important context of the first of the Ten Commandments, we note the concept of God "punishing children for the iniquity of their parents to the third and fourth generation of those who reject me, but showing steadfast love to the thousandth generation of those who love me and keep my commandments" (Ex. 20:5-6; 4:6-7).

20. (Pseudo-Clementine) *Homilies* III, 20. This concept of prior incarnations of Jesus plays an important role also in Manichaean and Mandaean teaching and later in certain forms of Islamic faith. Cf. C.H. Dodd, *Interpretation of the Fourth Gospel*, Cambridge: Cambridge University Press, 1955, pp. 122, 239. According to the *Homilies*, the one who became Jesus of Nazareth, the Christ, had been incarnated as Adam, Enoch, Noah, Abraham, Isaac, Jacob, Moses, and lastly, Jesus. Moses is at times eliminated from this list, making Jesus the seventh in the series. Actually, the list appears to be rather a selective genealogy or a symbolic listing because, according to the canonical Scriptures, Abraham and Isaac, and also Isaac and Jacob, were respectively living on the earth at the same time. Cf. F.L. Cross, *The Early Christian Fathers*, London: Gerald Duckworth, 1960, pp. 98-99; W.D. Davies, *Paul and Rabbinic Judaism*, London: S.P.C.K., 1955, pp. 50-51. We should note that if we are to take seriously this Jewish Christian affirmation of Jesus as Adam, who though, as Luke states (Lk. 3:38), he was son of God, did fall, there is strong reason to believe that in his final incarnation as Jesus of Nazareth, as the Christ, he had become quite without sin (cf. Heb. 4:15; 5:8).

21. Cf. Morton Smith, *The Secret Gospel*, New York: Harper & Row, 1973, pp. 14-17; *Clement of Alexandria and a Secret Gospel of Mark*, Cambridge, MA: Harvard University Press, 1973, pp. 452-

453. In the letter Clement refers to the "hierophantic teaching of the Lord" and to certain sayings of Jesus which, when rightly interpreted, "lead the hearers into the inmost sanctuary of that truth hidden by seven [veils]." The main purpose of the letter, however, was clearly Clement's intent to demonstrate that the Carpocratian interpretation of this teaching in the direction of sexual libertinism had no support in the text of the "Secret Gospel." Frank Kermode has written in his perceptive study of Mark that "parable . . . may proclaim a truth as a herald does, and at the same time conceal truth like an oracle." *The Genesis of Secrecy,* Cambridge, MA: Harvard University Press, 1979, p. 47. F.F. Bruce accepts the letter as probably Clement's, but questions whether the "Secret Gospel" is truly Marcan. *The 'Secret Gospel' of Mark,* London: Athlone Press, 1974, pp. 3-20. I cannot follow Morton Smith in his ascription of the term magician to Jesus of Nazareth. Cf. *Jesus the Magician,* New York: Harper & Row, 1981, *passim.*

22. Cf. Hugh Anderson, *The Gospel of Mark,* London: Oliphants, 1976, pp. 208-216. Bruce Vawter has argued convincingly for consideration of Ezekiel as a primary element in the background of Jesus' usage of the term "son of man." "Ezekiel and John," *The Catholic Biblical Quarterly* XXVI, 3 (1964), pp. 451-455. Geza Vermes affirms the same on the basis particularly of Aramaic linguistic studies, *Jesus the Jew,* Philadelphia: Fortress Press, 1981, pp. 160-191. Vermes also reports that Jewish charismatics, notably Hanina ben Dosa, who was active around the middle of the first century C.E., were also proclaimed as a son of God by a heavenly voice, *ibid.,* pp. 206-210. It should be noted that in Mark, as Marcus Borg points out, there is no human proclamation of Jesus as son of God, only heavenly voices (as at Jesus' baptism and transfiguration, 1:11; 9:7, or by evil spirits, 3:11; 5:7), except the Roman centurion at the cross (15:39). Marcus J. Borg, *Jesus, a New Vision, op. cit.,* p. 18.

23. Cf. David Hill, *The Gospel of Matthew,* London: Oliphants, 1972, pp. 64-65. Neither Mark nor Luke has this particular interpretation (Mk. 2:12; Lk. 5:26).

24. Recent studies have shown that Luke is more to be interpreted in the context of unbroken continuity with the tradition of Israel than was formerly thought. Cf. Jacob Jervell, *Luke and*

the People of God, Minneapolis: Augsburg, 1972, pp. 41-74; David L. Tiede, *Prophecy and History in Luke-Acts,* Philadelphia: Fortress Press, 1980, pp. 8-11.

25. Cf. G.S. Kirk and J.E. Raven, *The Presocratic Philosophers,* Cambridge: Cambridge University Press, 1960, pp. 186-187. The prologue (Jn. 1:1-18) as a whole seems to echo the creation story of Genesis 1, and the term *Logos* may be presumed to have affinities also with the Hebrew *Dabar* (Word) of God.

26. Cf. W.F. Arndt and F.W. Gingrich, *A Greek-English Lexicon of the New Testament,* Chicago: University of Chicago Press, 1960, pp. 716-718.

27. Cf. Raymond E. Brown, *The Gospel According to John,* I, Garden City, New York: Doubleday, 1966, pp. 4-5. Origen distinguishes between *ho Theos* (with the definite article) as the uncreated first Cause *(Autotheos)* and *Theos* (without the article) as the Logos "made God by participation." This is the Logos who "by being with God is at all times God, not possessing that of himself but by his being with the Father." This is "the first-born of all creation, who is the first to be with God, and to attract to himself divinity." He "is a being of more exalted rank than the other gods beside him, of whom God is the God . . . It was by the offices of the first-born that they became gods." *Commentarius in Johannem* II, 2.

28. The Greek text of John 1:18, for which the NRSV gives as the preferred reading, "God the only Son, who is close to the Father's heart," is probably to be read "unique God" *(monogenes Theos),* meaning something like "the uniquely divine One." Cf. Kurt Aland *et al.,* eds., *The Greek New Testament,* 3rd ed., Stuttgart: United Bible Societies, 1975, p. 322. The term *ton monogenē* is used of Isaac in Heb. 11:17 to mean a special son but, of course, not Abraham's only son; Ishmael was born first and circumcised as a sign of participation in the Abrahamic covenant before Isaac was born (Gen. 17:23-27). Cf. Wis. 7:22, where the word is used to denote the unique quality of Wisdom. We may note that Israel was called the "first-born" of God in a special but not exclusive sense (cf. Ex. 4:22; Jer. 31:9; Sir. 36:11; in the Septuagint the term is *prototokos* or *protogonos).* Karl Rahner develops the thesis that while the incarnation of God in Jesus Christ is a unique event, it

happens not as "a sort of marvel or something heteronomous," but in the context of human nature that is in its essence constituted to receive such. Rahner has manifested a high anthropology from his earliest writings and came to affirm that "the fundamental act of transcendence" constitutes the essence of being human. This is also to speak of "man's fundamental tendency towards absolute closeness to God." *Sacramentum Mundi*, III, New York: Herder and Herder, 1969, p. 116; *Hominisation*, New York: Herder and Herder, 1965, pp. 87-93.

29. Cf. Ernest F. Scott, "Philippians," *The Interpreter's Bible*, XI, George A. Buttrick, ed., New York: Abingdon, 1955, pp. 48-49.

30. Cf. Hugh Ross Mackintosh, *The Doctrine of the Person of Jesus Christ*, New York: Charles Scribner's Sons, 1915, pp. 71-74, 85, 101, 114-115; I Cor. 3:23; 11:3; 15:28. Justin Martyr, *The First Apology* 13.

31. The Greek for "first-born" of all creation *(prototokos)* reminds one of what may be the better reading for Mt. 1:25: *ton hyion autes ton prototokon*, cf. Lk. 2:7. In Colossians 2:9 we find the pregnant phrase, "in him the whole fullness of deity *(theotes)* dwells bodily." Paul appears to be saying that the highest level of divinity *(pleroma)* is resident in Christ Jesus, that Jesus is one with the Most High. Cf. Eduard Lohse, *Colossians and Philemon*, Philadelphia: Fortress Press, 1971, pp. 94-101.

32. Cf. Frank Chamberlin Porter, *The Mind of Christ in Paul*, New York: Charles Scribner's Sons, 1932, pp. 45-91. In Romans 8:15-16 we find this theme succinctly summarized, "When we cry, 'Abba! Father!' it is that very Spirit bearing witness with our spirit that we are children of God, and if children, then heirs, heirs of God and joint heirs with Christ—if, in fact, we suffer with him so that we may also be glorified with him."

33. The Jewish Christian *Gospel of the Ebionites* (early second century) affirms that Jesus had pre-existed, to be sure as a created being, like one of the archangels but greater than they, the one who "ruled over the angels and all that was created by the Almighty." By divine election he came to be called Son of God, from the coming down upon him of Christ [sic] in the form of a dove at his baptism from John. Epiphanius, *Adversus Haereses* XXX, 16. Cf. Edgar Hennecke, *New Testament Aprocrypha*, I,

Wilhelm Schneemelcher, ed., Philadelphia: Westminster, 1963, pp. 157-158.

34. Hebrews 3:1-2 (Jesus as the apostle, the "appointed" of God; the Greek for "appointed," however, is *to poiesanti auton,* which in fact properly means that God "made" or "created" the Son, as Robert Jewett has so translated); 12:24; 13:20; 10:20; 1:3 (10:12); 7:25; 12:25, 2:11-12, 17. Cf. Brooke Foss Westcott, *The Epistle to the Hebrews,* Grand Rapids, MI: Wm. B. Eerdmans, 1951, pp. 425-428; Hugh Montefiore, *A Commentary on the Epistle to the Hebrews,* London: Adam & Charles Black, 1964, pp. 4-5; Robert Jewett, *Letter to Pilgrims,* New York: Pilgrim Press, 1981, pp. 49-53.

35. I would remind my readers of an earlier reference to the case of Evan Roberts, the leader of the great Welsh revival of 1904-'05, who was clearly the possessor of supernormal insight, whether called "the reading of hearts" or "psychic phenomena," and unquestioningly approved of by conservative evangelicals, David Matthews, *I Saw the Welsh Revival,* Chicago: Moody Press, 1951, pp. 38-45. I would add that there is no need to continue the tradition from ancient times wherein pagans ascribed miracles wrought in Christian context to magical or demonic sources and Christians did the same for both pagans and disapproved Christian groups. Cf. Harold Remus, *Pagan-Christian Conflict over Miracle in the Second Century,* Phil.: Philadelphia Patristic Foundation, 1983, pp. 52-72.

36. Amos 1:1; 7:1, 4, 7; 9:1; Hos. 1:2; 3:1; Joel 2:28-29; Obad. 1; Mic. 1:1; Nah. 1:1; Hab. 1:1; Zech. 1:7-21. The prophets are frequently recorded as "seeing" the word of God. Cf. Alfred Guillaume, *Prophecy and Divination,* New York: Harper, 1938, pp. 111, 152-154, 198, 349-353; John Skinner, *Prophecy and Religion,* Cambridge: The University Press, 1922, pp. 185-200.

37. It is not without significance that there is supportive evidence from clairvoyant sources for the historic Christian belief in the virgin birth of Jesus. Cf. Richard H. Drummond, *Unto the Churches,* Virginia Beach, VA: A.R.E. Press, 1978, pp. 88-95.

38. Cf. Lyall Watson, *Supernature,* New York: Bantam, 1974, *passim.* I myself have written briefly on this theme. See the chapter "On Discerning the Times" in my *Unto the Churches, op. cit.,*

pp. 1-24. Cf. Arthur Koestler, *The Roots of Coincidence*, New York: Random House, 1972, pp. 50-77. Michael Polanyi has written sharply about the necessity to perceive the limitations of natural science, especially with regard to using it as a guide or "supreme interpreter of human affairs." See his *Personal Knowledge*, New York: Harper & Row, 1964, pp. 134-150.

39. Joseph's (Giuseppe's) experiences, of course, could not be hidden, and various pilgrims came to behold his "upliftings from the ground and prolonged flights." In 1645 the Spanish ambassador to the Vatican, the High Admiral of Castile, together with his wife and a large retinue, saw Joseph fly about twelve paces above their heads to the feet of a statue of Mary above the high altar of the church where they were. The Duke of Brunswick and Hanover, a Lutheran, became a Roman Catholic after twice seeing Joseph in ecstatic flights. It is worthy of note that Joseph was denounced to the Inquisition in Naples in 1638, was freed after three examinations but sent to the general of his order in Rome. He is said to have had an influence over animals even surpassing that of Francis of Assisi: sheep were reported to gather about him and listen to his prayers, a sparrow at a convent came and went at his word. Teresa of Avila (1515-1582) is also alleged, by her own witness as by that of others, to have had experiences of levitation. Cf. Robert D. Smith, *Comparative Miracles*, St. Louis: D. Herder, 1965, pp. 38-50. Smith discusses carefully some of the problems of evaluating evidence in these cases. Cf. Walter Nigg, *Great Saints*, Hinsdale, IL: Henry Regnery, 1948, p. 132.

40. Sidney Lee, *Dictionary of National Biography*, XXVII, New York: Macmillan, 1891, pp. 225-227. Home appears to have been a man of high personal as well as financial integrity.

41. Rufus Mosely, *Manifest Victory*, Plainfield, NJ: Logos International, 1971, pp. 143-144.

42. Arnold Schulman, *Baba*, New York: Pocket Books, 1973, pp. 13-14, 23-27, 108, 122, 131, 149, 169; cf. Howard Murphet, *Sai Baba, Man of Miracles*, Madras, India: Macmillan, 1975, *passim*. See also Murphet's *Sai Baba, Avatar*, New Delhi, India: Macmillan, 1978, especially pp. 68-85, 110-122, 213-232.

43. Schulman, *Baba, op. cit.*, pp. 70-71, 82-83, 93-95, 133, 149-151, 157. Howard Murphet describes the teachings of Baba

with greater fullness in his *Sai Baba, Man of Miracles, op. cit.,* pp. 190-208; *Sai Baba, Avatar, op. cit.,* pp. 58-67, 110-122, 172, 232, 236, 244-255, 261. A carefully critical, valuable study is that by the Icelandic social scientist Erlendur Haraldsson, *Modern Miracles, an Investigative Report on Psychic Phenomena Associated with Sathya Sai Baba,* New York: Fawcett Columbine (Ballantine Books), 1988.

44. Cf. C. F. D. Moule, ed., *Miracles, Cambridge Studies in Their Philosophy and History,* London: A. R. Mowbray, 1966; C. S. Lewis, *Miracles, a Preliminary Study,* New York: Macmillan, 1947; David Hume, *An Enquiry Concerning Human Understanding,* LaSalle, IL: Open Court Publishing Co., 1938, pp. 112-138.

45. Schulman, *Baba, op. cit.,* p. 134. The language cited here may, of course, owe something to Schulman's own perceptions and modes of expression. For the social welfare and educational work, see Peggy Mason & Ron Laing, *Sathya Sai Baba, the Embodiment of Love,* London: Sawbridge Enterprises, 1982, pp. 195-214.

46. Mark 1:34, 44; 3:12; 4:11; 5:43; 7:36; 8:26; 9:9. Cf. Leslie D. Weatherhead, *Psychology, Religion and Healing,* New York: Abingdon, 1952, pp. 35-36.

47. The passage in Mk. 5:21-34 which tells of a woman who was healed of a flow of blood apparently without Jesus' conscious effort seems to imply on Jesus' part an openness to help and heal others that functioned even on a subconscious level. It appears that healing power could flow out from him apart from his conscious will in the case of this woman who by her faith and touch put herself in the way of the outflowing. We should note that Jesus' healing met not only the desired physical need, but worked also at other levels of need at the same time.

48. Krister Stendahl, "Your Kingdom Come: Notes for Bible Study," *Your Kingdom Come,* Geneva: WCC, 1980, p. 76. Cf. Charles H. Talbert, *Reading Luke,* New York: Crossroad, 1982, pp. 58-62; Wolfhart Pannenberg, *Systematische Theologie,* Vol. I, Göttingen: Vandenhoeck & Ruprecht, 1988, pp. 69-70.

49. Cf. Smith, *Comparative Miracles, op. cit.,* p. 173. The reference, however, in Tertullian's *Adversus Iudaeos* IX, 31 (Quae operatum Christum nec vos diffitemini, etc.) to the Jews' ac-

knowledgment of these works of Jesus may be no more than the result of his reading of John 5:16, 18. We note a comparable ambiguity among rabbinic critics of the Hasidim or charismatic miracle workers, Honi (Onias) and Hanina ben Dosa, respectively, of the first century B.C.E. and a somewhat later contemporary of Jesus. Geza Vermes, *Jesus the Jew, op. cit.,* pp. 69-82.

50. If we may accept as a true report the statement in Mark 15:10 that Pilate knew the primary motive of the religious establishment of Israel for their opposition to Jesus to be envy, we can recognize such envy to be the resentment of religious professionals who were not able to do what a "nonprofessional" (from their point of view) could do. This understanding of Pilate, if true, constitutes further support of the facticity of Jesus' miracles.

51. Schulman, *Baba, op. cit.,* pp. 93-94, 167-168.

52. Cf. Alfred North Whitehead's perceptive words, "The reported sayings of Christ are not formularized thought. They are descriptions of direct insight." *Religion in the Making,* New York: Macmillan, 1926, pp. 56-57.

53. Cf. Henry Barclay Swete, *The Gospel According to St. Mark,* London: Macmillan, 1927, p. 35.

54. Lk. 5:1-11; Jn. 21:1-8 (in John the incident, while still associated with Peter, is transferred to a post-resurrection event). Cf. Mt. 4:18-22; Mk. 1:16-20.

55. Cf. Friedrich Rittelmeyer, *Rudolf Steiner Enters My Life,* London: Christian Community Press, 1963, pp. 42, 91-92; Guenther Wachsmuth, *The Life and Work of Rudolf Steiner,* New York: Whittier Books, 1955, pp. 340-341; Stewart C. Easton, *Rudolf Steiner: Herald of a New Epoch,* Spring Valley, NY: Anthroposophic Press, 1980, pp. 212-217.

56. Thomas Sugrue, *There Is a River,* New York: Dell Books, 1967, pp. 25, 120, 126, 129.

57. Charles Mortimer Carty, *Padre Pio: The Stigmatist,* St. Paul: Radio Replies Press, 1961, pp. 120-131, 56-82. Miracles of healing and of bilocation are also reported of Padre Pio.

58. Schulman, *op. cit.,* pp. 21, 66, 71-79, 105, 167-168. Like Padre Pio, Baba is also noted for his apparent experiences of bilocation, *ibid.,* pp. 23-25, 61. Like Edgar Cayce, he is capable of accurate medical diagnosis without formal medical examina-

tion; differently from Cayce, he is reported to have performed operations after having materialized the instruments, *ibid.*, pp. 50, 134-135. It may be in order to add that there are also reports of events in Baba's youth similar to the experience recorded of Jesus in the temple at the age of twelve (Lk. 2:41-51), *ibid.*, pp. 124, 130-131.

59. Ewert Cousins, tr., *Bonaventure,* New York: Paulist Press, 1978, p. 322, cf. pp. 180-181. The quotation is from Bonaventura's *The Life of St. Francis* XV, 2.

60. E. Allison Peers, *Mother of Carmel,* New York: Morehouse-Gorham, 1948, pp. 147-148. Comparable experiences are reported of Sathya Sai Baba, Schulman, *op. cit.,* pp. 96, 131.

61. *Eschatology* is a term which refers to consideration of the "last things," the terminus toward which Old Testament prophets came to see human history as moving, in conformity with the purposed end and design of the God of their faith. I do not use it here in the existentialist sense found in Rudolf Bultmann and his school. Apocalypse is a word taken from the Greek which means "revelation." It is used especially to denote literature which tells in cryptic language something of the mode and scope of the great end events. This literature is a relatively late development in the Old Testament period and flourished especially from the early second century B.C.E. into the first century C.E. Cf. John Bright, *The Kingdom of God,* New York: Abingdon, 1953, pp. 162-164; Donald C. Drummond, *The Bulletin of the Christian Research Institute of Meiji Gakuin University* X (March 1981), pp. 31-66. For an account of the shift away from the Germanic position, especially among North American scholars within the past two decades—British scholars have always held to a more mediating position—see Marcus J. Borg, *Jesus, a New Vision, op. cit.,* pp. 8-21. See also Borg's *Conflict, Holiness and Politics in the Teachings of Jesus,* New York: The Edwin Mellen Press, 1984, pp. 201-227.

62. Paul D. Hanson contends—rightly, I believe—that the visionary dimension of religious experience commonly regarded as characteristic of Jewish apocalyptic can be traced back to the earliest periods of Israel's history as an integral part of the roles of her prophetic figures. Hanson thus sees the classic Hebrew prophets as "the ones who forged the visionary and realistic [i.e.,

attempting to translate vision into the political, social, economic realities of the time] aspects of the religious experience into one tension-filled whole, allowing Yahwism to develop into an ethical religion in many ways unique in the ancient world." *The Dawn of Apocalyptic,* rev. ed., Philadelphia: Fortress Press, 1979, pp. 1-31.

63. Gustav Dalman states that the Hebrew term for kingdom (*malkuth*), when used with reference to God, consistently meant throughout the Old Testament and in later Jewish literature God's kingly rule, the sovereignty of God, as distinguished from geographical territory ruled (cf. I Sam. 12:12; Ps. 103:19; 145:13), *The Words of Jesus,* Edinburgh: T. & T. Clark, 1909, pp. 92-94. Gerhard von Rad has shown that the concept of linear time in any absolute sense is foreign to the Old Testament. The eschatological expectations of the prophets envisage divine saving activity in the future that will be more or less analogous to that of the past. They do not appear to be concerned with the end of time or of history in the modern sense of the term but, differently from the earlier perspectives of Israel, see the future divine activity as decisive for the future of Israel *and* of all humankind, even for the "fixed orders of creation." *Old Testament Theology,* II, New York: Harper & Row, 1965, pp. 99-125. Cf. Zech. 14:9. An ethically less sensitive expression of this expectation is seen in the Jewish work, probably written in the first half century of our era, *The Testament of Moses* 10:1-10.

64. Cf. John Bright, *A History of Israel, op. cit.,* pp. 433-434. James H. Charlesworth contends that "Jewish messianology"— especially when bearing apocalyptic expectations—became a significant part of Jewish religious and ideological activity only in the early first century B.C.E. "and not before." He also contends that there was no "coherent and normative messianology" prevalent among Palestinian Jews from that time through the following three centuries. This conclusion leads him further to say that certainly not all, and perhaps most, Jews during this period were not looking for the coming of the Messiah. "From Messianology to Christology: Problems and Prospects," *The Messiah,* James H. Charlesworth, ed., Minneapolis: Augsburg Fortress, 1992, pp. 3-35. Charlesworth appears somewhat tendentious in his argu-

mentation, but his primary caution seems valid; i.e., we should not presume too facilely the presence of unified messianic expectations in the Jewish population of Palestine.

65. Cf. Bright, *The Kingdom of God, op. cit.,* pp. 168-170. It may be appropriate to mention at this point that in the apparently authentic teaching of Zoroaster (Zarathustra—ca. 628-551 B.C.E.) we find no absolute dualism but Ahura Mazdah, the "Wise Lord," as the One True God and supreme above all. This faith-understanding, however, was significantly altered in the Zoroastrianism of the second great Persian (Sassanian) Empire. Cf. R. C. Zaehner "Zoroastrianism," *The Concise Encyclopedia of Living Faiths,* New York: Hawthorn Books, 1959, pp. 209-210.

66. Ernst Käsemann, "The Eschatological Royal Reign of God," *Your Kingdom Come, op. cit.,* pp. 65-66.

67. The New Testament also uses the term *metanoia* in the sense of return to a right relationship with God, as in Acts 20:21. Edward Schillebeeckx has shown that Jesus' ministry, as John the Baptist's, was in the tradition of a series of *metanoia* or revivalist, Chasidic movements in Israel that may be traced back to the destruction of the First Temple (587 B.C.E.). And it came to be a part of the consciousness of these movements especially from the Maccabean period to transcend exclusive ethnocentric understandings of the Abrahamic covenant (cf. Mt. 3:7-10; Lk. 3:7-9; 4:16-30; Acts 10). *Jesus,* New York: Seabury Press, 1979, pp. 116-139. Cf. Donald C. Drummond, "Theological Comments on the Colossian Hymn (Col. 1:15-20)," *The Bulletin of the Christian Research Institute of Meiji Gakuin University* XV (March 1982), pp. 31-33.

68. Gustav Dalman states that it is not entirely certain that Jesus himself coupled his proclamation of the Kingdom of God with any form of the word *gospel, op. cit.,* pp. 102-106. But it is clear that the early Christian communities universally made the association, which practice was in fact, if not in word, owed to Jesus.

69. If we would be faithful to the New Testament witness, it is better not to say reconciliation with Yahweh as something "first" and then reconciliation with our fellow human beings as a temporally later event. There is, of course, a theological priority

to be assigned to the love—and the forgiveness—of God. No one can merit the love of God—in a sense we cannot merit the love of one another. There is always a mysterious spontaneity, freedom, generosity, involved in love. Yet, we egregiously distort the teaching of Jesus if we turn this theological priority into a temporal priority. Jesus' teaching of the Lord's Prayer in Matthew, with its emphasis by repetition of this key point, makes quite clear that while forgiveness of others may not be a formal condition of God's forgiveness of us, it is certainly a concomitant necessity, for without our forgiving others God's forgiveness of us does not work within us (Mt. 6:14-15). For a singularly perceptive and balanced treatment of this and concomitant issues regarding the Kingdom of God in both the Old and New Testaments see Patrick D'Souza, "Church and Mission in Relation to the Kingdom of God Especially in a Third World Context," *Toward a New Age in Mission,* II, Manila: Ateneo de Manila University, 1981, pp. 25-53.

70. Dale Patrick, "The Kingdom of God in the Old Testament," *The Kingdom of God in 20th-Century Interpretation,* Peabody, MA: Hendrickson Publishers, 1987, p. 70. In this same volume an article by Karl Paul Donfried stresses the presence in the Pauline literature (including Acts) of an understanding of the Kingdom of God (or of his Christ) as bearing both present and future aspects. "The Kingdom of God in Paul," *ibid.,* pp. 175-190.

71. Cf. John Dominic Crossan, *The Historical Jesus, the Life of a Mediterranean Peasant,* San Francisco: Harper Collins, 1991, pp. xii, 265-302.

72. The term *Kingdom of God* is found in Jewish prayers of the first century B.C.E., as in the Targums (Aramaic translations of the Hebrew text of the Bible). We noted the term in the Psalms of Solomon (17:3), which was written about 50 B.C.E. In this work the Kingdom of God is none other than the Kingdom of Wisdom, which is eternally present and available to anyone who heeds her call (cf. Crossan, *The Historical Jesus, op. cit.,* p. 290). Possibly of this period, or at the latest in the first century C.E., is the Jewish prayer, "May He establish His Kingdom during your life and during your days." It is clear from various materials that according to Jewish usage at the time of Jesus, the Kingdom of God was understood as a reality that in some mode could be "accepted" in

the present and its blessings enjoyed in the end "by those who have fulfilled the necessary conditions." C. H. Dodd, *The Parables of the Kingdom*, New York: Charles Scribner's Sons, 1961, pp. 21-35. Cf. Ps. 145:8-19; Wolfhart Pannenberg, *Theology and the Kingdom of God*, Philadelphia: Westminster, 1969, pp. 53-64.

73. Cf. John Wick Bowman, *The Intention of Jesus*, Philadelphia: Westminster, 1943, pp. 43-77; Norman Perrin, *The Kingdom of God in the Teaching of Jesus*, London: SCM Press, 1963, pp. 158-206. George Eldon Ladd contends that in the case of both Jesus and the Old Testament prophets the historical and the eschatological are mingled and the final eschatological event is seen through the "transparency" of contemporary history. *A Theology of the New Testament*, Grand Rapids, MI: Eerdmans, 1983, p. 198. Cf. Seiichi Yagi, *Pauro, Shinran, Iesu, Zen*, Kyoto: Hōzōkan, 1983, pp. 187-228; Marcus J. Borg, *Jesus, a New Vision, op. cit.*, pp. 8-21.

74. Cf. Norman Perrin, *Jesus and the Language of the Kingdom*, Philadelphia: Fortress Press, 1976, pp. 32-60; Joachim Jeremias, *New Testament Theology: Part I, The Proclamation of Jesus*, New York: Charles Scribner's Sons, 1971, pp. 100-102. Jeremias, however, still understood even *ephthasen* (Lk. 11:20; Mt. 12:28) as indicative of an eschatological future event, although he interpreted the term as meaning God "is already there."

75. I would contend that there is no reason to alter the plain meaning of the Greek of Lk. 17:21, which is that "the Kingdom of God is within you" (*entos hymon*—when the expression "in your midst" is desired in Greek, other phrases are used, as in Jn. 1:26; 14:25). As Charles Talbert has put it, "In Luke-Acts the presence of the Spirit is the 'already' of the kingdom" (*Reading Luke, op. cit.*, pp. 131, 134). It is now held by a number of scholars that some sections of the extracanonical *Gospel According to Thomas* may be dated back to the period 50-100 C.E. Here we find the affirmation that "the Kingdom is within you and it is without you" (Logion 25), that "the Kingdom of the Father is spread upon the earth and men do not see it" (117). As Elaine Pagels has put it, "In the gospel of *Thomas*, the Kingdom symbolizes a transformation in spiritual consciousness: it has become an interior reality." See Pagels, "The Orthodox Against the Gnostics: Confrontation and

Interiority in Early Christianity," *The Other Side of God*, Peter L. Berger, ed., Garden City, New York: Doubleday, 1981, pp. 61-73. With regard to the issue of "orthodox" Christianity being considered primarily representative of a "confrontation" type of religious posture over against one of "interiority" (this latter presumably characteristic of Hindu and Buddhist as well as Jewish and Christian Gnostic traditions), I would forthrightly assert that both Jesus and apostolic Christianity combined the two types. I further believe that the entire history of spirituality as of renewal in the Christian church is rooted in varying combinations of the two types. An article by Stevan Davies has given additional weight to the significance of the passages in the gospel of Thomas. Davies sees the key point of this gospel to be the identification of the Wisdom of God, as in the later pre-Christian Jewish tradition, with the Kingdom of God, an identification which may have characterized Jesus' own teaching. And central to both is the understanding that the reality concerned is present here and now, to be sought and found. "Thomas—The Fourth Synoptic Gospel," *Biblical Archaeologist* XLVI, 1(Winter 1983), pp. 6-14. We note a similar position taken by Origen, *De Oratione* XXV, 1-3. Frithjof Schuon writes of Jesus' "insistence upon inwardness" and of the "inwardness" of his message. *Survey of Metaphysics and Esoterism*, Bloomington, IN: World Wisdom Books, 1986, pp. 96, 107. See also Marcus J. Borg, *Meeting Jesus Again for the First Time, op. cit.*, pp. 29, 86-87; Marcus J. Borg, *Jesus in Contemporary Scholarship*, Valley Forge, Pa.: Trinity Press International, 1994, pp. 150-155.

76. Günther Bornkamm, *Jesus of Nazareth, op. cit.*, pp. 69-75.

77. See Raymond E. Brown, *The Gospel According to John* (I-XII), I, 2nd ed., Garden City, NY: Doubleday, 1983, pp. cxv-cxxi. All the synoptic gospels record that Jesus himself dissociated the person of the Messiah from Davidic physical descent and by implication from a political-military rule like David's (Mk. 12:35-37; Mt. 22:41-46; Lk. 20:41-44). The genealogies, however, in both Matthew and Luke indicate that at least some early Christians held Jesus to have been of Davidic descent (Mt. 1:6; Lk. 3:31). So do Rom. 1:3; II Tim. 2:8; Rev. 22:16; cf. Jn. 7:41-42.

78. Cf. Charles E. Carlston, *The Parables of the Triple Tradition*, Philadelphia: Fortress Press, 1978, pp. 162-167, n.b. ftn. 10, p. 163. Carl Gustav Jung noted that modern rationalism likes to make the "within" subsidiary to the "outer." "Psychological Aspects of the Mother Archetype," *Collected Works of C. G. Jung*, IX, New York: Bollingen, 1959, p. 101.

79. Cf. Mt. 5:21-22, 27-28, 44; 6:14-15, 22-23; 12:34; 15:8, 18-20; 18:35; 22:37-40; 25:13 (and parallel passages in the other gospels). See also I Cor. 13; 14:20; 16:13-14; II Cor. 11:3; Gal. 5:19-24; 6:7-9; Phil. 2:5; 4:8; Col. 3:14-15; Jas. 3:17; 4:8; I Pet. 1:13, 22; 2:1; 3:4; 5:8; I Jn. 2:9-10; 4:7-12; II Jn. 5-6; Rev. 2:4, 23; 16:15.

80. The entire volume of *Your Kingdom Come (op. cit.)*, the Report on the World Conference on Mission and Evangelism held at Melbourne, Australia, May 12-25, 1980, under the auspices of the Commission on World Mission and Evangelism of the WCC, is an example of this mentality. Stephen Neill, in his *Colonialism and Christian Missions*, New York: McGraw-Hill, 1966, has shown that the ethical practices of the older evangelicalism as well as of Roman Catholics form a more complex pattern than has in more recent years been thought.

81. Cf. C. G. Jung, "The Personal and the Collective Unconscious," *The Basic Writings of C. G. Jung*, Violet S. de Laszlo, ed., New York: Random House, 1959, pp. 107-118, also pp. 119-143. Cf. Reinhold Niebuhr, *The Nature and Destiny of Man*, II, New York: Charles Scribner's Sons, 1949, pp. 184-212.

82. Cf. W. O. E. Oesterley, *The Gospel Parables in the Light of Their Jewish Background*, New York: Macmillan, 1936, pp. 57-72. I feel the augumentation of Bernard Brandon Scott on this issue to be quite strained, *Hear Then the Parable*, Minneapolis: Augsburg Fortress Press, 1989, pp. 321-329.

83. Cf. Carlston, *op. cit.*, pp. 40-45. We may also take note of the imagery in pre-Christian Wisdom literature of personified divine Wisdom taking the initiative to seek and cry out to persons (Prov. 1:20-21; 8:1-4; Wis. 6:16).

84. Cf. Ralph Waldo Emerson, "Compensation," *Essays and English Traits*, Harvard Classics V, New York: Collier & Son, 1909, pp. 89-107. In this context we may aptly recall the pregnant phrase of G. B. Caird that Jesus had a "mighty vein of granite in

his character," *Saint Luke*, Harmondsworth, England: Penguin Books, 1973, p. 126.

85. The Lucan variations of this material have been denoted as the Sermon on the Plain (Lk. 6:17-49). Cf. John Wick Bowman & Roland W. Tapp, *The Gospel from the Mount*, Philadelphia: Westminster, 1957, pp. 22-25, 143-150.

86. We find in the Matthean version of Jesus' parable of the marriage feast sharply personalized language used of the working of the process, which the teaching of Jesus as recorded in the synoptic gospels as a whole suggests is a completely just working of cause and effect, each appropriate to the other. Matthew cites Jesus as saying that "the king [God] was enraged. He sent his troops, destroyed those murderers and burned their city" (Mt. 22: 1-14). Luke's account, however, shows notable differences from Matthew's more allegorical format. In Luke the "owner of the house" is angry at the rejections of his invitation, but is far less graphic in his identification of consequences (Lk. 14:15-24). It is worthy of note, on the other hand, that Matthew uses the parable to make the point of an original total inclusiveness of divine calling which, however, must be followed by appropriate ethical response. "For many are called, but few are chosen" (elect—*eklektoi*). The point is that all are called, but they must then work to become worthy of their calling (Mt. 22:10-14). Cf. Günther Bornkamm, *Jesus of Nazareth, op. cit.*, pp. 18-19, who notes that in the Lucan account the slave of the master is sent to those in the town and then to those *outside* the town. In a wondrously inclusive way he is to bring in even "the poor, the crippled, the blind, and the lame."

87. Cf. Edersheim, *op. cit.*, II, pp. 221-223; Leon Morris, *The Gospel According to St. Luke*, Grand Rapids, MI: Wm. B. Eerdmans, 1975, pp. 221-222. It is highly significant that in this Lucan collection of warnings of the consequences of ethical activity-being, Jesus is recorded as affirming the principle of proportionate judgment in the sense both of degrees of punishment and of a "time limit" to punishment (Lk. 12:47-48, 59; cf. Mt. 5:26, 16:15; 18:34; I Cor. 3:10-15; I Pet. 3:18-20). Joseph A. Fitzmeyer, however, reminds us that in Luke, in discussion of the theme of reception and rejection in the Kingdom, the "narrow door" of vs.

13:24 becomes what he translates as a "locked door" in 13:25. But the NRSV translation "shut the door" is probably preferable, inasmuch as communication continues between the parties. There is no mention in the text of reopening the door for the conversation to be heard, but the term "lock" seems out of keeping with the Gospel of Luke. *The Gospel According to Luke X-XXIV,* New York: Doubleday, 1985, pp. 1020-1023.

88. Mt. 7:2; 10:26; 16:27; Lk. 12:47-48; Jn. 5:14; 8:34; Acts 24:25; Rom. 2:6; II Cor. 5:10; 9:6, 10; 11:15; Gal. 5:15; 6:7-10; Eph. 6:8; Col. 3:25; II Thess. 1:6; Heb. 2:2; Jas. 1:13; 3:16; 5:4; I Pet. 1:17; 3:12; II Pet. 2:13, 16; Rev. 2:23; 14:8, 13; 18:6; 20:12-13; 22:12. In the Old Testament the principle of compensatory ethical judgment, of sowing and reaping, lies at the basis of the entire prophetic tradition. It is expressed in particularly graphic form in Deuteronomy 27-28, is found throughout the book of Proverbs, and expressed or implied in every prophetic book.

89. Cf. George A. Buttrick, *The Parables of Jesus,* New York: Harper, 1928, pp. 240-250; cf. Buttrick, *God, Pain and Evil,* Nashville, TN: Abingdon, 1966, pp. 56-83; John B. Cobb, Jr., "Process Theology and an Ecological Model," *Pacific Theological Review* XV, 2 (Winter 1982), pp. 24-29; Paul Tillich, *The Shaking of the Foundations,* Harmondsworth, England: Penguin Books, 1969, pp. 109-112.

90. It should be noted that a few Jewish thinkers had brought these two separate verses of the Torah together into one religious focus well before the time of Jesus. Such is clearly the case in *The Testaments of the Twelve Patriarchs,* which was probably composed in the reign of John Hyrcanus (135-104 B.C.E.)—Issachar 5:2; Dan. 5:3; Benjamin 3:3. Less clear are the references in *The Book of Jubilees,* 20:7, 10; 36:4-6, composed about the same time. Philo, whom we have noted as approximately a contemporary of Jesus (ca. 20 B.C.E.-50 C.E.), specifically identifies the "two main heads" *(kephalaia)* of Jewish faith to be the duty of piety and holiness toward God and the duty of love *(philanthropia)* and justice *(dikaiosynē)* toward human beings (*The Special Laws* II, 63). Cf. Leonard Swidler, "The Jewishness of Jesus, Some Religious Obligations for Christians," *Journal of Ecumenical Studies* XVIII, 1 (Winter 1981), pp. 104-113.

91. The language of George A. Buttrick on this theme is, I believe, singularly beautiful as well as perceptive. "If we insert two adjectives, the saying is clear: 'Whosoever will save his [lower] life shall lose his [higher] life.' There seem to be a thousand roads to travel. Actually there are but two: for when we say a man is kind, we imply that he could have been cruel; and when we say of Lincoln that 'he belongs to the ages,' we infer that he could have lived for the moment . . . But we must clearly understand that a cross is no self-mutilation. The higher self cannot live unless the lower self is nailed down to die. The Cross is the plucking off of poor buds that one fine bud may come to flower; it is the pruning of the tree that there may be an abundant harvest." *The Interpreter's Bible*, VII, New York: Abingdon-Cokesbury, 1951, p. 455.

92. See Sherman E. Johnson, "The Gospel According to Matthew," *The Interpreter's Bible*, VII, *op. cit.*, p. 452. Cf. Günther Bornkamm, "End-Expectation and Church in Matthew," *Tradition and Interpretation in Matthew*, Bornkamm, Barth, & Held, Philadelphia: Westminster, 1963, pp. 38-51, 270-271; Paul S. Minear, *Images of the Church in the New Testament*, Philadelphia: Westminster, 1975, pp. 221-267.

93. The witness of Edgar Cayce on this theme is, "The period of resurrection—here we find that in which ye *all* may glory. For without the fact of His overcoming death, the whole of the experience would have been as naught" (5749-10). Cf. Richard H. Drummond, *Unto the Churches, op. cit.*, pp. 173-180.

94. Cf. Charles E. Carlston, *The Parables of the Triple Tradition, op. cit.*, pp. 178-190.

95. Stevan L. Davies, *The Gospel of Thomas and Christian Wisdom*, New York: Seabury, 1983, pp. 5-6, 14-17.

96. Cf. David Hill, *The Gospel of Matthew*, London: Oliphants, 1972, pp. 219-221; Pierre Bonnard, *L'Evangile selon Saint Matthieu*, Neuchatel: Delachaux & Niestlé, 1970, pp. 183-184. R.T. France, *Matthew, Evangelist and Teacher*, Grand Rapids, MI: Zondervan Publishing House, 1989, p. 137.

97. Cf. Sherman E. Johnson, *The Interpreter's Bible*, VII, *op. cit.*, pp. 387-390; Michael Grant, *Jesus, an Historian's Review of the Gospels, op. cit.*, p. 82.

98. Cf. David Hill, *The Gospel of Matthew, op. cit.,* pp. 204-209; Wolfgang Trilling, *Das Evangelium Matthäus* I, Düsseldorf: Patmos-Verlag, 1965, pp. 252-259.

99. The language of these Maccabean passages is surprisingly specific. As a part of the persecutions initiated by Antiochus IV Epiphanes (175-163 B.C.E.), the youngest of seven sons to be killed is recorded as saying before the king and his own mother that he, like his brothers, was giving up "body and life [soul]" for the laws of his forefathers. He went on to pray that God would speedily show mercy to his people and that through himself and his brothers *(en moi de kai tois adelphois)* God would stay his wrath which had justly fallen on their whole nation (II Macc. 7:37-38). In IV Maccabees 6:27-29 we find prayer that the blood of the martyr may be a purifying sacrifice *(katharsion)* and punishment *(dikē)* on behalf of all the people, that his soul be a compensation for them *(antipsychon auton).* In a later passage the affirmation is made that "the divine providence delivered Israel from her various mistreatments through the blood of those devout persons and the expiating effect of their death" *(tou hilasteriou tou thanatou auton,* IV Macc. 17:22); II Maccabees was written after 125 B.C.E., but before the beginning of Roman rule in 63 B.C.E.; IV Maccabees, however, was evidently written sometime between 18 and 37 C.E., probably by a Jew of the Diaspora.

100. C.K. Barrett, "The Background of Mark 10:45," *New Testament Essays,* Manchester: University of Manchester Press, 1959, pp. 1-18. Barrett does not specifically identify the "creative mind" here with Jesus himself, but he evidently expects his readers to consider the identification as at least a lively possibility.

101. W.J. Moulder, "The Old Testament Background and the Interpretation of Mark X, 45," *New Testament Studies,* XXIV, 1 (October 1977), pp. 120-127.

102. Karl Kertelge, "Der dienende Menschensohn (Mk. 10:45)," *Jesus und der Menschensohn,* R. Pesch, R. Schnackenburg, & O. Kaiser, eds., Freiburg: Herder, 1975, pp. 225-239.

103. Martin Hengel, *The Atonement,* Philadelphia: Fortress Press, 1981, pp. 1-22. It is worthy of note that concepts of the afterlife (Hades, Sheol) which occur in Homer and in the earliest strata of the Old Testament participate in a comparable develop-

ment-change in sophistication of understanding over subsequent centuries. With reference to early Christian appreciation of Gentile self-sacrifice, see I Clement 55, 1.

104. Plutarch, *Pelopidas* XX, 3-XXII, 2.

105. E.g., Jürgen Roloff, "Anfänge der soteriologischen Deutung des Todes Jesu (Mk. X, 45 und Lk. XXII, 27)," *New Testament Studies*, XIX, 1(October 1972), pp. 38-64. Roloff discusses Mk. 10:45 in connection with Lk. 22:27 and sets forth the double thesis that the soteriological understanding of the death of Jesus developed in the early Palestinian Jewish Christian community in intimate association with the Eucharistic meal and that the atoning significance of Jesus' death was perceived as also implicit in Jesus' service of others, especially "sinners" and "the lost," throughout his earthly ministry. Roloff, however, feels that it is hardly to be questioned *(dürfte kaum fraglich sein)* that a soteriological interpretation of Jesus' death goes back to the earthly Jesus himself. He believes also that there is no reason to question that Mk. 10:45 was formulated in free reference *(in freier Anlehnung)* to Isa. 53:10 ff. Peter Stuhlmacher commits himself without reservation to the conclusion that the earthly Jesus himself understood his life, suffering, and death as that of the messianic atoning agent of God witnessed to *"eindringlich und verheissungsvoll"* in Deutero-Isaiah. "Existenzstellvertretung für die Vielen: Mk. 10:45 (Mt. 20:28)," *Werden und Wirken des Alten Testaments*, Festschrift für Claus Westermann zum 70. Geburtstag, Göttingen: Vandenhoeck & Ruprecht, 1980, pp. 412-427. It is appropriate to cite the insistence of the Jewish Christian Jakób Jocz (1906-1983) that a central element in the worship of historic Israel—represented by the temple, as well as by earlier practices—were the sacrifices offered for expiation of the sins of the people. Arthur F. Glasser, "The Legacy of Jakób Jocz," *International Bulletin of Missionary Research*, Vol. 17, No. 2 (April 1993), pp. 66-71.

106. The textual evidence for comparable language in Luke 22:19 is somewhat ambiguous, but the statement "This is my body which is being given for you (plural)" may be the best reading. Cf. Kurt Aland *et al.*, *The Greek New Testament*, 3rd ed., Stuttgart: United Bible Societies, 1975, pp. 302-303.

107. Edward Schillebeeckx cites three strands apparent in the New Testament understanding of the suffering and death of Jesus. These are that Jesus died the death of a prophetic martyr, that Jesus' death forms an integral element in the larger compass of the divine plan and work of salvation, and that his death has "a saving efficacy" under God in a somewhat more distinctive way. There is, of course, a sense in which the Gospel of Mark belongs to the third category and that of Luke to the second, but the apparently universal liturgical practice of the Eucharist in the early Christian community together with its liturgical formula of the redemptive, atoning significance of Jesus' death constitute weighty evidence for such understanding, even with some variations, being almost universal in the church of the first generation. The textual evidence for accepting all or almost all of Luke 22:19-20 is very strong. Cf. Schillebeeckx, *Jesus*, New York: Seabury, 1979, pp. 272-319.

108. It is significant for Paul's understanding of the gospel and of the nature of the salvation which he believed God through Jesus Christ conveys that we note precisely his use of language in I Corinthians 15:1-2. Paul writes of "the good news that I proclaimed to you, which you in turn received, in which also you stand, through which also you are being saved, if you hold firmly to the message that I proclaimed to you—unless you have come to believe in vain" (NRSV). The phrase "you are being saved" in the Greek is in the present continuative tense (*sodsesthe*) and means an ongoing process.

109. Cf. Martin Hengel, *The Atonement, op. cit.*, pp. 33-39; Helmut Koester, *History and Literature of Early Christianity,* Philadelphia: Fortress Press, 1982, pp. 88-89.

110. We may note that Paul also uses language which denotes "all who are led by the Spirit of God" as sons of God. In the same passage he goes on to denote such as children *(tekna)* of God and then "joint heirs *(synkleronomoi)* with Christ," language which seems to suggest that those who are obedient to the Spirit of God are younger brothers and sisters of the Elder Brother (Rom. 8:14-17). Significantly indicative of the principle of continuum are also Paul's exhortations to believers that they should imitate him and the Lord, even as they have already imitated the churches of

Judea (I Thess. 1:6, 2:14). Paul, of course, saw the Lord Jesus as the prime example both for himself and for all (Phil. 2:5-11; cf. I Tim. 1:16).

111.   David A. Kerr has written that in the case of Paul and indeed of other apostles, ancient or modern, "The readiness thus to suffer is, alone, that which liberates the apostles from the restrictive nature of culture, to become a witness by participation in the truth of the message of *'God* in Christ reconciling the world to himself.'" "The Problem of Christianity in Muslim Perspective: Implications for Christian Mission," *International Bulletin of Missionary Research,* V, 4 (October 1981), pp. 160-161. Kerr draws upon the earlier perceptions of Kosuke Koyama, who emphasized the necessary missionary quality of being "nurtured in his life-participation in the apostolic existence of reviled-bless, persecuted-endure, slandered-conciliate" (cf. I Cor. 4:9-13). "What Makes a Missionary," *Mission Trends No. 1,* Gerald H. Anderson & Thomas F. Stransky, eds., New York: Paulist Press, 1974, p. 129. Origen affirms that "the powers of evil do suffer defeat by the death of the holy martyrs." He speaks of how many receive benefit therefrom "by an influence we cannot describe." *Commentarius in Johannem* VI, 36.

112.   It is significant that various contemporary African theologians are making much of the theme of "sharing in the redeeming work of Christ." See Burgess Carr, "The Relation of Union to Mission," *Mission Trends No. 3, Third World Theologies,* Gerald H. Anderson & Thomas F. Stransky, eds., New York: Paulist Press, 1975, p. 168. Cf. Kenneth D. Kaunda, "The Challenge of Our Stewardship in Africa," *ibid.,* pp. 172-173; Manas Buthelezi, "Daring to Live for Christ," *ibid.,* pp. 176-179, 180. Significant examples of substitutionary and highly effective curative suffering for others are found also outside the Judeo-Christian tradition. See Howard Murphet, *Sai Baba, Man of Miracles, op. cit.,* pp. 127-130, 138-140; Paramahansa Yogananda, *Autobiography of a Yogi,* Los Angeles: Self-Realization Fellowship, 1959, pp. 208-212. For a careful analysis of the material in Luke-Acts, see Charles H. Talbert, *Reading Luke, op. cit.,* pp. 206-225. Talbert in general would restrict Luke's intent to a rather narrow interpretation of the term "martyrdom," but even though there is no explicit association in

Luke-Acts between the forgiveness of sins and Jesus' death on the cross, Talbert himself affirms that somehow the latter event "would have beneficial effects" for others (*ibid.*, p. 209). Cf. Eduard Schweizer, *Luke, a Challenge to Present Theology*, Atlanta: John Knox Press, 1982, pp. 53-55, 77, 86; *The Good News According to Luke*, Atlanta: John Knox Press, 1984, pp. 338-340. It is possible that with the term "the new covenant" (Lk. 22:20), Jesus is applying the language of the prophet Jeremiah (31:31-34; 32:40), with its rich intimations of depth of personal relationship with Yahweh, to his own ministry of suffering for others. Noteworthy also is the fact that the Qumran community thought of themselves as the people of the new covenant, as did the Christian community (I Cor. 11:25; II Cor. 3:6; Heb. 8:6-13; 10:15-17). Cf. William L. Holladay, *Jeremiah, a Fresh Reading*, New York: Pilgrim Press, 1990, pp. 128-132.

113. Richard H. Drummond, *Toward a New Age in Christian Theology*, Maryknoll, New York: Orbis Books, 1985, pp. 25-26.

114. Cf. Richard C. Martin, *Islam, a Cultural Perspective*, Englewood Cliffs, NJ: Prentice-Hall, 1982, pp. 12-14; Frithjof Schuon, *Understanding Islam*, Baltimore, MD: Penguin Books, 1972, pp. 157-159.

115. Hermann Beckh, *From Buddha to Christ*, Edinburgh: Floris Books, 1977, pp. 8, 16-18.

116. *Ibid.*, pp. 13-14, 19-25, 29-35. Cf. Rudolf Steiner, *From Buddha to Christ*, Spring Valley, NY: Anthroposophic Press, 1978, pp. 15-22, 34-45, 61-93.

117. Rudolf Steiner, *An Autobiography*, Blauvelt, New York: Rudolf Steiner Publications, 1977, pp. 28-29, 53-70, 151-154. Cf. A.P. Shepherd, *A Scientist of the Invisible*, London: Hodder & Stoughton, 1975, pp. 29-48.

118. Johannes Steiner, *Therese Neumann, op. cit.*, pp. 27, 51-62; 158-182. Therese is noted also for her being able to subsist without nourishment, without either food or water, except for a daily communion wafer, and remain in good health from 1927 until her death in 1962. Cf. Anne Catherine Emmerich, *The Dolorous Passion of Our Lord Jesus Christ, op. cit.*, pp. vi-vii.

119. Cf. Richard H. Drummond, *Unto the Churches, op. cit.*, pp. 79-205; "Edgar Cayce: Christian Mystic and Bible Expositor,"

op. cit., pp. 146-163. All the persons cited in the paragraphs just above in our text may properly be designated as "spirit persons" in the sense of that term as used by Marcus J. Borg, *Meeting Jesus Again for the First Time*, *op. cit.*, pp. 31-39.

120. Albert Schweitzer, *The Quest of the Historical Jesus*, New York: Macmillan, 1959, p. 403. Schweitzer's words, the last paragraph of his book, have become memorable: "He comes to us as One unknown, without a name, as of old, by the lake-side. He came to those men who knew Him not. He speaks to us the same word: 'Follow thou me!' and sets us to the tasks which He has to fulfill for our time. He commands. And to those who obey Him, whether they be wise or simple, He will reveal Himself in the toils, the conflicts, the sufferings which they shall pass through in His fellowship, and, as an ineffable mystery, they shall learn in their own experience Who He is."

121. Cf. Huston Smith, *Forgotten Truth, the Primordial Tradition*, New York: Harper & Row, 1977; *Beyond the Post-Modern Mind*, New York: Crossroad, 1982; Jacob Needleman, *A Sense of the Cosmos*, Garden City, NY: Doubleday, 1975; Frithjof Schuon, *The Transcendent Unity of Religions*, New York: Harper & Row, 1975; Marco Pallis, *A Buddhist Spectrum*, New York: Seabury, 1981.

122. Cf. Karl Rahner, *Foundations of Christian Faith*, New York: Seabury, 1978, pp. 250-255. If readers wish to find a specific term to identify the particular christological position which I myself take in this book, may I suggest one from the spectrum of views given by J. Peter Schineller, viz., "Christocentric Universe, Inclusive Christology." "Christ and Church: A Spectrum of Views," *Theological Studies*, XXXVII, 4 (December 1976), pp. 552-555.

123. Leon Morris, *The Gospel According to St. Luke*, Grand Rapids, MI: Wm. B. Eerdmans, 1975, pp. 37-38.

124. We may properly note that the conclusion of Jesus' parable of the workers in a vineyard who worked different lengths of time but were all paid the same is affirmation of God's desire to be more generous than the religious tradition normally expected or thought proper (Mt. 20:1-16). A brilliant treatment of this theme of the utter generosity and open-endedness of God's love in the teaching and practice of Jesus, seen in the context of com-

parison with insights from Zen Buddhism, is the article by Silvio E. Fittipaldi, "Zen-Mind, Christian-Mind, Empty-Mind," *Journal of Ecumenical Studies* XIX, 1 (Winter 1982), pp. 69-84. Cf. Marcus A. Borg, *Jesus, a New Vision, op. cit.*, pp. 100-103.

Part III

1. Rudolf Steiner, *From Buddha to Christ*, Spring Valley, NY: Anthroposophic Press, 1978, pp. 62-71, 83-84, 92-100. Cf. Rudolf Steiner, *The Gospel of St. Luke*, London: Rudolf Steiner Press, 1975, pp. 37-75. Hans Küng, Josef van Ess, Heinrich von Stietencron, Heinz Bechert, *Christianity and the World Religions*, Garden City, NY: Doubleday, 1986, pp. 440-443. A critique of Küng's alleged ecclesiastical presumption, especially as he develops these points in a later book (*Global Responsibility*, London: SCM Press, 1991), is offered by a Western freelance journalist working in Hong Kong, Liam Fitzpatrick, "Book Review," *Inter-Religio*, No. 21(Summer 1992), pp. 38-42.

2. James George Frazer, *The Golden Bough*, abr. ed., New York: Macmillan, 1939, pp. 691-701.

3. For Paul's emphasis that transformation involves process—time, patience, and effort—see Rom. 8:18-27; I Cor. 1:18; II Cor. 3:18; 4:16; Phil. 3:10-16; Col. 3:10. A contemporary German Roman Catholic scholar writes of what he calls "transformation of identity" as a "mystical spiritual process," as "an ever-new orientation and openness toward the divine spirit," Eckard Wolz-Gottwald, "Mysticism and Ecumenism: On the Question of Religious Identity in the Religious Dialogue," *Journal of Ecumenical Studies*, Vol. 32, No. 1(Winter 1995), pp. 30-34.

4. Cf. E.A. Burtt, *The Teachings of the Compassionate Buddha*, New York: New American Library, 1960, pp. 207-212; Karl Ludwig Reichelt, *Truth and Tradition in Chinese Buddhism*, Shanghai: The Commercial Press, 1927; B.H. Streeter & A.J. Appasamy, *The Message of Sadhu Sundar Singh: A Study in Mysticism on Practical Religion*, New York: Macmillan, 1921, pp. 86-123.

5. *Vinaya-Piṭaka, Mahāvagga* I, 11,11.

6. *Anguttara-Nikāya* IV, 279-287; cf. *ibid.*, II, 63-67; III, 44-

47. See Hajime Nakamura, *Shūkyō to Shakai Rinri,* Tokyo: Iwanami Shoten, 1967, pp. 81-85.

7. *Vinaya-Piṭaka, Mahāvagga* I, 46-47.

8. *Thera-gāthā* 620-631. Cf. the account of the ordination of the cowherd Nanda in *Sanyutta-Nikāya* IV, 181. See also the early *Sutta-Nipāta* 136.

9. *Dīgha-Nikāya* XVI, 6, 2.

10. In the story of Visakha in Buddhaghosa's commentary on *Dhammapada* 53, the statement is made that Indian maidens are commonly considered but "goods for sale." Henry Clarke Warren, *Buddhism in Translations,* New York: Atheneum, 1963, pp. 456-457.

11. *Dīgha-Nikāya* II, 141. Cf. *Anguttara-Nikāya* I, 1; I, 27; I, 77; II, 80.

12. Cf. Yutaka Iwamoto, *Bukkyō Nyūmon,* Tokyo: Chūō-kōronsha, 1964, pp. 104-113.

13. *Dīgha-Nikāya* II, 95-98.

14. *Theri-gāthā* 252-270.

15. Jn. 8:1-11. The ambiguity inherent in the account of the incident involving Ambapāli may be one factor in subsequent ambiguities in later Buddhist history, as, for example, in Japanese Buddhism. We note that in the case of the Japanese pioneer prophet of the True Pure Land School (*Jōdo Shinshū*) Shinran (1173-1262), some of his followers came to belittle common morality as well as to deny its salvific value. Shinran severely reproved these followers for their immorality and insisted that faith in Amida Buddha (the context is, of course, the Pure Land Schools of the Mahāyāna tradition) is not intended to free believers from ethical responsibility. Cf. Toshihide Akamatsu, *Shinran,* Tokyo: Yoshikawa Hirobumi Kan, 1965, pp. 229, 242-252, 284.

16. *Theri-gāthā* 63-66.

17. E.g., Yutaka Iwamoto, *op. cit.,* pp. 104-113.

18. Marcus J. Borg, *Jesus, a New Vision,* San Francisco: Harper & Row, 1987, p. 101. See his extended treatment of this theme over pp. 129-142, also Borg, *Meeting Jesus Again for the First Time,* San Francisco: Harper, 1994, pp. 46-68.

19. Borg identifies as sharing his view that Jesus' acceptance of outcasts was the primary reason for his rejection by the Jewish

establishment: Norman Perrin, *Rediscovering the Teaching of Jesus,* NewYork: Harper & Row, 1967, pp. 102-108, andWilliam R. Farmer, "An Historical Essay on the Humanity of Jesus," in *Christian History and Interpretation,* Farmer *et al.,* eds., Cambridge: Cambridge University Press, 1967, pp. 103-104. Significant also is the Jewish scholar Geza Vermes's contention that in his acceptance of the socially ostracized, Jesus differed "from both his contemporaries and even his prophetic predecessors." *Jesus the Jew,* Philadelphia: Fortress Press, 1981, p. 224.

20. Cf. Marcus Borg, *Jesus, a New Vision, op. cit.,* pp. 91-93, 131-142.

21. The Greek text simply says "our place" and, in the context of the author's occasional use of more than one level of meaning in his words, may mean the "place" of the establishment as much as the temple in Jerusalem.

22. Borg, *op. cit.,* pp. 16, 97-124.

23. Millard C. Lind, "Refocusing Theological Education to Mission: The Old Testament and Contextualization," *Missiology* X, 2 (April 1982), pp. 141-148.

24. Cf. Tilman Vetter in *Dialogue and Syncretism,* Jerald D. Gort *et al.,* eds., Grand Rapids, MI: William B. Eerdmans, 1989, p. 132.

25. Cf. Richard H. Drummond, *Toward a New Age in Christian Theology,* Maryknoll, NY: Orbis Books, 1985, pp. 2-14.

26. Hans WalterWolff, *Joel and Amos,* Philadelphia: Fortress Press, 1977, pp. 347-348.

27. Patrick Kalilombe, "The Salvific Value of African Religions," in *Mission Trends No. 5,* Gerald H. Anderson & Thomas F. Stransky, eds., NewYork: Paulist Press, 1981, pp. 50-68.

28. Choan-Seng Song, "Theology of the Incarnation," in *Asian Voices in Christian Theology,* Gerald H. Anderson, ed., Maryknoll, NY: Orbis Books, 1976, pp. 147-153.

29. Choan-Seng Song, "From Israel to Asia: A Theological Leap," in *Mission Trends No. 3,* Gerald H. Anderson &Thomas F. Stransky, eds., NewYork: Paulist Press, 1976, pp. 212-222. Cf. Song, *Christian Mission in Reconstruction,* Maryknoll, NY: Orbis Books, 1977, pp. 174-276.

30. Cf. Samuel Angus, *The Religious Quests of the Graeco-*

Roman World, New York: Charles Scribner's Sons, 1929, pp. 54, 98. The Old Testament itself gives us clear examples of both tendencies. The vision of Second Isaiah looks toward the remnant of Israel as a light to the nations in order that the salvation of Yahweh may "reach to the end of the earth" (Isa. 49:6; 45:22). In Deuteronomy, however, the prophecy for Joseph is to the end that, like a wild ox, "he gores the peoples, driving them to the ends of the earth" (Deut. 33:17; cf. the function of Gentiles as agents of curse, Deut. 28:49, 64-68). The Septuagint adds to the Hebrew of Deut. 33:19, which might originally have had some positive missionary significance, the promise that Joseph's tribes, Zebulun and Issachar, will utterly destroy the nations. The extracanonical *Book of Jubilees* (late second century B.C.E.) speaks in an apparently total way of the uncleanness and shame of the Gentiles, who will be to Israel "an offence and a tribulation and a snare" (I, 9, 21-25). See also John Bright, *The Kingdom of God*, Nashville: Abingdon, 1953, pp. 160-162. John Dominic Crossan stresses the important background role of what he calls "inclusive Judaism" in the later relatively swift spread of Christian faith in the Gentile world. "It took both the ideological orientation and practical missionary experience of inclusive Judaism as well as the enabling vision and abiding presence of Jesus to create that effect." *The Historical Jesus, the Life of a Mediterranean Jewish Peasant*, San Francisco: Harper Collins, 1991, p. 422.

31. Philo, *ton hierotaton Platona, Every Good Man Is Free*, 13.

32. It may have taken centuries of faith-experience under Yahweh for the people of Israel to come to understand that their election and covenant with Yahweh necessarily involved mission to others. This understanding, however, came to clear focus in Second Isaiah in his perception that the restoration of Israel is not an end in itself, "It is too light a thing that you should be my servant to raise up the tribes of Jacob and to restore the survivors of Israel; I will give you as a light to the nations, that my salvation may reach to the end of the earth" (Isa. 49:6; cf. Zeph. 3:9; Isa. 25:6-8).

33. The synoptic gospels all tell us of Jesus' sending "the twelve" or inner core of his disciples on separate missionary jour-

neys fairly early in his public ministry without his physical presence, in order to teach, heal the sick, and exorcise unclean spirits. This mission charge was probably aimed primarily at Jews alone, but only Matthew says that it was so confined (Mt. 10:5-6). Luke writes of another mission charge, that of seventy disciples sent out at a later time (cf. Mk. 6:7-13; Mt. 10:1-23; Lk. 9:1-6; 10:1-12).

34. We do not have space to discuss the details of the incident of Jesus' healing the daughter of a woman in the area of Tyre and Sidon, one of the several times when Jesus took some of his disciples with him on trips outside Jewish Palestine. The mother is called a Canaanite by Matthew (15:21-28), a Greek woman, "of Syrophoenician origin" by Mark (7:24-30). In both gospels Jesus is cited as addressing the mother with language implying that Gentiles are "dogs" in comparison with the "children" of Israel. Many contemporary biblical scholars prefer to attribute language of this kind to the presence in the early Palestinian Christian church of elements who preferred to restrict the Christian mission to Jews and Jewish proselytes (cf. the reference previously made in our text to Peter's conversion from this mentality as described in Acts 10:1-48). In the Matthean account Jesus is described as responding to the mother's wit and charming initiative in the warmest way, "Woman, great is your faith! Let it be done for you as you wish" (15:28); Mark's language is somewhat less gracious (7:29). For those who are open to such materials, however, it may be of some significance that Edgar Cayce restricts the use of the term "dogs" to the mother alone and assigns as much initiative and charm to Jesus as to the mother (cf. readings 1159-1; 2364-1; 585-2).

35. This statement is also found in Lk. 9:50. The thought negatively phrased occurs in Mt. 12:30; Lk. 11:23; cf. Num. 11:27-29.

36. We may say of Jesus' use of the Hebrew Scriptures as recorded in the Gospel of Matthew that it is both selective and, on occasion, corrective. See Mt. 5:17-48.

37. Marcus J. Borg, *Jesus, a New Vision, op. cit.*, pp. 133-135. We may properly note that in archaic societies the evidence suggests that "women were coequal with men because they had in-

dispensable economic, cultural, and religious roles." The tensions between matriarchal and patriarchal tendencies in human experience are indeed ancient. Cf. Denise Lardner Carmody, *Women and World Religions,* Nashville, TN: Abingdon, 1979, pp. 19-38, 156-168; Leonard Swidler, *Women in Judaism,* Metuchen, NJ: The Scarecrow Press, 1976, pp. 4-28.

38.   Charles E. Carlston, "Proverbs, Maxims, and the Historical Jesus," *Journal of Biblical Literature,* Vol. 99, No. 1, (March 1980), pp. 95-96.

39.   A.N. Wilson, *Jesus,* New York: W.W. Norton, 1992, pp. 241-242. We should recall that Paul implies that Jesus appeared first to Cephas (Peter), "then to the twelve" (I Cor. 15:4-6). Incidentally, with regard to the issues of methodology in biblical research that we discussed earlier, Wilson gives it as his opinion that "subjectivity is the only criterion of Gospel truth."

40.   Cf. Denise L. Carmody, *op. cit.,* pp. 45-91; 113-136; Leonard Swidler, *Biblical Affirmations of Women,* Philadelphia: Westminster Press, 1979, pp. 139-157, 339-351.

41.   Richard H. Drummond, *Toward a New Age in Christian Theology, op. cit.,* pp. 200-201.

42.   Cf. Karl Ludwig Reichelt, *Truth and Tradition in Chinese Buddhism,* Shanghai: The Commercial Press, 1927, *passim;* Shōkō Watanabe, *Shin Shakuson Den,* Tokyo: Daihōrinkaku, 1967, pp. 15-27.

43.   *Vinaya-Piṭaka, Mahāvagga* VIII, 20, 1-3.

44.   This translation in the NRSV, "members of my family," is the result of an attempt to avoid the allegedly sexist language of the older translation "these my brethren" (as indeed the Greek text has it). In either case the meaning does not refer to blood relatives of the speaker, but to an all-inclusive human solidarity, and from there to a larger cosmic solidarity with the Maker of all, as with the whole of his creation.

45.   *Thera-gāthā* 557-566. The early Buddhist texts are not always fully consistent with reference to this as to other issues. For a brief discussion of certain of these problematics see Richard H. Drummond, *Gautama the Buddha,* Grand Rapids, MI: William B. Eerdmans, 1974, pp. 110-112.

46.   *Vinaya-Piṭaka, Mahāvagga* I, 11, 1.

47. Buddhaghosa, *Sumaṅgula-Vilāsini* I, 45-47.

48. In the chief account of the utterances made shortly before his death, the Buddha is said to have specifically denied his ever having made any distinction between exoteric and esoteric doctrine (*Digha-Nikāya* II, 100).

49. *Sanyutta-Nikāya* IV, 314-316. We may recall that Jesus' similar parable (Mk. 4:2-20 and parallels) should properly be named a parable of soils. Cf. George A. Buttrick, *The Parables of Jesus*, New York: Harper, 1928, p. 41.

50. E.g., Günther Bornkamm, "End-Expectation and Church in Matthew," Bornkamm, Barth, Held, *Tradition and Interpretation in Matthew*, Philadelphia: Westminster, 1963, pp. 38-51.

51. Gerhard Lohfink quotes, in agreement, the Danish New Testament scholar Johannes Munck to the effect that "Jesus came precisely to Israel because his mission was for the entire world." *Jesus and Community*, John P. Galvin, tr., Philadelphia: Fortress Press, 1984, p. 137.

52. *Vinaya-Piṭaka, Cullavagga* VII, 1-5.

53. Cf. Donald J. Goergen, O.P., *A Theology of Jesus, I: The Mission and Ministry of Jesus*, Wilmington, DE: Michael Glazier, 1986, pp. 91-106.

54. Cf. Richard H. Drummond, *Gautama the Buddha, op. cit.*, pp. 197-200. The Buddha was not a social reformer of modern kind, nor a prophet of confrontation style like Nathan before David. We find him, however, willing to criticize King Prasenajit of Kośala for his prejudice against women and consistently conducting himself with independent dignity before the rulers of kingdoms with whom he had some contact. His recorded criticism of Brāhman religious professionals was at points scathing, and while he did not declaim in public places against social evils, he completely transcended the caste system, as we have seen, in both his order of monks and in his teaching with regard to the spiritual and moral potential of all persons.

55. Cf. Hugh Anderson, *The Gospel of Mark*, New Century Bible Commentary, Grand Rapids, MI: Wm. B. Eerdmans, 1981, pp. 205-217.

56. The phrase quoted is from William L. Lane, *The Gospel of Mark*, The New International Commentary on the New Testa-

ment, Grand Rapids, MI: Wm. B. Eerdmans, 1974, pp. 291-292.

57. Donald J. Goergen writes that Jesus was both unmessianic and messianic, but concludes that he was indeed the Messiah, yet "in a different, unexpected way." That is, "Jesus did not think of himself as the Messiah in any way that was understood within the Judaism of his day." *A Theology of Jesus, I: The Mission and Ministry of Jesus, op. cit.,* pp. 157-170.

58. The reference to II Cor. 10:1 seems appropriate because it is evidently a phrase—"the meekness and gentleness of Christ"—that the apostle Paul believed to be the most aptly summarizing characterization of the risen Christ whom he knew in his own experience. We should note again in this context that there is no evidence in the gospel accounts that Jesus intended to lead his disciples into any kind of physically violent reprisal against the emerging opposition. As Richard A. Horsley has contended, "Jesus, while not necessarily a pacifist [cf. Lk. 22:50—the account indicates that at least one of Jesus' disciples carried a sword—to be correlated with Jn. 18:36], actively opposed violence, both oppressive and repressive, both political-economic and spiritual." Horsley makes the further point, however, that in Jesus' opposition to violence in all its forms, whether personal or institutional, in other modes he "entered actively into the situation of violence, and even exacerbated the conflict" (cf. Mk. 1:26; Mt. 10:34-36). *Jesus and the Spiral of Violence,* San Francisco: Harper & Row, 1987, pp. 318 ff.

59. A.E. Harvey argues that the term *christos,* meaning "anointed" and carrying a variety of consequent meanings, was in fact applied to Jesus during his lifetime. *Jesus and the Constraints of History,* Philadelphia: Westminster Press, 1982, pp. 33, 79-84, 135-142.

60. I recall my longtime friend in Japan, a colleague at Meiji Gakuin University in Tokyo, Professor Shiro Abe, saying in my hearing in September of 1986 that a central aspect of the Christian understanding of salvation is "*zasetsu kara no kaifuku.*" This phrase can properly be translated, I believe, by the English "recovery (or restoration) from failure." There is a further poignancy in the Japanese original in that the term *zasetsu* can mean "complete collapse."

61. This is not the place to go into detail, but mention should be made that the issues revolving around failure on the plane of human history still remain as significant differences of understanding among the historic faiths of Judaism, Christianity, and Islam. Mainstream Judaism has regarded it as integral to the role of Messiah that he bring in the messianic kingdom on earth—as a "success story." Muḥammad and historic Islam have believed that an authentic prophet of God will ultimately succeed on the plane of human history. Cf. *Qur'ān* 22:15.

62. *Vinaya-Piṭaka, Mahāvagga* I, 5, 4-13.

63. *Sanyutta-Nikāya* I, 139; *Dīgha-Nikāya* III, 77. Cf. James Fredericks, "The Metanoetics of Interreligious Encounter," *Inter-Religio*, No. 16 (Fall 1989), pp. 45-46.

64. The variations in the Greek text of this passage as found in some manuscripts and church Fathers suggest that many early Christians wrestled with the issues involved. Almost all variations, however, point to a focus.

65. Perhaps the older translation of the RSV, "seek first," is preferable to "strive first."

66. Joseph M. Kitagawa, *Religions of the East*, Philadelphia: Westminster Press, 1960, p. 186.

67. A further example of the "lurking presence" of a focus is perceptible in the Japanese Buddhist philosopher Masao Abe's "definitions" or descriptive statements of the Ultimate Reality of his faith-system, which he names "Boundless Openness" or "Formlessness." Abe regards this Reality as the ultimate ground of all else, Truth itself. At first approach this Reality would appear as utterly without quality or focus. But as Abe goes on, he reveals that this Reality is characterized by a "dynamic activity constantly emptying everything, including itself. It is formless by negating every form [=negating absoluteness to particular forms?], and yet without remaining in formlessness, takes various forms freely by negating its own formlessness." Abe identifies this "dynamically formless Dharma" as also performing a *critical* function in that, while all-embracing—for example, of particular religious forms in human history—"it is at the same time constantly emptying them—even asking them to abnegate themselves and return to itself ('Boundless Openness') as their ultimate ground." Abe does

not identify this activity as having ethical quality, but in the context of the history of religions, one can hardly avoid such a conclusion. Abe frequently uses the New Testament term *kenosis* (emptying—cf. Phil. 2:7, where the term clearly has the ethical meaning of self-sacrificial activity for the sake of others) to denote this activity and implies, without claiming, a noble ethical quality to reside therein, whether the activity be that of "Boundless Openness" or of particular forms in the cosmos. Masao Abe, "A Dynamic Unity in Religious Pluralism: A Proposal from the *Buddhist* Point of View," *The Experience of Religious Diversity*, John Hick & Hasan Askari, eds., Brookfield, VT: Gower Publishing Co., 1987, pp. 163-190.

68. Yamada (surname) Reirin & Kuwada Hidenobu, *Zen to Kirisuto Kyō*, Tokyo: Chōbunsha, 1967, pp. 35-58, 77-80, 167. A more recent statement by the widely published Japanese Rinzai Zen monk-scholar Ryōmin Akizuki is sharply illuminative of the same point. He writes, "whoever got the idea that Zen is a religion of 'self-power' is wrong. As long as religion is religion, it must not be a religion of self-power. For one cannot live on one's own." "Christian-Buddhist Dialogue," *Inter-Religio*, No. 14 (Fall 1988), pp. 47-48. The Belgian Roman Catholic priest-scholar Jan Van Bragt makes the same point with the reference to the Buddha himself and to the whole of subsequent Buddhism. Van Bragt would interpret Dharma as Other-Power and affirm that "Even in Sākyamini's case, rather than saying that he grasped the truth, it is more fitting to say that the Dharma revealed itself to him ... No, Buddhism cannot exist as a self-power path. Even for Zen there is no liberation by self-power, if this is understood as power of the ego." "Salvation and Enlightenment: Pure Land Buddhism and Christianity," *Bulletin of the Nanzan Institute for Religion and Culture*, No. 14 (Summer 1990), p. 36. See also the perceptive article by a Dutch scholar who links the modern French philosopher Jacques Derrida, Plato's Socrates (in the *Timaeus*) and Zen Buddhism. Her positive appreciation of the concept of "emptiness," the "empty," in, for example, the modern Kyoto School of Zen philosophy, leads her to see emptiness as a *field of possibilities*, as giving *glow* to the concrete phenomena of our world. And yet "a thing is never in itself, it is dependent

on the 'open' that lets it be." Emptiness is really openness. Ilse N. Bulhof, "Towards a 'Postmodern' Spirituality," *Studies in Interreligious Dialogue,* Vol. 5, No. 1 (1995), pp. 18-19, 25.

69. Cf. Richard H. Drummond, *A History of Christianity in Japan,* Grand Rapids, MI: William B. Eerdmans, 1971, pp. 195-196.

70. The term *ransom* in New Testament context has its focus of meaning on power effective to secure liberation, not on payment of money or other valued goods to an owner with legal right of possession. Thus theories of the atonement suggesting Jesus' death as a kind of literal ransom payment to the devil or as an offering to God to mollify his anger are spiritually below the level of New Testament thought.

71. Rudolf Steiner, *From Jesus to Christ,* London: Rudolf Steiner Press, 1973, p. 69.

72. Guenther Wachsmuth, *The Life and Work of Rudolf Steiner,* New York: Whittier Books, 1955, pp. 309-311, 327. This is the massive biography of Steiner translated from the German by Olin D. Wannamaker and Reginald E. Raab.

73. Cf. Stewart C. Easton, *Man and World in the Light of Anthroposophy,* Spring Valley, NY: The Anthroposophic Press, 1982, pp. 201-203, 185-186. Readers are asked to study the series of articles by a number of contemporary American thinkers on the theme of "Rudolf Steiner and American Thought." *ReVision* XIII, 4 (Spring 1991); XIV, 1(Summer 1991).

74. The numbers following references to Edgar Cayce represent, first, the person who received a "reading" from Cayce, and, second, the number of reading when more than one was given to the same person. These readings are available to the general public as copies in the library of the Association for Research and Enlightenment, Inc., in Virginia Beach, Virginia.

Bibliography

Abe, Masao, "A Dynamic Unity in Religious Pluralism: A Proposal from the *Buddhist* Point of View," *The Experience of Religious Diversity*, John Hick & Hasan Askari, eds., Brookfield, VT: Gower Publishing Co., 1987.

Abhidharma.

Akamatsu, Toshihide, *Shinran*, Tokyo: Yoshikawa Hirobumi Kan, 1965.

Akizuki, Ryōmin, "Christian-Buddhist Dialogue," *Inter-Religio*, No. 14 (Fall 1988).

Aland, Kurt, *et al.*, eds., *The Greek New Testament*, 3rd ed., Stuttgart: United Bible Societies, 1975.

Amore, Roy C., "Giving and Harming: Buddhist Symbols of Good and Evil," *Developments in Buddhist Thought: Canadian Contributions to Buddhist Studies*, Waterloo, Ontario: Canadian Corporation for Studies in Religion, 1979.

Anderson, Gerald H., & Stransky, Thomas F., eds., *Christ's Lordship and Religious Pluralism*, Maryknoll, NY: Orbis Books, 1981.

_____ , *Mission Trends Nos. 1, 2, 3, 4, 5*, New York: Paulist Press, 1974, 1975, 1976, 1979, 1981.

Anderson, Hugh, *The Gospel of Mark*, Grand Rapids, MI: Wm. B. Eerdmans, 1981.

Angus, Samuel, *The Religious Quests of the Graeco-Roman World*, New York: Charles Scribner's Sons, 1929.

Anguttara-Nikāya.

Ariarajah, S. Wesley, "Towards a Theology of Dialogue," *Interreligious Dialogue: Facing the Next Frontier*, Richard W. Rousseau, ed., Montrose, PA: Ridge Row Press, 1981.

Arndt, W.F., & Gingrich, F.W., *A Greek-English Lexicon of the New Testament*, Chicago: University of Chicago Press, 1960.

Arnold, Edwin, *The Light of Asia*, Boston: Robert Brothers, 1891.

Augustine, *Enchiridion.*

_____ , *In Epistolam Joannis ad Parthos.*

_____ , *Speculum.*

Balthasar, Hans Urs von, *A Theology of History*, New York: Sheed & Ward, 1963.

Bareau, André, *Die Religionen Indiens*, C.M. Schroeder, ed., Stuttgart: Kohlhammer Verlag, 1964.

Barfield, Owen, *Saving the Appearances, a Study in Idolatry*, New York: Harcourt, Brace and World, n.d.

Barrett, C.K., "The Background of Mark 10:45," *New Testament Essays*, Manchester: University of Manchester Press, 1959.

Beckh, Hermann, *From Buddha to Christ*, Edinburgh: Floris Books, 1977.

Bellow, Saul, *Humboldt's Gift*, Harmondsworth, Middlesex: Penguin Books, 1977.

_____ , *Newsweek*, September 1, 1975.

Benz, Ernst, *Indische Einflüsse auf die frühchristliche Theologie*, Wiesbaden: Verlag der Akademie der Wissenschaften und der Literatur in Mainz, 1951.

Berkhof, Hendrickus, *Christian Faith*, Grand Rapids, Michigan: Wm. B. Eerdmans, 1979.

Berry, Thomas, "Religious Studies and the Global Community of Man," *Interreligious Dialogue: Facing the Next Frontier*, Richard W. Rousseau, ed., Montrose, PA: Ridge Row Press, 1981.

Bhagavad-Gītā.

Bleeker, C.J., *Christ in Modern Athens*, Leiden: E.J. Brill, 1965.

Bloesch, Donald G., *Essentials of Evangelical Theology*, San Francisco: Harper & Row, 1978, I.

Bonaventura, *The Life of St. Francis.*

Bonnard, Pierre, *L'Evangile selon Saint Matthieu*, Neuchatel: Delachaux et Niestlé, 1970.

Book of Jubilees, The.

Borg, Marcus J., *Conflict, Holiness and Politics in the Teachings of Jesus*, New York: The Edwin Mellen Press, 1984.

_____ , *Jesus, a New Vision*, San Francisco: Harper & Row, 1987.

_____ , *Jesus in Contemporary Scholarship*, Valley Forge, Pa.: Trinity Press International, 1994.

_____ , *Meeting Jesus Again for the First Time*, San Francisco: Harper, 1994.

_____ , "The Historian, the Christian and Jesus," *Theology Today*, Vol. 52, No. 1 (April 1995).

Bornkamm, Günther, "End-Expectation and Church in Matthew," *Tradition and Interpretation in Matthew*, Bornkamm,

Barth, *et al.*, Philadelphia: Westminster, 1963.

_____ , *Jesus of Nazareth*, New York: Harper & Row, 1975.

Bouquet, A.C., *The Christian Faith and Non-Christian Religions*, New York: Harper and Brothers, 1958.

Bowden, John, *Voices in the Wilderness*, Naperville, Illinois: SCM Press, 1977.

Bowman, John Wick, *The Intention of Jesus*, Philadelphia: Westminster, 1943.

Bowman, John Wick, & Tapp, Roland W., *The Gospel from the Mount*, Philadelphia: Westminster, 1957.

Boyd, James W., "The Path of Liberation from Suffering in Buddhism," *Buddhism and Christianity*, Geffré & Dhavamony, eds., New York: Seabury Press, 1979.

Braaten, Carl E., & Harrisville, Roy A., *Kerygma and History*, New York: Abingdon Press, 1962.

Bright, John, *A History of Israel*, Philadelphia: Westminster, 1959.

_____ , *The Kingdom of God*, Nashville: Abingdon, 1953.

Brihadāranyaka Upaniṣad.

Bro, Harmon, H., "The Seer and His Gift," *The A.R.E. Journal* XVI, 4 (July 1981).

_____ , *A Seer Out of Season, the Life of Edgar Cayce*, New York: New American Library, 1989.

Brown, Raymond E., *The Gospel According to John*, I, II, The Anchor Bible, Garden City, NY: Doubleday, 1966.

Brown, W. Norman, *Man in the Universe, Some Cultural Continuities in India*, Berkeley: University of California Press, 1966.

Brownlee, W.H., "John the Baptist in the New Light of Ancient Scrolls," *The Scrolls and the New Testament*, Krister Stendahl, ed., New York: Harper, 1957.

Bruce, F.F., *The 'Secret Gospel' of Mark*, London: Athlone Press, 1974.

Buddhacarita.

Buddhadāsa Indapañño, *Buddha Dhamma for Students*, Bangkok: M.P., 1966.

_____ , *Christianity and Buddhism*, Bangkok: Karn Pim Pranakorn, 1968.

Buddhaghosa, *Sumañgula-Vilāsinī*.

Bulhof, Ilse N., "Towards a 'Postmodern' Spirituality," *Studies in*

Interreligious Dialogue, Vol. 5, No. 1 (1995).

Bultmann, Rudolf, *Faith and Understanding*, London: SCM Press, 1969.

_____ , *Kerygma and Myth, a Theological Debate*, London: S.P.C.K., 1953.

Burtt, E.A., *The Teachings of the Compassionate Buddha*, New York: The New American Library, 1960.

Buthelezi, Manas, "Daring to Live for Christ," *Mission Trends No. 3, Third World Theologies*, Gerald H. Anderson & Thomas F. Stransky, eds., New York: Paulist Press, 1975.

Butterworth, G.W., ed., *Origen on First Principles*, Gloucester, Mass.: Peter Smith, 1973.

Buttrick, George A., *Christ and History*, New York: Abingdon, 1963.

_____ , *God, Pain and Evil*, Nashville: Abingdon, 1966.

_____ , ed., *The Interpreter's Bible*, New York: Abingdon-Cokesbury, 1951.

_____ , *The Parables of Jesus*, New York: Harper, 1928.

Cadbury, H.J., *Jesus: What Manner of Man?* New York: Macmillan, 1947.

Caird, G.B., *Saint Luke*, Harmondsworth, England: Penguin Books, 1973.

Calvin, John, *Institutes of the Christian Religion*, I, II, John T. McNeill, ed., Ford Lewis Battles, tr., Philadelphia: Westminster, 1960.

Campbell, Joseph, *The Hero with a Thousand Faces*, Princeton: Princeton Univ. Press, 1973.

Campi, Emilio, *Voices of Unity*, Ans. J. van der Bent, ed., Geneva: WCC, 1981.

Capra, Fritjof, "Ancient Buddhism in Modern Physics," *New Realities*, I, 1 (1977).

_____ , *The Law of Physics*, Berkeley, CA: Shambhala Publications, 1975.

_____ , *The Turning Point*, New York: Bantam Books, 1988.

Carlston, Charles E., *The Parables of the Triple Tradition*, Philadelphia: Fortress Press, 1978.

_____ , "Proverbs, Maxims, and the Historical Jesus," *Journal of Biblical Literature*, Vol. 99, No. 1 (March 1980).

Carmody, Denise Lardner, *Women and World Religions*, Nashville: Abingdon, 1979.

Carr, Burgess, "The Relation of Union to Mission," *Mission Trends No. 3, Third World Theologies*, Gerald H. Anderson & Thomas F. Stransky, eds., New York: Paulist Press, 1975.

Carty, Charles Mortimer, *Padre Pio: The Stigmatist*, St. Paul: Radio Replies Press, 1961.

Cayce, Edgar Evans, & Cayce, Hugh Lynn, *The Outer Limits of Edgar Cayce's Power*, New York: Harper and Row, 1971.

Chadwick, Henry, *Early Christian Thought and the Classical Tradition*, London: Oxford University Press, 1966.

Chāndogya Upaniṣad.

Charlesworth, James H., "From Messianology to Christology," *The Messiah*, James H. Charlesworth, ed., Minneapolis: Augsburg Fortress, 1992.

Childe, Gordon, *What Happened in History?* Harmondsworth, Middlesex: Penguin Books, 1961.

Clement of Alexandria, *Stromateis.*

Cobb, John B., Jr., *Beyond Dialogue, Toward a Mutual Transformation of Christianity and Buddhism*, Philadelphia: Fortress Press, 1982.

_____ , *Christ in a Pluralistic Age*, Philadelphia: Westminster Press, 1975.

_____ , "Process Theology and an Ecological Model," *Pacific Theological Review* XV, 2 (Winter 1982).

_____ , & Ives, Christopher, eds., *The Emptying God, a Buddhist-Jewish-Christian Conversation*, Maryknoll, NY: Orbis Books, 1991.

Conze, Edward, *Buddhism: Its Essence and Development*, New York: Harper and Brothers, 1959.

_____ , *Buddhist Thought in India*, Ann Arbor: University of Michigan Press, 1967.

_____ , "The Mahāyāna," *Concise Encyclopedia of Religious Faiths*, R.C. Zaehner, ed., New York: Hawthorn Books, 1959.

Corless, Roger, "A Christian Perspective on Buddhist Liberation," *Buddhism and Christianity*, Geffré & Dhavamony, eds., New York: Harper, 1959.

Cousins, Ewert, tr., *Bonaventure*, New York: Paulist Press, 1978.

_____ , "The Trinity and World Religions," *Journal of Ecumenical Studies*, VII, 3 (Summer 1970).

Covell, Ralph R., *Confucius, the Buddha and Christ*, Maryknoll, NY: Orbis Books, 1986.

Cox, Harvey, "The Battle of the Gods? A Concluding Unsystematic Postscript," *The Other Side of God*, Peter L. Berger, ed., Garden City, NY: Doubleday, 1981.

_____ , *Feast of Fools*, Cambridge: Harvard University Press, 1969.

Cross, F.L., *The Early Christian Fathers*, London: Gerald Duckworth, 1960.

Crossan, John Dominic, *The Historical Jesus, the Life of a Mediterranean Jewish Peasant*, San Francisco: Harper Collins, 1991.

Cullavagga (Vinaya-Piṭaka).

Dahl, Nils Astrup, "The Problem of the Historical Jesus," in Braaten, Carl E., & Harrisville, Roy A., *Kerygma and History*, New York: Abingdon Press, 1962.

Dalman, Gustav, *The Words of Jesus*, Edinburgh: T. & T. Clark, 1909.

Daniélou, Jean, *Origéne*, Paris: La Table Ronde, 1948.

Davids, Mrs. Rhys (Caroline Augusta Foley), *The Book of the Gradual Sayings*, I, F.L. Woodward, tr., London: Luzac, 1970.

_____ , *The Book of the Kindred Sayings*, I, London: Luzac, 1950.

Davies, Stevan L., *The Gospel of Thomas and Christian Wisdom*, New York: Seabury, 1983.

_____ , "Thomas—The Fourth Synoptic Gospel," *Biblical Archaeologist* XLVI, 1 (Winter 1983).

Davies, W.D., *Paul and Rabbinic Judaism*, London: S.P.C.K., 1955.

Dawe, Donald G., "Christian Faith in a Religiously Plural World," *Christian Faith in a Religiously Plural World*, Maryknoll, NY: Orbis, 1978.

_____ , "Religious Pluralism and the Church," *Journal of Ecumenical Studies* XVIII, 4 (Fall 1981).

Dhammapada.

Didache.

Dīgha-Nikāya.

Dodd, C.H., *Interpretation of the Fourth Gospel*, Cambridge: Cambridge University Press, 1955.

_____ , *The Parables of the Kingdom*, New York: Charles Scribner's Sons, 1961.

Donfried, Karl Paul, "The Kingdom of God in Paul," *The Kingdom of God in 20th-Century Interpretation*, Peabody, MA: Hendrickson Publishers, 1987.

Drummond, Donald C., "Eschatological Time in Jewish Apocalyptic and John's Apocalypse," *The Bulletin of the Christian Research Institute of Meiji Gakuin University*, X (March 1981).

_____ , "Theological Comments on the Colossian Hymn (Col. 1:15-20)," *The Bulletin of the Christian Research Institute of Meiji Gakuin University*, XV (March 1982).

Drummond, Richard H., "Authority in the Church: An Ecumenical Inquiry," *The Journal of Bible and Religion* XXXIV, 4 (October 1966).

_____ , "Christian Theology and the History of Religions," *Journal of Ecumenical Studies* XII, 3 (Summer 1975).

_____ , "Edgar Cayce: Christian Mystic and Bible Expositor," *The A.R.E. Journal* XVI, 4 (July 1981).

_____ , *Gautama the Buddha*, Grand Rapids, Michigan: Wm. B. Eerdmans, 1974.

_____ , *A History of Christianity in Japan*, Grand Rapids, Michigan: Wm. B. Eerdmans, 1971.

_____ , *Toward a New Age in Christian Theology*, Maryknoll, NY: Orbis Books, 1985.

_____ , "Toward Theological Understanding of Islam," *Journal of Ecumenical Studies* IX, 4 (Fall 1972).

_____ , *Unto the Churches*, Virginia Beach, Virginia: A.R.E. Press, 1978.

D'Souza, Patrick, "Church and Mission in Relation to the Kingdom of God Especially in a Third World Context," *Toward a New Age in Mission*, II, Manila: Ateneo de Manila University, 1981.

Dubarle, Dominique, "Buddhist Spirituality and the Christian Understanding of God," *Buddhism and Christianity*, Claude Geffré & Mariasusai Dhavamony, eds., New York: Seabury Press, 1979.

Duff, J. Wight, *A Literary History of Rome*, New York: Charles Scribner's Sons, 1932.

Dumoulin, Heinrich, "Buddhism—A Religion of Liberation," *Buddhism and Christianity,* Claude Geffré & Mariasusai Dhavamony, eds., New York: Seabury Press, 1979.
_____ , *A History of Zen Buddhism,* New York: Random House, 1963.
Dutt, Sukumar, *The Buddha and Five After-Centuries,* London: Luzac, 1957.

Easton, Stewart C., *Man and World in the Light of Anthroposophy,* Spring Valley, NY: The Anthroposophic Press, 1982.
_____ , *Rudolf Steiner: Herald of a New Epoch,* Spring Valley, NY: Anthroposophic Press, 1980.
Eccles, Sir John, *The Neurophysiological Basis of Mind,* London: Oxford University Press, 1953.
Eddy, Sherwood, *You Will Survive After Death,* New York: Rinehart, 1959.
Edersheim, Alfred, *The Life and Times of Jesus the Messiah,* I, II, New York: Longmans, Green, 1912.
Edmunds, Francis, *Anthroposophy, a Way of Life,* East Sussex, England: Carnant Books, 1982.
Eichrodt, Walther, *Theology of the Old Testament,* 6th ed., Philadelphia: Westminster, 1961.
Eilert, Håkan, *Boundlessness,* Århus, Denmark: Forlaget Aros, 1974.
Eliade, Mircea, *A History of Religious Ideas II,* Chicago: University of Chicago Press, 1982.
_____ , *The Quest, History and Meaning in Religion,* Chicago: University of Chicago Press, 1975.
Emerson, Ralph Waldo, "Compensation," *Essays and English Traits,* (Harvard Classics V), New York: Collier and Son, 1909.
Emmerich, Anne Catherine, *The Dolorous Passion of Our Lord Jesus Christ,* London: Burns, Oates and Washbourne, 1930.
Epiphanius, *Adversus Haereses.*

Farmer, William R., "An Historical Essay on the Humanity of Jesus," in *Christian History and Interpretation,* Farmer *et al.,* eds., Cambridge: Cambridge University Press, 1967.
al Faruqi, Isma'il R., "Prospects for Dialogue," *The Sacred Heart*

Messenger, Vol. 102, No. 9 (September 1967).

Ferré, Nels F., *The Universal Word,* Philadelphia: Westminster, 1969.

Finality of Jesus Christ in the Age of Universal History, The, Geneva: WCC Bulletin, Division of Studies VIII, 2 (Autumn 1962).

Fiorenza, Elisabeth Schüssler, *In Memory of Her,* New York, NY: Crossroad Publishing, 1989.

Fittipaldi, Silvio E., "Zen-Mind, Christian-Mind, Empty-Mind," *Journal of Ecumenical Studies* XIX, 1 (Winter 1982).

Fitzmeyer, Joseph A., S.J., *The Gospel According to Luke X-XXIV,* New York: Doubleday, 1985.

Fitzpatrick, Liam, "Book Review," *Inter-Religio,* No. 21 (Summer 1992).

Forster, Roger T., & Marston, Paul V., *God's Strategy in Human History,* Wheaton, Illinois: Tyndale House, 1974.

France, R. T., *Matthew, Evangelist and Teacher,* Grand Rapids, MI: Zondervan, 1989.

Frazer, James George, *The Golden Bough,* abr. ed., New York: Macmillan, 1939.

Fredericks, James, "The Metanoetics of Interreligious Encounter," *Inter-Religio,* No. 16 (Fall 1989).

Gaer, Joseph, *The Lore of the New Testament,* Boston: Little Brown, 1952.

Geffré, Claude, & Dhavamony, Mariasusai, eds., *Buddhism and Christianity* (A Concilium book), New York: Seabury, 1979.

Gilkey, Langdon, *Society and the Sacred,* New York: Crossroad, 1981.

von Glasenapp, Helmut, *Die nichtchristlichen Religionen,* Frankfurt am Main: Fischer Bucherei, 1957.

Glasser, Arthur F., "The Legacy of Jakób Jocz," *International Bulletin of Missionary Research,* Vol. 17, No. 2 (April 1993).

Glover, T.R., *The Jesus of History,* New York: Association Press, 1922.

Gnilka, Joachim, *Das Evangelium nach Markus,* Zürich: Benziger, 1978.

Goergen, Donald J., O.P., *A Theology of Jesus, I: The Mission and Ministry of Jesus,* Wilmington, DE: Michael Glazier, 1986.

Goetz, Ronald, "Joshua, Calvin, and Genocide," *Theology Today* XXXII, 3 (October 1975).

Govinda, Lama Anagarika, *The Psychological Attitude of Early Buddhist Philosophy,* London: Rider, 1969.

Grant, Frederick C., "The Gospel According to Mark, Exegesis," *The Interpreter's Bible,* VII, George A. Buttrick, ed., New York: Abingdon-Cokesbury, 1951.

Grant, Michael, *Jesus, an Historian's Review of the Gospels,* New York: Charles Scribner's Sons, 1977.

Gregory Thaumatourgos, *Panegyric on Origen.*

Guardini, Romano, *The Lord,* Chicago: Henry Regnery, 1954.

Guillaume, Alfred, *Prophecy and Divination,* New York: Harper, 1938.

Hanson, Paul D., *The Dawn of Apocalyptic,* rev. ed., Philadelphia: Fortress Press, 1979.

Haraldsson, Erlendur, *Modern Miracles, an Investigative Report on Psychic Phenomena Associated with Sathya Sai Baba,* New York: Fawcett Columbine (Ballantine Books), 1988.

Harnack, Adolf von, *Essays on the Social Gospel,* London: Williams and Norgate, 1907.

Harvey, A.E., *Jesus and the Constraints of History,* Philadelphia: Westminster Press, 1982.

Hemleben, Johannes, *Rudolf Steiner,* Sussex, England: Henry Goulden, 1975.

Hengel, Martin, *Acts and the History of Earliest Christianity,* Philadelphia: Fortress Press, 1980.

_____ , *The Atonement,* Philadelphia: Fortress Press, 1981.

Hennecke, Edgar, *New Testament Apocrypha,* I, II, Wilhelm Schneemelcher, ed., Philadelphia: Westminster, 1963.

Hill, David, *The Gospel of Matthew,* London: Oliphants, 1972.

Holladay, William L., *Jeremiah, a Fresh Reading,* New York: Pilgrim Press, 1990.

Homilies (Psuedo-Clementine).

Horsley, Richard A., *Jesus and the Spiral of Violence,* San Francisco: Harper & Row, 1987.

Hossfeld, Paul, "Jesus (der Christus) und Siddhārtha Gautama (der Buddha)," *Theologie und Glaube* LXIV, 4-5 (1974).

Hume, David, *An Enquiry Concerning Human Understanding,*

LaSalle, IL: Open Court Publ. Co., 1938.
Humphreys, Christmas, *Buddhism*, Harmondsworth, Middlesex: Penguin Books, 1958.

Ingram, Paul D., "Two Western Models of Interreligious Dialogue," *Journal of Ecumenical Studies*, Vol. 26, No. 1 (Winter 1989).
Interpreter's Bible, George A. Buttrick, ed., New York: Abingdon-Cokesbury, 1951.
Irenaeus, *Adversus Haereses*.
_____ , *Epideixis.*
Iwamoto, Yutaka, *Bukkyō Nyūmon*, Tokyo: Chūōkōronsha, 1964.

James, E.O., *The Cult of the Mother Goddess*, New York: Barnes & Noble, 1959.
_____ , *From Cave to Cathedral*, New York, Praeger, 1965.
James, William, *The Varieties of Religious Experience*, New York: The New American Library, 1961.
Jaspers, Karl, *The Origin and Goal of History*, New Haven: Yale University Press, 1959.
Jeremias, Joachim, *New Testament Theology: Part I, The Proclamation of Jesus*, New York: Charles Scribner's Sons, 1971.
_____ , *The Parables of Jesus*, rev. ed., New York: Charles Scribner's Sons, 1963.
_____ , *The Problem of the Historical Jesus*, Philadelphia: Fortress Press, 1964.
Jerome, *Letters (Epistula ad Demetriadem)*.
Jervell, Jacob, *Luke and the People of God*, Minneapolis: Augsburg, 1972.
Jewett, Robert, *Letter to Pilgrims*, New York: Pilgrim Press, 1981.
Johnson, Robert C., *Authority in Protestant Theology*, Philadelphia: Westminster, 1959.
Johnson, Sherman E., "The Gospel According to Matthew," *The Interpreter's Bible*, VII, George A. Buttrick, ed., New York: Abingdon-Cokesbury, 1951.
Josephus, Flavius, *Antiquities of the Jews.*
Jung, Carl Gustav, "The Personal and the Collective Unconscious," *The Basic Writings of C.G. Jung*, Violet S. de Laszlo, ed., New York: Random House, 1959.

_____ , "Psychological Aspects of the Mother Archetype," *Collected Works of C. G. Jung*, IX, New York: Bollingen, 1959.

Justin Martyr, *The First Apology.*

_____ , *The Second Apology.*

Kalilombe, Patrick, "The Salvific Value of African Religions," in *Mission Trends No. 5*, Gerald H. Anderson & Thomas F. Stransky, eds., New York: Paulist Press, 1981.

Käsemann, Ernst, "The Eschatological Royal Reign of God," *Your Kingdom Come*, Geneva: WCC (CWME), 1980.

Kaunda, Kenneth D., "The Challenge of Our Stewardship in Africa," *Mission Trends No. 3, Third World Theologies*, Gerald H. Anderson & Thomas F. Stransky, eds., New York: Paulist Press, 1975.

Keith, Arthur Berriedale, "The Age of the Rigveda," *The Cambridge History of India*, I, Cambridge: Cambridge University Press, 1922.

_____ , *The Religion and Philosophy of the Veda and Upanishads*, Cambridge: Harvard University Press, 1923.

Kermode, Frank, *The Genesis of Secrecy*, Cambridge, MA: Harvard University Press, 1979.

Kerr, David A., "The Problem of Christianity in Muslim Perspective: Implications for Christian Mission," *International Bulletin of Missionary Research*, V, 4 (October 1981).

_____ , "What Makes a Missionary," *Mission Trends No. 1*, Gerald H. Anderson & Thomas F. Stransky, eds., New York: Paulist Press, 1974.

Kertelge, Karl, "Der dienende Menschensohn (Mk. 10:45)," *Jesus und der Menschensohn*, R. Pesch, R. Schnackenburg, & O. Kaiser, eds., Freiburg: Herder, 1975.

Khin Maung Din, "Some Problems and Possibilities for Burmese Christian Theology Today," *Christianity and the Religion of the East*, Richard W. Rousseau, ed., Montrose, PA: Ridge Row Press, 1982.

King, Winston L., *Buddhism and Christianity*, Philadelphia: Westminster Press, 1962.

_____ , *In the Hope of Nibbana*, LaSalle, Illinois: The Open Court Publishing Co., 1964.

Kirk, G.S., & Raven, J.E., *The Presocratic Philosophers*, Cambridge: Cambridge University Press, 1960.

Kitagawa, Joseph M., *Religions of the East*, Philadelphia: Westminster Press, 1960.

Kiyota, Minoru, *Gedatsukai: Its Theory and Practice*, Los Angeles: Buddhist Books International, 1982.

Koester, Helmut, "History and Development of Mark's Gospel (From Mark to Secret Mark and 'Canonical' Mark)," *Colloquy on New Testament Studies: A Time for Reappraisal and Fresh Approaches*, Bruce Corley, ed., Macon, GA: Mercer University Press, 1983.

_____ , *History and Literature of Early Christianity*, Philadelphia: Fortress, 1982.

Koestler, Arthur, *The Roots of Coincidence*, New York: Random House, 1972.

Koyama, Kosuke, "Theocentric Christology: A Response to S. Mark Heim," *Journal of Ecumenical Studies*, Vol. 24, No. 1 (Winter 1987).

_____ , "What Makes a Missionary," *Mission Trends No. 3, Third World Theologies*, Gerald H. Anderson & Thomas F. Stransky, eds., New York: Paulist Press, 1975.

Koyasu, Michiko, *Myunhen no Shōgakusei*, Tokyo: Chūōkōronsha, 1977.

Küng, Hans, *et al.*, *Christianity and the World Religions*, Garden City, NY: Doubleday and Co., 1986.

_____ , *Global Responsibility*, London: SCM Press, 1991.

Ladd, George Eldon, *A Theology of the New Testament*, Grand Rapids, MI: Wm. B. Eerdmans, 1983.

Lanczkowski, Günter, "Das Heilsziel des Nirvāṇa in der Lehre des Buddhas," *Asien Missioniert im Abendland*, Kurt Hutten & Siegfried von Kortzfleisch, eds., Stuttgart: Kreuz-Verlag, 1962.

Lane, William L., *The Gospel of Mark*, Grand Rapids, MI: Wm. B. Eerdmans, 1974.

Lee, Sydney, *Dictionary of National Biography*, XXVII, New York: Macmillan, 1891.

Levi (H. Dowling), *The Aquarian Gospel of Jesus the Christ*, Santa Monica, California: DeVorss and Co., 1969.

Lewis, C.S., *Miracles, a Preliminary Study,* New York: Macmillan, 1947.

Lind, Millard C., "Refocusing Theological Education to Mission: The Old Testament and Contextualization," *Missiology* X, 2 (April 1982).

Lohfink, Gerhard, *Jesus and Community,* John P. Galvin, tr., Philadelphia: Fortress Press, 1984.

Lohse, Eduard, *Colossians and Philemon,* Philadelphia: Fortress Press, 1971.

Luther's Works.

Mackintosh, Hugh Ross, *The Doctrine of the Person of Jesus Christ,* New York: Charles Scribner's Sons, 1915.

Mahābhārata.

Mahā Parinibbāna Sutta.

Mahāvagga (Vinaya-Piṭaka).

Majjhima-Nikāya.

Malina, Bruce J., *The Gospel of John in Sociolinguistic Perspective,* Berkeley, CA: Center for Hermeneutical Studies in Hellenistic and Modern Culture, 1985.

Malina, Bruce J., & Rohrbaugh, Richard L., *Social Science Commentary on the Synoptic Gospels,* Minneapolis: Augsburg Fortress, 1992.

March, W. Eugene, "Because the *Lord* Is Lord: Old Testament Covenant Imagery and Ecumenical Commitment," *Austin Seminary Bulletin* XCVI (March 1981).

Martin, Richard C., *Islam, a Cultural Perspective,* Englewood Cliffs, NJ: Prentice-Hall, 1982.

Mascaró, Juan, tr., *The Upanishads,* Harmondsworth, Middlesex: Penguin Books, 1971.

Mason, Peggy, & Laing, Ron, *Sathya Sai Baba, the Embodiment of Love,* London: Sawbridge Enterprises, 1982.

Matthews, David, *I Saw the Welsh Revival,* Chicago: Moody Press, 1951.

McDannell, Colleen, & Bernhard Lang, *Heaven—A History,* New Haven: Yale University Press, 1988.

McDermott, Robert A., *et al.,* "Rudolf Steiner and American Thought," *ReVision,* Vol. XIII, No. 4 (Spring 1991); Vol. XIV, No. 1 (Summer 1991).

McNeil, John T., *The History and Character of Calvinism*, New York: Oxford University Press, 1954.

Mendenhall, George E., "Law and Covenant in Israel and the Ancient Near East," *The Biblical Colloquium*, Pittsburgh, 1955.

Metzger, Bruce Manning, *The Text of the New Testament, Its Transmission, Corruption and Restoration*, 2nd ed., New York: Oxford University Press, 1968.

Migne, J.P., *Patrologia Graeca*.

Milindapañha.

Minear, Paul S., *Images of the Church in the New Testament*, Philadelphia: Westminster, 1975.

Moltmann, Jürgen, *The Church in the Power of the Holy Spirit*, New York: Harper and Row, 1977.

Montefiore, Hugh, *A Commentary on the Epistle to the Hebrews*, London: Adam & Charles Black, 1964.

Morris, Leon, *The Gospel According to St. Luke*, Grand Rapids, Michigan: Wm. B. Eerdmans, 1975.

Mosely, Rufus, *Manifest Victory*, Plainfield, New Jersey: Logos International, 1971.

Moulder, W.J., "The Old Testament Background and the Interpretation of Mark X, 45," *New Testament Studies*, XXIV, 1 (October 1977).

Moule, C.F.D., ed., *Miracles, Cambridge Studies in Their Philosophy and History*, London: A.R. Mowbray, 1966.

Muṇḍaka Upaniṣad.

Murphet, Howard, *Sai Baba, Avatar*, New Delhi, India: Macmillan, 1978.

_____ , *Sai Baba, Man of Miracles*, Madras, India: Macmillan, 1975.

Nakamura, Hajime, *Gōtama Budda*, Tokyo: Shunshūsha, 1978.

_____ , *Shūkyō to Shakai Rinri*, Tokyo: Iwanami Shoten, 1967.

Needleman, Jacob, *A Sense of the Cosmos*, Garden City, NY: Doubleday, 1975.

Neill, Stephen, *Colonialism and Christian Missions*, New York: McGraw-Hill, 1966.

Nemeshegyi, Peter, "Notions de Dieu et Expériences de Dieu en Asie," New York: Seabury Press, *Concilium*, 123, 1977.

Niebuhr, Reinhold, *The Nature and Destiny of Man*, I, II, New York: Charles Scribner's Sons, 1949.

Niesel, Wilhelm, *The Theology of Calvin*, Philadelphia: Westminster, 1956.

Nigg, Walter, *Great Saints*, Hinsdale, Illinois: Henry Regnery, 1948.

Nikhilananda, Swami, *The Upanishads*, New York: Harper & Row, 1963.

Nishitani, Keiji, "The Personal and the Impersonal in Religion," *The Eastern Buddhist*, III, 2 (October 1970).

Norbu, Thubten, Jigme, & Turnbull, Colin M., *Tibet*, New York: Simon & Schuster, 1968.

Notovitch, Nicolas, *The Unknown Life of Jesus Christ*, J.H. Connelly & L. Landsberg, trs., New York: Gordon Press, 1974.

Nottingham Statement, The, Over Wallop, Hampshire, The United Kingdom: BAS Printers, 1977.

Oesterly, W.O.E., *The Gospel Parables in the Light of Their Jewish Background*, New York: Macmillan, 1936.

Origen, *Commentarius in Cantica Canticorum*.

_____ , *Commentarius in Johannem*.

_____ , *Contra Celsum*.

_____ , *De Oratione*.

_____ , *De Principiis*.

Pagels, Elaine, *The Gnostic Gospels*, New York: Random House, 1979.

_____ , "The Orthodox Against the Gnostics: Confrontation and Interiority in Early Christianity," *The Other Side of God*, Peter L. Berger, ed., Garden City, NY: Doubleday, 1981.

Pallis, Marco, *A Buddhist Spectrum*, New York: Seabury Press, 1981.

Pannenberg, Wolfhart, *Systematische Theologie*, Vol. I, Göttingen: Vandenhoeck & Ruprecht, 1988.

_____ , *Theology and the Kingdom of God*, Richard John Neuhaus, ed., Philadelphia: Westminster, 1969.

_____ , *Theology and the Philosophy of Science*, Francis McDonagh, tr., Philadelphia: Westminster, 1976.

Pannikar, Raimundo, *The Silence of God, the Answer of the Buddha*, Maryknoll, NY: Orbis Books, 1989.

318

_____ , *The Unknown Christ of Hinduism,* London: Darton, Longman & Todd, 1964.

Patrick, Dale, "The Kingdom of God in the Old Testament," *The Kingdom of God in 20th-Century Interpretation,* Peabody, MA: Hendrickson Publishers, 1987.

Peat, F. David, *Synchronicity,* New York: Bantam Books, 1988.

Peers, E. Allison, *Mother of Carmel,* New York: Morehouse-Gorham, 1948.

Peper, Christian B., ed., *An Historian's Conscience, the Correspondence of Arnold J. Toynbee and Columba Cary-Elwes, Monk of Ampleforth,* Boston: Beacon Press, 1986.

Perrin, Norman, *Jesus and the Language of the Kingdom,* Philadelphia: Fortress Press, 1976.

_____ , *The Kingdom of God in the Teaching of Jesus,* London: SCM Press, 1963.

_____ , *Rediscovering the Teaching of Jesus,* New York: Harper & Row, 1967.

_____ , *What Is Redaction Criticism?* Philadelphia: Fortress Press, 1978.

Pettinato, Giovanni, "The Royal Archives of Tell Mardikh-Ebba," *The Biblical Archaeologist,* May 1976.

Philo Judaeus, *Every Good Man Is Free.*

_____ , *On the Comtemplative Life.*

_____ , *Special Laws.*

Pieris, Aloysius, S.J., *Love Meets Wisdom, a Christian Experience of Buddhism,* Maryknoll, NY: Orbis Books, 1988.

Piggot, Stuart, *Prehistoric India,* Harmondsworth, Middlesex: Penguin Books, 1961.

Plato, *Apology.*

_____ , *Laws.*

_____ , *Phaedo.*

Plinius, Gaius Secundus, *The Letters of Pliny.*

Plutarch, *Pelopidas.*

Polanyi, Michael, *Personal Knowledge,* New York: Harper & Row, 1964.

_____ , *The Tacit Dimension,* Garden City, NY: Doubleday, 1967.

Porter, Frank Chamberlin, *The Mind of Christ in Paul,* New York: Charles Scribner's Sons, 1932.

Powell, Ralph Austin, *Freely Chosen Reality,* Washington, D.C.: University Press of America, 1983.

Puryear, Herbert Bruce, "Religion and Spirituality," *Covenant,* Virginia Beach: A.R.E. Press, 1981.

Qur'ān.

Rad, Gerhard von, *Old Testament Theology,* New York: Harper & Row, 1965.

_____ , *Wisdom in Israel,* Nashville: Abingdon, 1972.

Radhakrishnan, Sarvapalli, *Eastern Religions and Western Thought,* New York: Oxford University Press, 1960.

Rahner, Karl, "Das Christentum und die nichtchristlichen Religionen," *Schriften zur Theologie,* V, Einsiedeln: Benziger, 1964.

_____ , *Foundations of Christian Faith,* New York: Seabury Press, 1978.

_____ , *Hominisation,* New York: Herder and Herder, 1965.

_____ , "Incarnation," *Sacramentum Mundi,* III, New York: Herder and Herder, 1969.

_____ , *Theological Investigations,* Baltimore, MD: Helican Press, 1966.

Rahula, Walpola, *What the Buddha Taught,* Bedford, England: Gordon Fraker, 1959.

Rāmāyana.

Ramsey, Paul, *Reinhold Niebuhr,* Charles W. Kegley & Robert W. Bretal, eds., New York: Macmillan, 1956.

Raymond of Capua, *The Life of St. Catherine of Siena,* George Lamb, tr., New York: P.J. Kennedy, 1960.

Recognitions (Pseudo-Clementine).

Reichelt, Karl Ludwig, *Truth and Tradition in Chinese Buddhism,* Shanghai: The Commercial Press, 1927.

Remus, Harold, *Pagan-Christian Conflict over Miracle in the Second Century,* Philadelphia: Philadelphia Patristic Foundation, 1983.

Renan, Ernest, *The Life of Jesus,* New York: Washington Square Press, 1963.

Rittelmeyer, Friedrich, *Rudolf Steiner Enters My Life,* London: Christian Community Press, 1963.

Robinson, James M., *A New Quest of the Historical Jesus*, Philadelphia: Fortress Press, 1983.

Robinson, John A.T., *In the End, God*, London: James Clarke, 1950.

_____ , *Redating the New Testament*, Philadelphia: Westminster Press, 1976.

Robinson, Richard H., & Willard L. Johnson, *The Buddhist Religion*, 2nd ed., Encino, California: Dickenson Publishing Co., 1977.

Roloff, Jürgen, "Anfänge der soteriologischen Deutung des Todes Jesu (Mk. X, 45 und Lk. XII, 27)," *New Testament Studies*, XIX, 1 (October 1972).

Roszak, Theodore, *The Making of a Counter Culture*, Garden City, NY: Doubleday, 1968.

Rousseau, Richard W., ed., *Christianity and the Religions of the East*, Montrose, PA: Ridge Row Press, 1982.

_____ , *Interreligious Dialogue: Facing the Next Frontier*, Montrose, PA: Ridge Row Press, 1981.

Sabatier, Paul, *Life of St. Francis of Assisi*, New York: Charles Scribner's and Sons, 1911.

Saldanha, Chrys, *Divine Pedagogy, a Patristic View of Non-Christian Religions*, Roma: Libreria Ateneo Silesiano, 1984.

Samartha, S.J., "More Than an Encounter of Commitments," *International Review of Missions* LIX, 236 (October 1970).

Sanders, E.P., *Jesus and Judaism*, Philadelphia: Fortress Press, 1985.

Sanyutta-Nikāya.

Satapatha-Brāhmana.

Schillebeeckx, Edward, *Christ, the Sacrament of the Encounter with God*, New York: Sheed and Ward, 1963.

_____ , *Jesus*, New York: Seabury Press, 1979.

Schineller, J. Peter, "Christ and Church: A Spectrum of Views," *Theological Studies*, XXXVII, 4 (December 1976).

Schulman, Arnold, *Baba*, New York. Pocket Books, 1973.

Schumann, Hans Wolfgang, *Buddhism*, Wheaton, Illinois: Theosophical Publishing House, 1974.

Schuon, Frithjof, *Survey of Metaphysics and Esoterism*, Gustavo Polit, tr., Bloomington, IN: World Wisdom Books, 1986.

_____ , *The Transcendent Unity of Religions*, New York: Harper & Row, 1975.

_____ , *Understanding Islam*, Baltimore, MD: Penguin Books, 1972.

Schweinitz, Helmut von, *Buddhismus und Christentum*, München: Ernst Reinhardt Verlag, 1955.

Schweitzer, Albert, *The Quest of the Historical Jesus*, New York: Macmillan, 1959.

Schweizer, Eduard, *The Good News According to Luke*, Atlanta: John Knox Press, 1984.

_____ , *Luke, a Challenge to Present Theology*, Atlanta: John Knox Press, 1982.

Scott, Ernest F., "Philippians," *The Interpreter's Bible*, XI, George A. Buttrick, ed., New York: Abingdon, 1955.

Sen, K.M., *Hinduism*, Baltimore, Maryland: Penguin Books, 1961.

Shepherd, A.P., *A Scientist of the Invisible*, London: Hodder & Stoughton, 1975.

Skinner, John, *Prophecy and Religion*, Cambridge: The University Press, 1922.

Smith, Huston, *Beyond the Post-Modern Mind*, New York: Crossroad, 1982.

_____ , *Forgotten Truth, the Primordial Tradition*, New York: Harper & Row, 1977.

Smith, Morton, *Clement of Alexandria and a Secret Gospel of Mark*, Cambridge, MA: Harvard University Press, 1973.

_____ , *Jesus the Magician*, New York: Harper & Row, 1981.

_____ , *The Secret Gospel*, New York: Harper & Row, 1973.

Smith, Robert D., *Comparative Miracles*, St. Louis: D. Herder, 1965.

Song, Choan-Seng, *Christian Mission in Reconstruction*, Maryknoll, NY: Orbis Books, 1977.

_____ , "From Israel to Asia: A Theological Leap," in *Mission Trends No.3*, Gerald H. Anderson & Thomas F. Stransky, eds., New York: Paulist Press, 1976.

_____ , *Jesus, the Crucified People*, New York: Crossroad, 1990.

_____ , "Theology of the Incarnation," in *Asian Voices in Christian Theology*, Gerald H. Anderson, ed., Maryknoll, NY: Orbis Books, 1976.

Spangler, David, "The Ethics of Emergence: The Phenomenon of

Cultural Transformation," *The A.R.E. Journal* XVIII, 2 (March 1983).

Sperry, Roger, "Changed Concepts of Brain and Consciousness: Some Value Implications," *Synopsis*, The Isthmus Institute Lecture Series, December 3-4, 1982.

Stadler, Anton P., "Dialogue: Does It Complement, Modify or Replace Mission?" *Interreligious Dialogue: Facing the Next Frontier*, Richard W. Rousseau, ed., Montrose, PA: Ridge Row Press, 1981.

Stcherbatsky, Fedor, *Buddhist Logic*, New York: Dover, 1962.

Steiner, Johannes, *Therese Neumann*, Staten Island, NY: Alba House, 1967.

Steiner, Rudolf, *Aus der Akasha-Forschung, das Fünfte Evangelium*, Dornach (Switzerland): Rudolf Steiner, 1975.

_____ , *An Autobiography*, Blauvelt, New York: Rudolf Steiner Publications, 1977.

_____ , *Christianity as Mystical Fact and the Mysteries of Antiquity*, New York: Anthroposophic Press, 1972.

_____ , *The Course of My Life*, New York: Anthroposophic Press, 1957.

_____ , *From Buddha to Christ*, Spring Valley, NY: Anthroposophic Press, 1978.

_____ , *From Jesus to Christ*, London: Rudolf Steiner Press, 1973.

_____ , *The Gospel of St. Luke*, London: Rudolf Steiner Press, 1975.

_____ , *Knowledge of the Higher Worlds and Its Attainment*, New York: Anthroposophic Press, 1947.

_____ , *Manifestations of Karma*, London: Rudolf Steiner Press, 1976.

Stendahl, Krister, "Notes for Three Bible Studies," *Christ's Lordship and Religious Pluralism*, Gerald H. Anderson & Thomas F. Stransky, eds., Maryknoll, NY: Orbis Books, 1981.

_____ , ed., *The Scrolls and the New Testament*, New York: Harper, 1957.

_____ , "Your Kingdom Come: Notes for Bible Study," *Your Kingdom Come*, Geneva: WCC, 1980.

Stock, Augustin, "Limits of Historical-Critical Exegesis," *Biblical*

Theology, Bulletin XIII, 1 (January 1983).
Streeter, B.H., & Appasamy, A.J., *The Message of Sadhu Sundar Singh,* New York: Macmillan, 1921.
Stuhlmacher, Peter, "Existenzstellvertretung für die Vielen: Mk. 10:45 (Mt. 20:28)," *Werden und Wirken des Alten Testaments,* Festschrift für Claus Westermann zum 70. Geburtstag, Göttingen: Vandenhoeck und Ruprecht, 1980.
Suetonius, Gaius Tranquillus, *Divus Claudius.*
Sugrue, Thomas, *There Is a River,* New York: Dell, 1967.
Sutta Nipāta, Woven Cadences of Early Buddhists, E.M. Hare, tr., London: Oxford University Press, 1947.
Suzuki, Beatrice Lane, *Mahayana Buddhism,* London: Macmillan, 1927.
_____ , *Mahayana Buddhism,* London: Allen & Unwin, 1959.
Śvetāśvatara Upaniṣad.
Swete, Henry Barclay, *The Gospel According to St. Mark,* London: Macmillan, 1927.
Swidler, Leonard, *Biblical Affirmations of Women,* Philadelphia: Westminster Press, 1979.
_____ , "The Jewishness of Jesus, Some Religious Obligations for Christians," *Journal of Ecumenical Studies* XVIII, 1 (Winter 1981).
_____ , "Preface: The Critical Divide," *Journal of Ecumenical Studies* XIX, 2 (Spring 1982), p. 1.
_____ , *Women in Judaism,* Metuchen, NJ: The Scarecrow Press, 1976.

Tacitus, P. Cornelius, *Annals.*
Talbert, Charles H. *Reading Luke,* New York: Crossroad, 1982.
Tawney, Richard Henry, *Religion and the Spirit of Capitalism,* Gloucester, Mass.: Peter Smith, 1962.
Taylor, John V., *The Primal Vision,* Philadelphia: Fortress, 1964.
Teilhard de Chardin, Pierre, *The Future of Man,* New York: Harper, 1964.
_____ , *The Phenomenon of Man,* New York: Harper, 1959.
Tertullian, *Ad Nationes.*
_____ , *Adversus Iudaeos.*

_____ , *De Oratione.*

_____ , *De Praescriptione Haereticorum.*

Testament of Moses, The.

Testaments of the Twelve Patriarchs, The.

Thelle, Notto R., "The Legacy of Karl Ludwig Reichelt," *International Bulletin of Missionary Research,* V, 2 (April 1981).

Thera-gāthā.

Theri-gāthā.

Thomas, Edward J., *The Life of the Buddha as Legend and History,* New York: Barnes & Noble, 1952.

Thomas, Gospel According to.

Tiede, David L., *Prophecy and History in Luke-Acts,* Philadelphia: Fortress Press, 1980.

Tillich, Paul, *Biblical Religion and the Search of Ultimate Reality,* Chicago: University of Chicago Press, 1965.

_____ , *Christianity and the Encounter of the World Religions,* New York: Columbia University Press, 1963.

_____ , *The Future of Religions,* Jerald C. Brauer, ed., New York: Harper & Row, 1966.

_____ , *The Shaking of the Foundations,* Harmondsworth, England: Penguin Books, 1969.

Ting, K.H., "The Church in China," Geneva: WCC, *A Monthly Letter on Evangelism* 3 (March 1983).

Toward a New Age in Mission: The Good News of God's Kingdom to the People of Asia, International Congress on Mission, I, II, III, Manila: Theological Conference Office, 1981.

Toynbee, Arnold J., *East to West,* New York: Oxford University Press, 1958.

Tracy, David, *The Analogical Imagination,* New York: Crossroad, 1981.

_____ , & John B. Cobb, Jr., *Talking About God,* New York: Seabury, 1983.

Trilling, Wolfgang, *Das Evangelium Matthäus,* Düsseldorf: Patmos-Verlag, 1965.

Udāna.

Van Bragt, Jan, "Salvation and Enlightenment: Pure Land Buddhism and Christianity," *Bulletin of the Nanzan Institute for Religion and Culture*, No. 14 (Summer 1990).

_____ , "The Challenge to Christian Theology from Kyoto-school Buddhist Philosophy," *Studies in Interreligious Dialogue*, 1, 1, (1991).

Vawter, Bruce, "Ezekiel and John," *The Catholic Biblical Quarterly* XXVI, 3 (1964), pp. 451-455.

Vedas.

Vermes, Geza, *Jesus the Jew*, Philadelphia: Fortress Press, 1981.

Vernoff, Charles E., "The Suffering Servant and the Holocaust: Toward a Theology of Judaism and Christianity," unpublished article.

Vetter, Tilman, "John B. Cobb, Jr., and the Encounter with Buddhism," *Dialogue and Syncretism*, Jerald D. Gort *et al.*, eds., Grand Rapids, MI: Wm. B. Eerdmans, 1989.

Vinaya-Piṭaka.

Virgil, *Bucolica, Ecloga.*

Visser t'Hooft, W.A., *No Other Name*, Philadelphia: Westminster, 1963.

Visuddhi-Magga.

Voices of Unity, Ans J. van der Bent, ed., Geneva: WCC, 1981.

Vos, Frits, "The Discovery of the Special Nature of Buddha: Sudden Enlightenment in Zen," *Buddhism and Christianity*, Geffré & Dhavamony, eds., New York: Seabury Press, 1979.

Wachsmuth, Guenther, *The Life and Work of Rudolf Steiner*, New York: Whittier Books, 1955.

Walker, Williston, *A History of the Christian Church*, Robert T. Handy *et al.*, rev. 3rd ed., New York: Charles Scribner's Sons, 1970.

Warren, Henry Clarke, *Buddhism in Translations*, New York: Atheneum, 1963.

Watanabe, Shōkō, *Shin Shakuson Den*, Tokyo: Daihōrinkaku, 1967.

Watson, Lyall, *Supernature*, New York: Bantam, 1974.

Weatherhead, Leslie D., *Psychology, Religion and Healing*, New York: Abingdon, 1952.

_____ , *The Will of God*, Nashville: Abingdon, 1978.

Weber, Max, *The Protestant Ethic and the Spirit of Capitalism*, New York: Charles Scribner's Sons, 1958.

Weisheipl, James A., *Friar Thomas D'Aquino, His Life, Thought and Work*, Garden City, NY: Doubleday, 1974.

Wesley, John, *The Works of John Wesley*, Grand Rapids, MI: Baker Book House, 1978.

Westcott, Brooke Foss, *The Epistle to the Hebrews*, Grand Rapids, MI: Wm. B. Eerdmans, 1951.

_____ , & Hort, Fenton John Anthony, *The New Testament in the Original Greek*, New York: Macmillan, 1961.

Wheeler, Sir Mortimer, *Early India and Pakistan*, New York: Frederick A. Praeger, 1959.

Whitehead, Alfred North, *Religion in the Making*, New York: Macmillan, 1926.

Wilson, A.N., *Jesus*, New York: W.W. Norton, 1992.

Wisdom of Solomon.

Wolff, Hans Walter, *Joel and Amos*, Philadelphia: Fortress Press, 1977.

Wolz-Gottwald, Eckard, "Mysticism and Ecumenism: On the Question of Religious Identity in the Religious Dialogue," *Journal of Ecumenical Studies*, Vol. 32, No. 1 (Winter 1995).

Yagi, Seiichi, "Christ and Buddha," *Journal of Ecumenical Studies*, Vol. 27, No. 2 (Spring 1990).

_____ , *Pauro, Shinran, Iesu, Zen*, Kyoto: Hōzōkan, 1983.

Yamada, Reirin, & Kuwada, Hidenobu, *Zen to Kirisuto Kyō*, Tokyo: Chōbunsha, 1967.

Yogananda, Paramahansa, *Autobiography of a Yogi*, Los Angeles: Self-Realization Fellowship, 1959.

Your Kingdom Come, Geneva: WCC (CWME), 1980.

Zaehner, R.C., ed., *Concise Encyclopedia of Living Faiths*, New York: Hawthorn Books, 1959.

Zago, Marcello, "L'équivalent de 'Dieu' dans le bouddhisme," *Église et Théologie* VI (1975).

Zenger, Erich, "Jahwe und die Götter," *Theologie und Philosophie* XLIII (1968).

Zimmer, Heinrich, *Philosophies of India*, Cleveland: World Publishing Co., 1961.

Index

matic) 268 fn. 22, 273 fn. 49
Son of God, 268 fn. 22
Bengali, 5
Benz, Ernst, 250 fn. 18
Bhagavad-Gitā, 250 fn. 19
Bhārhut, 257 fn. 87
Bible, 64, 73, 200, 202, 235 f.
  Hebrew, 201, 267 fn. 19, 295 fn. 36
Biblical studies, xii, 244
Bihar, 186
Bilocation, 150, 169
Bodh-gāya, 20
Bodhi,
  See Enlightenment
Bodhisattva(s), 49
Bolle, Kees W., xv
Borg, Marcus J., 72 f., 193, 195 f., 197,
  211, 252 fn. 39, 268 fn. 22, 292 fn.
  19
  Another world, 72 f.
  World of Spirit, 72
Bornkamm, Gunther, 120, 264 fn. 7,
  282 fn. 86
Bouquet, A.C., 248 fn. 2
Brāhman (priestly) caste, 7, 9, 187,
  222 f., 259 fn. 103, 297 fn. 54
Brāhman (Utimate Reality), 8, 51
Brahmanism, 9-11, 22
Brahmā Sahampati, 40
Brihadaranyaka Upaniṣad, 7, 10, 11
Bronze Age, 4
Brown, Raymond E., 121
Brunswick and Hanover, Duke of,
  272 fn. 39
Buckley, William F., 72
Buddha (Gautama), xi, xiv, xvi, xix,
  1-3, 8-13, 14-31, 32-58, 61, 69 ff.,
  76 ff., 79, 85, 92, 122, 128, 134,
  143, 146, 150, 167, 178, 180 f.,
  183-192, 204, 209, 211 f., 216 f.,
  221 ff., 225, 227, 232-236, 240 f.,
  243, 252 fn. 39, 252 fn. 47, 253 fn.
  51-53, 254 fn. 56, 256 fn. 85, 87,
  257 fn. 90, 258 fn. 102, 259 fn.
  103, 106, 260 fn. 110, 111, 265 fn.
  12, 266 fn. 19, 297 fn. 48, 54, 300
  fn. 68
  And women, 188-191
  Buddhas, 15, 40, 261 fn. 120, 263
  fn. 132

Śākyamuni (sage of the Śākyas),
  300 fn. 68
Siddhārtha (the Buddha's personal name) 1, 14, 17-23, 25,
  69, 79 f., 253 fn. 52, 260 fn. 111
Sumedha (previous incarnation), 80
Tathāgata, 54 f., 260 fn. 110, 261
  fn. 120
Universal Buddhahood, 16
Buddhacarita ("biography" of Buddha), 16
Buddhaghosa, 16, 38, 221, 262 fn.
  126, 292 fn.10
Buddhism, xii, xvi, 10, 11, 20, 33, 74,
  168, 184 f., 191, 199, 233, 254 fn.
  56, 255 fn. 75, 265 fn. 11, 292 fn.
  15
  Mahāsanghika, 15
  Mahāyāna, 16, 33, 36, 49 f., 57 f.,
  157, 164, 168, 191, 217, 237 f.,
  241, 256 fn. 79, 260 fn. 108,
  110, 292 fn. 15, 300 fn. 68
  Mind Only School Zen, 51, 237
  ff., 260 fn. 110, 290 fn. 124,
  300 fn. 68
  Pure Land Schools, xvi, 49, 220,
  256 fn. 79, 263 fn. 132, 292 fn.
  15
  Sarvāstivāda, 15
  Shingon (Mikkyō), 263 fn. 133
  Soto Zen, 237
  Theravāda, 15, 16, 33, 50
Buddhist-Christian dialogue, 237
Buddhist studies, xii, 70
  Japanese Buddhologists, xiii
Bultmann, Rudolf, 65, 264 fn. 5, 275
  fn. 61
Burma, 248 fn. 1
Buttrick, George A., 284 fn. 91

Caird, G.B., 281 fn. 84
Caligula (emperor), 265 fn. 8
Calvary, 167
Capernaum, 101, 213, 219
Caphtor, 201
Carlson, Jeffery, 247 fn. 2
Carlston, Charles E., 212
Carmody, Denise Lardner, 249 fn. 14
Carpocratian, 268 fn. 21

Catherine of Siena, 169
Cayce, Edgar, 24 f., 102, 245, 274 fn.
58, 284 fn. 93, 295 fn. 34, 301 fn.
74
Celibacy, 27
Cessation *(Nirodha)*, 45 f.
Chadwick, Henry, 250 fn. 18
Chandhu-dāro, 4
Chāndogya Upaniṣad, 7
Charlesworth, James H., 276 fn. 64
Chasidic movements, 277 fn. 67
Children, 211, 218 f.
China, 2, 3, 191, 248 fn. 1, 260 fn. 110
Chinese (language, texts), xii, xiii
Christianity, xii, 58, 82, 184, 204, 280
fn. 75, 299 fn. 61
    Anglican, 82,
    Eastern Orthodox, 70, 82
    Roman Catholic, 82, 220
Christianity and the World Religions,
179
Christology, 241
Church *(ecclesia)*, 145-148, 224, 226,
230
    And salvation, 148
    Asa sign, 146, 148
    First fruits *(aparchen)*, 147
Chuza, 212
Clairaudience, 94
Clairvoyance, 92 ff., 101 f., 112, 168
f., 171, 271 fn. 37
Claudius (emperor), 67
Clement of Alexandria, xiv, 83, 243,
267 fn. 21
Colossians, Letter to, 119, 144, 146
Comte, Auguste, xiv
Confucius, 2
Conze, Edward, 70 ff., 168, 260 fn.
109, 265 fn. 13
Corinth, 215
Corinthians, First Letter to, 138, 146,
287 fn. 108
Corinthians, Second Letter to, 182,
298 fn. 58
Corless, Roger, 263 fn. 132
Covenant (berith), 198 f., 269 fn. 28,
277 fn. 67, 288 fn. 112
    Universal (cosmic), 198-202
Craving (inordinate desire), 44-46,
48, 257 fn. 92

Crossan, John Dominic, xvi ff., 263
fn. 1, 294 fn. 30
Cullman, Oscar, 201
    History of Salvation School, 201

Dahl, Nils Astrup, 65
Dai Chōwa (Great Harmony), 238
Daimonion, 266 fn. 17
Dai Uchū (Great Universe), 238
Dalman, Gustav, 277 fn. 68
Daniel, 107, 156
David, 80, 83, 107
Davids, Rhys (Mrs.), 34, 39
Davies, Stevan, 280 fn. 75
Demons (unclean spirits), 74, 266
fn. 17
Dependent origination,
    See *Pratityasamutpāda*
Derrida, Jacques, 300 fn. 68
Deutero-Isaiah, 2
Deuteronomy, 200, 283 fn. 88, 294
fn. 30
Deva,
    See God
Devadatta, 225
Dhamma,
    See *Dharma*
Dhammapada, 48, 292 fn. 10
Dharma (law, teaching), xvi, 19, 27,
29 f., 35, 38-42, 44 ff., 48, 50, 56 f.,
69, 85, 113, 126, 180, 184 f., 221 f.
232, 234 ff., 240, 254 fn. 54, 255
fn. 74, 256 fn. 76, 257 fn. 88, 259
fn. 103, 260 fn. 111, 263 fn. 132,
299 fn. 67, 300 fn. 68
    As Truth, 41 f.
    Deity and personalism, 32, 56 f.
    Dhamma, 25, 28
    Dhammo, 256 fn. 76
    Dharmakāya, 260 fn. 110
    Dharma(s) (elements of being),
    39, 45
    Dhr (root word for dharma), 38
    Object of worshipful respect, 40
    Reminiscent of Hebrew Law and
    Wisdom, 41
Dharmakāya,
    See *Dharma*
Dharma-Nirvāṇa, 50, 56 f., 113
Donfried, Karl Paul, 278 fn. 70

Dorian(s), 4
Dravidian(s), 5, 7, 10
Duḥkha,
 See Suffering
Dumoulin, Heinrich, 256 fn. 87

Easton, Stewart C., 244
Ebed Yahweh (Servant of Yahweh),
 See Jesus Christ
Ebionites, Gospel of the, 270 fn. 33
Egypt, 3, 200 f.
Ehipassikam (come and see), 56
Ekatta (self-at-one), 26, 52
Elektoi (elect, chosen), 282 fn. 86
Elements of existence (being),
 See Dharma(s)
Elijah, 103, 200
Elisha, 93, 171
Elohim,
 See God
Emmerich, Anna Katherina, 169 f.,
 245
Emptiness, 300 fn. 68
Enlightenment, 19, 20 f., 25, 69, 80,
 190 f., 251 fn. 29, 32, 258 fn. 97,
 260 fn. 110
Enlightenment (Age of), 171
Enoch, I, 107, 110
 Enoch, II, 205
Entos hymon (within you), 279 fn. 75
Ephesians, Letter to, 146
Ephesus, 196
Ephthasen, 279 fn. 74
Epithymia (desire, passion), 257 fn.
 92, 266 fn. 18
Eschatology (last things), 113, 115,
 118, 121, 208, 275 fn. 61
 Realized, 113, 121
Essene(s), 90, 115, 205
Eternal life, 133
Ethiopian(s), 201
Euripides, 157
Evil, 22, 44 f., 55, 74 ff., 108
 Satan, 76, 99, 110, 163
Exodus, 200
Extrasensory perception, 92
 Paranormal perception, 101
 Transnormal intuition, 92 f.
Ezekiel, 2, 94, 108, 204, 267 fn. 19,
 268 fn. 22

Ezra, 204
 Ezra IV, 107

Failure, 230 f., 298 fn. 60, 299 fn. 61
 Zasetsu (complete collapse), 298
 fn. 60
Finland, 96
Fitzmeyer, Joseph A., 282 fn. 87
Flesh,
 See Paul
Forgione, Francesco (Padre Pio),
 102, 274 fn. 58
Forgotten Truth, 172
Form *(morphē)*,
 See Jesus Christ
Four Noble Truths, 23, 25, 27, 42 f.
Francis of Assisi, 103, 169, 220, 272
 fn. 39
Frazer, James (Sir), 182
From Buddha to Christ, 167

Galatians, Letter to, 132, 133, 144
Ganges River, 2, 8, 19, 30, 186, 189
Genesis, 198 ff., 266 fn. 16, 269 fn. 25
Gerasene, 105
Gethsemane, 129, 165
God, xiv, 71-76, 81, 87-90, 93 f., 97 ff.,
 102 ff., 107-110, 114-121, 129,
 133 f., 137-140, 141 f., 145, 152 f.,
 163 f., 171 f., 181, 183, 192, 195 f.,
 198 f., 203 f., 207 ff., 214, 224, 226,
 228, 230 f., 234, 239, 244, 246, 254
 fn. 56, 267 fn. 19, 269 fn. 27, 28,
 270 fn. 32, 277 fn. 65, 278 fn. 69,
 283 fn. 90, 285 fn. 99, 286 fn. 105,
 287 fn. 108, 288 fn. 111, 290 fn.
 124
 Abba (Father), 154, 270 fn. 32
 Aeon (god of this world), 74
 Angels and archangels, 73 f., 89,
 112, 235, 270 fn. 33
 As King, 115 f., 119 f., 126, 129
 Authority of, 116-120
 Cherubim and seraphim, 73, 235
 Children (tekna) of, 287 fn. 110
 Deva, 33, 184, 233, 235
 Elohim, 74
 Father, 81, 85-90, 99, 101, 111 f.,
 117 ff., 126-129, 133, 135,
 151-154, 161, 181, 192, 206,

332

fn. 133, 299 fn. 67
Unitive, 8
United Bible Societies, 62
Universal concatenation of all things,
  See *Pratityasamutpāda*
Upaniṣad, 6-13, 19, 33, 44, 249 fn. 11, 13, 250 fn. 19
Upanishads,
  See *Upaniṣad*
Urdu, 5
Uruvilvā, 20

Vacchagotta, 54
Vaiśāli, 19, 189
Vaisya(s), 9
Vakkali, 261 fn. 111
Van Bragt, Jan, 265 fn. 13, 300 fn. 68
Vattagāmani, King, 15
Vawater, Bruce, 268 fn. 22
Vedānta, 10, 54
Veda(s), 5, 6, 10, 11, 249 fn. 13, 250 fn. 19
  Vedic, 5, 6, 7, 8, 9, 17, 22, 47
Vedic,
  See Veda(s)
Vermes, Geza, 268 fn. 22, 293 fn. 19
Vibhuti (ashes), 97
Videha, 189
Vimutti,
  See Liberation
Vinaya (discipline), 19
Viññaṇassa ("mind-at-work"), 255 fn. 63
Visakha, 292 fn. 10
Von Glasenapp, Helmut, 21
Von Rad, Gerhard, 257 fn. 93

Weber, Max, 185
  Protestant ethic, 185
Weiss, Johannes, 106
Westcott, Brooke Foss, 64
Whithead, Alfred North, 274 fn. 52
Wilson, A.N., 214 f., 296 fn. 39
Wisdom (Hebrew), 41, 77, 85, 225, 269 fn. 28, 281 fn. 83
  And *Logos*, 41, 85
Wisdom of Solomon, 41, 205
Women, 211-219, 295 fn. 36
World of Spirit, 72, 78

Xenophanes, 2

Yagi, Seiichi, 252 fn. 39, 255 fn. 68
Yahweh,
  See God
Yamada, Reirin, 237 ff.
Yamaka, 54
Yama (lord of death), 55
Yangtze River, 3
Yasodhara (the Buddha's wife), 17, 19
Yoga, 70 f.
Yogasutra, 265 fn. 12
Your Kingdom Come, 281 fn. 80

Zacchaeus, 194 f.
Zarathustra (Zoroaster), 2, 150, 277 fn. 65
Zealot(s), 115, 205
Zen,
  See Buddhism
Zeus, 158
Zimmer, Heinrich, 16
Zoroastrian(s), 2, 74

341

What Is A.R.E.?

The Association for Research and Enlightenment, Inc. (A.R.E.®), is the international headquarters for the work of Edgar Cayce (1877-1945), who is considered the best-documented psychic of the twentieth century. Founded in 1931, the A.R.E. consists of a community of people from all walks of life and spiritual traditions, who have found meaningful and life-transformative insights from the readings of Edgar Cayce.

Although A.R.E. headquarters is located in Virginia Beach, Virginia—where visitors are always welcome—the A.R.E. community is a global network of individuals who offer conferences, educational activities, and fellowship around the world. People of every age are invited to participate in programs that focus on such topics as holistic health, dreams, reincarnation, ESP, the power of the mind, meditation, and personal spirituality.

In addition to study groups and various activities, the A.R.E. offers membership benefits and services, a bimonthly magazine, a newsletter, extracts from the Cayce readings, conferences, international tours, a massage school curriculum, an impressive volunteer network, a retreat-type camp for children and adults, and A.R.E. contacts around the world. A.R.E. also maintains an affiliation with Atlantic University, which offers a master's degree program in Transpersonal Studies.

For additional information about A.R.E. activities hosted near you, please contact:

A.R.E.
67th St. and Atlantic Ave.
P.O. Box 595
Virginia Beach, VA 23451-0595
(804) 428-3588

A.R.E. Press

A.R.E. Press is a publisher and distributor of books, audiotapes, and videos that offer guidance for a more fulfilling life. Our products are based on, or are compatible with, the concepts in the psychic readings of Edgar Cayce.

We especially seek to create products which carry forward the inspirational story of individuals who have made practical application of the Cayce legacy.

For a free catalog, please write to A.R.E. Press at the address below or call toll free 1-800-723-1112. For any other information, please call 804-428-3588.

A.R.E. Press
Sixty-Eighth & Atlantic Avenue
P.O. Box 656
Virginia Beach, VA 23451-0656

About the Author

Richard Henry Drummond was born and reared in California. He received the degrees of bachelor of arts and master of arts in classics from the University of California, Los Angeles, the former degree with highest honors *(summa cum laude)*. He received his Ph.D., also in classics, from the University of Wisconsin, before proceeding to theological studies. He studied at major seminaries in the Lutheran and Presbyterian-Reformed traditions and was ordained as a Presbyterian minister in 1947.

Drummond served seventeen years as a field and educational missionary in Japan, beginning in 1949. His latest period of service in that land was over the years 1986-'87. For many years he contributed a weekly column in Japanese for *Kurisuto Kyo Shimpo* and served as Japan correspondent for *The Christian Century*. He has taught courses in New Testament studies, history of religions, missiology, and classics at International Christian University, Meiji Gakuin University, and at Tokyo Union Theological Seminary.

Having taught thirty years at the University of Dubuque Theological Seminary, he became the first incumbent of the chair as Florence Livergood Warren Professor of Comparative Religions. As professor emeritus, he has continued to teach part-time at the same school. He has also served as adjunct or visiting professor at Aquinas Institute of Theology (Dubuque, Iowa), Atlantic University (Virginia Beach, Va.), Divine Word College (Epworth, Iowa), Luther Theological Seminary (St. Paul, Minn.), Old Dominion University (Norfolk, Va.), and Wartburg Theological Seminary (Dubuque, Iowa).

He is the author of six published books and many articles in both English and Japanese. One of his books, *Gautama the Buddha, an Essay in Religious Understanding,* was published also in Dutch. Two books, *Unto the Churches* and *Toward a New Age in Christian Theology,* were published in Japanese. *A Life of Jesus the Christ* has been published in Spanish, French, and German.